A Comparative Analysis
of Regulatory Strategies in Accounting
and their Impact on Corporate Compliance

T0326445

Betriebswirtschaftliche Studien
Rechnungs- und Finanzwesen,
Organisation und Institution

Herausgegeben von
Prof. Dr. Dr. h.c. Wolfgang Ballwieser, München
Prof. Dr. Christoph Kuhner, Köln
Prof. Dr. Dr. h.c. Dieter Ordelheide †, Frankfurt

Band 54

Peter Lang

Frankfurt am Main · Berlin · Bern · Bruxelles · New York · Oxford · Wien

Gabi Ebbers

A Comparative Analysis of Regulatory Strategies in Accounting and their Impact on Corporate Compliance

Peter Lang
Europäischer Verlag der Wissenschaften

Die Deutsche Bibliothek - CIP-Einheitsaufnahme

Ebbers, Gabi:

A comparative analysis of regulatory strategies in accounting
and their impact on corporate compliance / Gabi Ebbers. -
Frankfurt am Main ; Berlin ; Bern ; Bruxelles ; New York ;
Oxford ; Wien : Lang, 2001
(Betriebswirtschaftliche Studien. Rechnungs- und
Finanzwesen, Organisation und Institution ; Bd. 54)
Zugl.: Bangor (Wales), Univ., Diss., 1998
ISBN 3-631-38245-6

ISSN 1176-716X
ISBN 3-631-38245-6
US-ISBN 0-8204-5417-6

© Peter Lang GmbH
Europäischer Verlag der Wissenschaften
Frankfurt am Main 2001
All rights reserved.

Printed in Germany 1 2 3 4 5   7

www.peterlang.de

FOREWORD

In Europe, there is an intensifying debate about the source and design of accounting regulation which is caused by the increasingly global activities of groups, their wish to be listed at the New York Stock Exchange, the SEC's resistance against accounting rules of foreign countries and the activities of the IASC. But still there is a lack of empirical evidence on the actual influence of accounting design on compliance in reporting practice.

This book - a doctoral thesis of the University of Wales – analyses whether compliance behaviour in financial reporting may be influenced by differences in regulatory sources and in the design of the regulations themselves. For empirical research, Gabi Ebbers uses a binomial logistic regression model to describe the relative odds of full compliance rather than regulatory avoidance by way of partial or "creative" compliance. The analysis is based on the accounting policies adopted by about 200 internationally listed companies registered in Europe and observes three accounting practices: the revaluation of fixed assets, the accounting of foreign transactions and consolidation. Three financial years: 1987, 1993 and 1995 were selected to observe the behaviour.

The empirical results suggest that the compliance behaviour is systematically associated with the differences in the regulation authorities. Specifically, the avoidance of regulation seems to be at its lowest when such regulation has been issued by a standard setting agency. There are contradicting reasons to explain this result. One might be that the standard setter may be more effective than legislation, the other might be that the finally adopted standards may be heavily influenced by the preparers of accounts during the standard setting process. The results also indicate that a combination of legislation and standard setting agencies as well as a mixture of prescriptive regulatory text with broader principles might be harmful to the users of financial reporting.

The study of Gabi Ebbers is an important step in understanding the relationship between accounting regulation forms and compliance behaviour. Taking her results as representative, the study has meaningful implications on accounting regulation policy. I wish this book a lot of readers. It is the last one in this series which also had full recommendations by my colleague and friend Dieter Ordelheide who tragically died on May 29th, 2000.

Munich, 19 August 2000   Wolfgang Ballwieser

ACKNOWLEDGEMENTS

This thesis has been accepted for the degree of Doctor of Philosophy at the University of Wales in May 1998.

Throughout my studies I have been guided by Professor Stuart McLeay to whom I am greatly indebted for his support. His advice and encouragement provided me with opportunities to study in many different countries and to participate in international research projects and conferences. These experiences greatly contributed not only to my research work but also to my personal development.

I am also grateful to Dr. Shanti Chakravarty for providing me with valuable remarks regarding my work. I would like to extend my thanks to Mr. Chris Burke for the financial support from the School of Accounting, Banking and Economics of the University of Wales in Bangor. In addition, I would like to express my thanks to all members of the staff and the Institute of European Finance (IEF) for their friendly assistance during the period of my research.

This thesis is dedicated to my parents without whose faithful support, encouragement and love this work would not have been endeavoured, let alone completed.

Bangor, May 1998   Gabi Ebbers

CONTENTS

CHAPTER 1

PART I

ACCOUNTING REGULATION

CHAPTER 2

REGULATION AND COMPLIANCE:

CHAPTER 3

REGULATORY STRATEGIES IN ACCOUNTING:

A REVIEW OF INSTITUTIONAL STRUCTURES AND

PART II

ACCOUNTING DIVERSITY IN EUROPE:

THREE REPRESENTATIVE AREAS OF ACCOUNTING POLICY

CHAPTER 4

REGULATORY STRATEGIES IN

CHAPTER 5

CHAPTER 6

CHAPTER 7

PART III

STATISTICAL MODELLING OF COMPLIANCE WITH

ACCOUNTING REGULATION

CHAPTER 8

A PROBABILITY MODEL OF COMPLIANCE IN

FINANCIAL REPORTING

LIST OF TABLES

LIST OF FIGURES

ABBREVIATIONS

AECA	Asociación Española de Contabilidad y Administración de Empresas
ASB	Accounting Standards Board
ASC	Accounting Standards Committee
CNC	Conseil National de la Comptabilité
CNC	Commission des Normes Comptables
CNCC	Compagnie Nationale des Commissaires aux Comptes
COB	Commission des Opérations de Bourse
CONSOB	Commissione Nazionale per le Società e la Borsa
CSPC	Commissione per la Statuizione dei Principi Contabili
CRC	Comité de la Réglementation Comptable
EC	European Community
ED	Exposure Draft
EU	European Union
FASB	Financial Accounting Standards Board
FRC	Financial Reporting Council
FRS	Financial Reporting Standard
FSR	Foreningen af Statsautoriserede Revisorer
GoB	Grundsätze ordnungsmäßiger Buchführung
HGB	Handelsgesetzbuch
ICAEW	Institute of Chartered Accountants in England and Wales
ICAC	Instituto de Contabilidad y Auditoria de Cuentas
ICAI	Institute of Chartered Accountants in Ireland
IdW	Institut der Wirtschaftsprüfer
IOSCO	International Organisation of Securities Commissions
IAS	International Accounting Standard

IASC	International Accounting Standards Committee
OEC	Ordre des Experts Comptables
PCG	Plan Comptable Général
PGC	Plan General de Contabilidad
RJ	Raad voor de Jaarverslaggeving
SEC	Securities and Exchange Commission
US GAAP	United States Generally Accepted Accounting Principles

ABSTRACT

This thesis analyses whether compliance behaviour in financial reporting may be influenced by differences in regulatory sources and in the design of the regulations themselves. A logistic binomial model is used to describe the relative odds of full compliance rather than regulatory avoidance by way of partial or creative compliance. The analysis is based on the accounting policies adopted by internationally listed companies registered in Europe where, despite the harmonising impact of the European company law directives, regulatory strategies in accounting continue to be diverse.

CHAPTER 1

INTRODUCTION

1.1 Objective

In accounting, whatever the regulatory strategy, effective control over corporate financial disclosure may be an elusive goal, not only as a result of *a priori* political bargaining over the choice of regulation but also through *a posteriori* manipulation of accounting rules by the regulated themselves, who, as noted by Power (1993), seek to preserve their ability to exercise discretion in interpretation. Such avoidance of regulatory control in accounting is known as creative compliance and, in the UK, is already well documented. (Griffith, 1986; Smith, 1992; Naser, 1994; Shah, 1996). The underlying objective of this thesis is to examine such compliance behaviour in a comparative context, and to investigate whether the avoidance of regulation is associated with the different regulatory strategies for accounting found in Western Europe.

1.2 Background

The approaches to the regulation of accounting vary considerably among European countries. First, the institutions issuing accounting regulations, and hence the authority of rules, differ from one country to another. Thus European companies are governed by a variety of regulatory instruments, depending on their country of incorporation. Accounting rules are more likely to be enacted in the form of parliamentary or governmental legislation in France, Germany, Belgium, Spain and Italy, while accounting standards issued by the accountancy profession are more prevalent in the UK, Ireland, the Netherlands and Denmark. Non-binding accounting regulations in the form of recommendations are common in most jurisdictions, but these take on more importance in certain countries because they fill a regulatory vacuum.

Furthermore, the variety of laws, standards and recommendations issued by national institutions is intensified by the different approaches taken to the design of the regulatory text. While some regulators adopt very precise rules which aim at a high level of uniformity in financial reporting, others prefer more open-textured rules which allow for individual circumstances to be taken into account. For example, with the 'true and fair view' a more judgemental approach was introduced into EC company law at the initiative of UK accounting regulators, which in turn met resistance by other European regulators who prefer detailed rules (van Hulle, 1997a).

In systematising different approaches to regulatory control in accounting, this thesis focuses on two aspects in particular. The first of these concerns the sources of authority of accounting rules, which may have full legal force, or summarise standard practice, or which may merely provide advice. The second aspect concerns the design of the regulatory text, whereby a rule may either tend towards precision or be more open-textured.

The issue of compliance is central to the political debate concerning regulatory form. Contemporary accounting reforms, which are particularly intensive in Europe and aim at restraining the creative compliance and non-compliance behaviour of companies, relate to both the institutional authority and the design of accounting regulation.

In France, for instance, the introduction of a new rule-making hierarchy in accounting has been accompanied by accusations of '*vagabondage comptable*', the argument being that the institutional structure of regulation must be changed in order to take effective action against non-compliant companies which shop around for suitable accounting policies (Henisse, 1997). The *Comité de la Réglementation Comptable* (CRC) instituted in 1996, which is a governmental body, has been given the power to issue legally binding accounting regulations without prior approval by the government. In addition, a law approved in March 1998 allows French companies whose securities are traded on a regulated EU or foreign stock exchange to use International Accounting Standards (IAS) under two conditions: the first, if the relevant IAS has been translated into French and the second, if it has been adopted by a ruling of the new CRC.

In Germany, on the other hand, the driving force behind the efforts to reform the financial reporting regime is that compliance with domestic regulations may have prevented German companies from gaining full advantage in international capital markets (Ebke, 1997). A bill which was passed by the lower house of parliament on 27 March 1998, exempts German companies which use either IAS or US GAAP to acquire capital on international stock exchanges from presenting their consolidated financial statements in accordance with German consolidation regulation (Frankfurter Allgemeine Zeitung, 28 March 1998). Further legislation will establish a *Bilanzrat*, set up by representatives of industry, the audit profession and academia, which will be a private accounting standardisation council with three main responsibilities: first, to develop

2

recommendations to reform existing German consolidation regulation; second, to advise the Ministry of Justice on this issue and third, to represent Germany at the IASC (Frankfurter Allgemeine Zeitung, 14 February 1998).

Thus, in contrast to France, Germany will opt for a privately organised standard setting agency to accommodate national accounting regulation to the forces of internationalisation. The French and German examples demonstrate that, even though national regulators accept the penetration of internationally accepted accounting rules into local regimes, the institutional arrangements and hence the sources of authority and the design of policies which regulate accounting will continue to differ between nation-states.

Paradoxically, compliance achievement is not necessarily the primary goal of a regulatory authority. In fact, such institutions may be established in ways which constrain their ability to act in an effective manner, resulting in regulatory capture by parties which then set the kind of rules with which they themselves are willing to comply.

With respect to regulatory design, national calls for change have also been motivated by a concern with non-compliance. In the UK, for example, proposals for less prescription in accounting regulation have been based on the view that a mechanistic cookbook approach to rule-making may actually encourage avoidance (Tweedie and Whittington, 1990). The dilemma of regulatory design is, however, that while detailed accounting regulation may enable companies to avoid control without violating the letter of the law (McBarnet and Whelan, 1991) as it cannot take account of all possible cases which might arise in practice, on the other hand broad concepts such as 'substance over form' and 'true and fair' which aim at reflecting commercial reality in corporate reports are open to judgement and hence to the risk of abuse.

Similarly, at the international level, the source and design of accounting regulation is currently a focus of tension and controversy. The current power struggle for international accounting policy harmonisation appears to be a battle between accounting jurisdictions that pursue different, if not contradictory, regulatory strategies for accounting. While EC directives negotiated by governments and implemented in national commercial legislation have the authority of law, IASs issued by the professional accountancy bodies of member countries of the IASC which do not necessarily represent their government, have no legal status. Thus, in spite of the EU Commission's change in regulatory strategy to permit multinational companies to adopt IASs if these are compatible with EC Directives (van Hulle, 1997b), such companies remain subject to differing national regulatory forms.

3

Moreover, the debate with regard to the detail of future global accounting standards is contentious (Accountancy, January 1998). The endorsement of IAS by the International Organisation of Securities Commissions (IOSCO) will depend not only on the successful completion of the IASC-IOSCO work programme by the end of 1998 (Flower, 1997) but also on the US Securities and Exchange Commission (SEC) approval which would prefer US GAAP to be the future internationally accepted accounting principles. If US GAAP were to become the future global standards, these would have a high level of detail and specificity, but if IAS were endorsed, they would be considerably less detailed and would integrate the overriding principle of substance over form.

1.3 Research implementation

This thesis investigates whether the compliance behaviour of European companies is associated with the differences from country to country in the institutional authority of regulation and the degree of formalism of the accounting rules to which they are subject. The analysis is based on the financial reporting practices of those European multinational companies which compete in international capital markets. Multinational corporations are particularly affected by the diversity of national financial reporting regimes, as they are subject to different rules of disclosure and measurement when competing for investors, clients and creditors in international markets. Indeed, multinational companies may have similar motivations to escape national governance by seeking alternative interpretations of accounting rules to achieve a competitive advantage.

Despite the fact that the source and design of accounting regulation is a focus of ever-intensifying regulatory debate at both the national and international level, there is a lack of empirical evidence on its actual influence on compliance in reporting practice. Therefore, the aim of the present research is to statistically evaluate the relationship between compliance behaviour and the different approaches to the regulation of accounting. For this purpose we shall develop a binomial probability model, where the addition of regulatory factors to the linear predictor will permit an assessment of the relative influence of alternative regulatory sources and alternative regulatory designs on the compliance behaviour of European multinational companies.

A more complete understanding of the different forms of regulatory control in accounting can be acquired when the instruments relating to specific areas of rule-making are compared. It becomes apparent that regulatory approaches vary, not only between countries but also between different areas of accounting policy within the same country. Accordingly, three key accounting areas were selected to describe the diversity of the institutional sources and the regulatory design of European accounting regulation. These were the valuation of assets (the revaluation of fixed assets), foreign currency reporting (the accounting for foreign transactions) and consolidation (the definition of a subsidiary).

For the empirical analysis, a survey of financial reporting practices with regard to these three accounting areas was carried out. The selection criterion for sample companies was whether in addition to a domestic stock exchange listing, companies were also quoted on another stock exchange elsewhere in or outside Europe. The countries in which such multinational companies were regulated were Belgium, Denmark, France, Germany, Ireland, Italy, the Netherlands, Spain and the United Kingdom.

Accounting policies published in the annual reports by these companies were examined for compliance with the relevant national regulations. The corporate accounting report contains maximum regulated enterprise accounting information. No means exist for obtaining additional regulated information from reporting companies over and above that contained in the financial reports. Those who have additional financial statement information obtained in the course of other relationships with a company are not allowed to exploit this information on the market (Bromwich and Hopwood, 1992). Furthermore, it is unlikely that either the management or the auditors of a company would convey information above that disclosed in the corporate reports, unless required to do so by an enforcement agency.

In order to control for changes in compliance behaviour over time, three financial years: 1987, 1993 and 1995, were selected for the empirical analysis. The starting year was taken as 1987. By 1993, financial statements could be expected to reflect the regulatory amendments brought in with the Fourth and Seventh Directives which by that year had been implemented in all of the countries under study. Also in 1993, a number of IAS were revised with the objective of narrowing options formerly contained therein. These revised standards became effective two years later in 1995. Moreover, in 1995 the IASC agreed with the IOSCO on a work programme, aiming at the recognition of IASs for companies listed on international stock exchanges. A change in EU regulatory strategy was also announced by the European Commission in 1995, allowing the use of IAS in consolidated financial statements for multinational companies, provided that they conform with the European Directives.

1.4 Main empirical results

The empirical analysis of this thesis suggests that the compliance behaviour of European companies is systematically associated with the differences in the institutional authorities which issue the relevant accounting regulation in Europe. Thus, which authority is issuing the regulation constitutes an important aspect of companies' compliance with the regulations themselves. This result was confirmed in all three areas under investigation: individually, combined, and after controlling for national differences in compliance behaviour. In fact, the source of the regulation outperformed country differences as a factor in compliance with the rules relating to each of the three accounting policies.

Specifically, the results of this study suggest that the avoidance of accounting regulation in financial reporting is at its lowest when such regulation has been issued by a standard setting agency. In contrast, regulatory avoidance in the form of either creative or partial compliance in financial reporting is higher when the governing rules have the authority of laws, enacted by legislature, the government or individual ministers in the form of delegated legislation. When an accounting subject is regulated by both legislation and a standard, the results suggest that creative and partial compliance in financial reporting is greater than in the cases where accounting policies are governed solely by either a standard setting agency or by law.

However, it will be seen that the standard setting agencies in Europe display individual national characteristics in terms of independence from government participation in the rule-making process and the degree of self-regulation by the profession. Different classifications of the factor 'regulatory source' take account of this fact and ensure that the empirical results do not depend on the assigned categories of this explanatory variable. The results of this study confirm that a comparatively greater proportion of companies unambiguously comply with standards issued by professional standard setting agencies. In the case that the government has the residual power to review the agency's rule-making, the avoidance of regulation in practice is higher.

There are two possible explanations of these results. On the one hand, a standard setting agency may be a more effective rule-maker in accounting since it concentrates expertise, while the legislature has neither the time nor the technical knowledge to engage in specialised regulatory policy. Moreover, maintaining a distance from the government may facilitate consultation with the preparers of accounts and thus contribute to more effective rule-making. In accounting, frequent technical amendments are necessary, and these impose not only heavy costs but also serious delays on parliamentary inspection. An alternative explanation is, however, that of regulatory capture by the standard setting agencies because the finally adopted standard follows a process of consultation and lobbying, and therefore the preparers of accounts may have influenced the rules with which they are willing to comply.

Our empirical results suggest that the degree of formalism in accounting regulation is a systematic explanatory factor for compliance only in certain policy areas. While the design of rules significantly affects compliance behaviour in the area of revaluation, there is no systematic relationship in the areas of foreign currency reporting and consolidation. Furthermore, regulatory design is less important in explaining compliance behaviour than is the authority issuing the regulation; but when country differences are taken into account, compliance behaviour is in fact significantly influenced by regulatory design.

Detailed accounting regulations generate a higher rate of compliance in reporting practice than do accounting rules which are drafted in open-textured terms. Hence, judgement in accounting regulation leads to a higher rate of creative compliance than formalism. However, when the regulator adopts a rule containing elements of both precise and open formulations, this can be associated with a greater tendency to avoid that regulation in reporting practice, when compared with either formal or judgemental policy expressions.

Thus, in spite of the criticism that very precise rules in accounting are likely to be avoided, by complying with the form rather than the substance of such rules, judgemental rules which are adaptable to the individual circumstances of a commercial transaction seem less optimal for the disclosure of financial information. In jurisdictions with prescriptive revaluation rules, most companies disclose policies in compliance with the content of such rules, even though it must be noted that instances of revaluation beyond those formalised in the legislation have occurred.

Notwithstanding earlier conclusions, the empirical results suggest that there are significant differences in national compliance behaviour although, as mentioned earlier, the source of regulation is a more important explanatory factor than country differences. The results indicate that during the investigation period compliance with national accounting regulations was significantly higher in Germany than in the rest of Europe. Conversely, compliance was lowest in France. This result supports earlier suggestions that the *vagabondage comptable* of French companies was evident during the investigation period while their German counterparts complied with the national requirements.

As a policy recommendation, it follows that standard setting agencies in accounting will be more effective rule-makers than the public legislators; but of particular importance would be to avoid the overlapping of standards and legislation as this leads to higher avoidance.

As a further policy recommendation, regulators should adopt a high degree of detail in accounting regulation, although it should be noted that the source of the regulation has a stronger impact on compliance behaviour than policy design and also that regulatory design is not a decisive factor for compliance in each of the accounting policy areas under study. Moreover, regulators should avoid mixing prescriptive regulatory text with broader principles as this again leads to higher avoidance. This result argues in favour of standards similar to US GAAP, rather than IAS, for future global accounting standards. However, it should be acknowledged that a high degree of detail might be difficult to pursue when integrating the objectives of different national accounting regimes.

1.5 Summary outline of the thesis

The first part of this thesis is concerned with the theme of accounting regulation. Chapter Two reviews the theory and evidence on accounting regulation. Following this literature review, Chapter Three describes the different regulatory strategies that have been pursued in the nine European countries under study. The analysis centres on the two dimensions of regulatory strategy which will serve as explanatory variables in the statistical analysis: that is, (i) the different national regulatory institutions and hence the sources of authority of accounting rules, and (ii) alternative regulatory design to control financial reporting in Europe.

The regulatory diversity of individual accounting areas forms the second part of this study. Chapter Four argues that each area of rule-making is influenced by different circumstances and emerges from a different set of actors over time. The three areas of accounting referred to earlier are compared in detail across the nine European jurisdictions under study. The revaluation of fixed assets comprises Chapter Five, Chapter Six deals with foreign currency accounting and the definition of a subsidiary is discussed in Chapter Seven. Each chapter traces the historical development of the accounting regulations in each of these areas and relates this to the existing diversity of the regulatory strategies across Europe. Each chapter also contains examples of policy disclosure and the results of a preliminary survey of compliance by those European companies which are subject to these different regulatory circumstances.

This part of the thesis provides a detailed evaluation of alternative regulatory design and the different regulatory instruments involved. In Chapter Five, asset revaluation illustrates the alternative regulatory design of detailed and prescriptive requirements on the one hand and open-textured and flexible rules on the other. That is, while price-level indexing approaches tend to authorise the restatement of defined assets in line with specified price indices on predetermined dates, the use of current values generally allows a company to exercise discretion with respect to the basis, the scope and the timing of revaluation. Chapter Six on foreign currency reporting provides a good example of the diversity amongst the sources of accounting regulation to which companies are subject in Europe. The various locations of accounting regulation can be traced to legal statute, professional standard, recommendation and expert interpretation. Chapter Seven also demonstrates the regulatory conflict between formalism and anti-formalism which has been at the roots of controversy . surrounding the drafting of the criteria defining group companies included in the Seventh Directive. The implications of different regulatory designs with regard to the concepts of legal and economic group control are described in detail. Unique combinations of the *de jure* and *de facto* criteria that define a subsidiary for consolidation have led to international variations of the boundaries of a consolidated group. While some jurisdictions define a group solely on the basis of legal criteria, other countries have adopted, either purely or in addition to this, an economic concept of group control. The complexity of the regulatory design of the parent-subsidiary relationship is evident in cases where economic control is presumed to exist under certain legal control rights. For the areas of consolidation and revaluation in addition to the law, supplementary standards have been issued in some countries.

The third part of the thesis develops and applies a probability model based on binomial logistic regression, with the aim of empirically evaluating the relationship between compliance behaviour in reporting practice and the relevant regulatory strategies for the three accounting policies across Europe. The theoretical development of the model forms Chapter Eight. Chapter Nine describes the data and research design and illustrates and explains the reasoning for classifying reported accounting policies into different forms of compliance: that is, full compliance, creative compliance, partial compliance and non-compliance. The analysis of accounting practice is based on a review of annual financial reports of about 200 European multinational companies for the years 1987, 1993 and 1995. The statistical analysis, which has been carried out by comparing nested linear logistic models, is described in Chapter Ten. In this Chapter, the results of the tests are presented together with an analysis of parameter estimates. The conclusions of the thesis are presented in Chapter Eleven which also provides a comparison of the probabilities of regulatory avoidance across alternative regulatory sources and the different countries involved.

PART I

ACCOUNTING REGULATION

CHAPTER 2

REGULATION AND COMPLIANCE:

THEORY AND EVIDENCE

2.1 Introduction

This chapter seeks to provide a review of the literature on accounting regulation. The review is not exhaustive, but focuses on the principal contributions which are considered to be relevant for the present research study. The summary of the literature on accounting regulation begins by identifying the principal extant accounting theories which offer competing explanations of accounting regulation. The first of these theories to emerge was the normative and conceptual framework approach in the 1960's. Alternative approaches were developed in the early 70's with the positive accounting theory approach and, in the late 70's, with parallel developments incorporating social, economic and political aspects in the accounting domain, in particular the accounting research known as critical accounting. This review will make reference to different empirical research studies which are based on these theories.

Secondly, the literature on public regulation as opposed to private regulation (professional self-regulation), will be referred to within a context of both legal theory and the regulation of accounting. Thirdly, the literature on substance versus form in rule formulation will be considered. Similarly to the previous section, the discussion will deal with both the legal theory perspective and the viewpoint of accounting regulation. Fourthly, a summary of the literature on creative compliance in financial reporting will be provided which, as will be seen, has been limited to a single country and refers to the UK case. Finally, references to comparative international studies on accounting regulation will be made.

2.2 Theories of accounting regulation

Normative Theory and the Conceptual Framework
There is a long tradition of accounting theory being concerned with the interests of the users of accounts (Sterling, 1972). While many theories have

concentrated on aiding shareholders in decisions concerning their income, wealth and utility (Edwards and Bell, 1961, Chambers, 1966, Sterling 1970, Beaver and Demski, 1974), this theoretical approach has influenced practice in the form of conceptual frameworks offered by professional bodies (FASB, 1978; Stamp, 1980; Macve, 1981; IASC, 1989).

Empirical research can be divided into studies which concentrate on individual shareholder usage of accounting reports and those which are concerned with the impact of accounting information on stock market prices, explicitly taking account of the effects of the aggregate behaviour of investors.

The individual shareholder usage of accounting reports has been assessed in two ways: firstly, by the application of techniques to measure the readability, and hence the understanding, of accounting reports (*e.g.* Adelberg, 1979); and, secondly, by shareholders' responses to questionnaires about the use of corporate reports (*e.g.* Lee and Tweedie, 1977). The prescriptions derived from this research include calls for accounting reports to be simplified and for accounting policy makers to concentrate on the needs of naive investors. Cooper and Sherer (1984, p.210) emphasise the concentration of these studies on the interest of individual shareholders only. "In effect, shareholders are depicted as individuals operating within an environmental vacuum and this allows the design of corporate accounting reports to be considered as if it were only of private interest. But the omission of any consideration for the immediate environment, the capital market, in which the shareholder class operates, ignores wider effects which may ensue from such prescriptions."

Empirical studies which seek to provide insights from aggregate shareholder use of corporate reports by investigating the relationship between published accounting information and stock market prices (*e.g.* Ball and Brown, 1969; Foster, 1978) indicate that while there is some information content in accounting earnings reports, this information is not 'timely' since market price changes precede the publication of accounting reports. Consequently, the private shareholder cannot make consistent gains by using such information. In addition to the problems in assessing the efficiency of information markets (Fama, 1976), the limited value of the capital market research literature in relation to the value of accounting reports, is the concentration on the shareholder perspective of accounting information. Furthermore, it appears inappropriate to suggest that capital market efficiency tests can be used to assess the desirability of alternative accounting measures or disclosures (Beaver and Demski, 1974; Gonedes and Dopuch, 1974).

It follows that, rather than being derived as a logical purpose, the conceptual framework studies make a fundamental assertion with regard to the purpose of accounting regulation and the reason for its existence: the "decision usefulness" of accounting data to the users of corporate reports. This criterion however, does not permit a choice between alternative accounting standards. Paradoxically, while regulators would like to attain decision usefulness of accounting data, no conceptual framework appears to exist to achieve this goal. In this sense the conceptual frameworks contain and perpetuate a number of myths (Miller, 1985).

Positive Accounting Theory

It was the weakness of the FASB conceptual framework and, furthermore, the political nature of the standard setting process that led Watts and Zimmerman (1978) to adopt a different approach to the study of accounting regulation, namely that of positive accounting theory. While Solomans (1978) argued that standard setters should resist pressures from political lobbyists and should have as a first priority the setting of "neutral" accounting standards, positive accounting theorists called, not for speculation on what standard setting should be (what Watts and Zimmerman deride as normative theorising) but, instead, for concentration on what standard setting is (positive) and how choices are made within existing structures.

Following Coase (1937), corporations are viewed as a set of inter-related contracts between participants. Applications of the contracting approach with its emphasis on agency relationships, have been used to provide explanations for the development of accounting standards. Watts (1977) was the first paper attempting to explain and predict accounting choices on the basis of both contracting and political process arguments. Subsequently, the accounting choice literature (Hagerman and Zmijewski, 1979; Leftwich, Watts and Zimmermann, 1981; Holthausen 1981; Leftwich, 1983) sought to predict accounting choices; for example, with regard to depreciation, inventory, taxes, debt contracts and other contracting costs, primarily on the basis of managers' incentives to choose among permitted accounting methods in order to increase their wealth at the expense of other parties to the firm and in the political process. Lobbying behaviour on accounting standards is modelled as dependent on managers' utility maximisation (Watts and Zimmermann, 1986). The effect of accounting regulation on management remuneration and total wealth is based on a contracting monitoring model of the firm where managers' self interest is constrained to minimise total agency cost and to align with shareholder interest. Positive accounting theory has led to a vast number of lobbying studies (Walker and Robinson, 1993).

However, positive accounting theory does not answer the question why accounting regulation exists at all and why it is manifested in a particular form. The theory is restrictive in that it sees accounting as a function of contracting costs, and unless an argument for the standardisation of contract terms as an economy of scale is advanced, it can see no reason for regulation (Neal, 1997). In fact, the positive accounting theorists have been the focus of extensive criticism including the criticism that positive theory is in fact normative and masks a conservative ideological bias (Tinker *et al.*, 1982; Christensen, 1983; Sterling, 1990). Another problem with the contracting approach is that its main concern is with users of corporate accounts. This approach may be able to address issues for private value, but it does not seem able to deal with the social value of corporate reports (Cooper and Sherer, 1984).

Social value approaches in accounting theory
United in their criticism that partial equilibrium approaches to valuing accounting reports have failed to model the total interaction between these reports and all individuals and classes in society, a number of theories address the issue of the social value of accounting information. Social value approaches attempt both to understand and to explain the production and use of accounting from an economy-wide perspective and hence directly address the broader issue of the social value of accounting information. This section reviews the general equilibrium approach to the economics of information and the analysis of economic consequences.

General equilibrium economic analysis seeks to identify the role of information amongst the welfare conditions which result in economic efficiency in the allocation of resources through time among all market participants. However, the use of the general equilibrium economic analysis to explain the functions of accounting in society and to provide criteria for evaluating alternative accounting systems is limited, not only as a result of its high level of generality and abstraction, but also because the welfare implications of the analysis remain unclear. Whereas Hirschleifer (1971) suggests that public information is socially useless, Ohlson and Buckman (1981) demonstrate how this information will affect the sharing of risk in an economy and thus have welfare implications. Demski (1974) on the other hand, argues that there are incentives for one individual to privately produce information in order to make gains at the expense of another who does not have this information.

Economic consequences analysis emerged as an alternative approach for understanding and valuing the role of accounting in a broader social context. The economic consequences literature examines the consequences of regulating financial information disclosure. Zeff (1978) shows that economic consequences arguments were involved in US standard setting prior to the FASB era and, also in the steps which were institutionalised to assure that parties fearing adverse economic consequences would have a voice in the new FASB standards setting process.

In contrast to the general equilibrium economic analysis, the economic consequences analysis tends to be empirical. However, even though the economic consequences literature seems to have the potential for assessing a wider range of effects of changes in the accounting measurement system, empirical studies have almost invariably evaluated such consequences solely in terms of the behaviour and the interest of the shareholder and manager class (Selto and Neumann, 1981). Many of the studies have attempted to assess the stock market reaction to changes in the content of published accounting information (Griffin, 1979; Lev, 1979). But as Foster (1980) has observed, the inconsistency of the results of these studies is indicative of the general failure of such tests to specify a theory of expected effects and hence to identify control variables.

Critical accounting theory

The lack of definite positions on the appropriate forms of accounting regulation which characterise neoclassical economic or marginalism analysis has led to the assimilation of radical alternative socio-political theories into the accounting literature. This has followed calls (Burchell et al., 1980; Tinker, 1980) for an understanding of how accounting systems operate in their social, political and economic contexts in order that "better" accounting systems might eventually be designed. The literature which forms part of this critical accounting theory can be divided into that based on a Marxist perspective (Tinker, 1985; Cooper and Sherer, 1984, Cooper and Hopper, 1990) and that based on a sociological perspective (Miller, 1986; Robson et al., 1994; Hoskin, 1994).

The strength of the Marxist school lies in the critical argument of existing paradigms. The critical accounting theorists reject prior exclusive shareholder orientation in the research on accounting policy choice and suggest an alternative approach, known as the political economy of accounting. Implicit in this approach is a notion of social welfare that focuses on society as an aggregate (rather than as an aggregation of individuals), an emphasis on distributive as well as exchange (allocative) dimensions of wealth and power and a concern with socially necessary rather than market determined production. However, from the recognition that accounting policy is essentially political, it does not follow that an improvement of accounting policy can necessarily be achieved. Rather, there is an implication that the politically determined nature of the value of accounting prevents such a resolution within accounting itself (Cooper and Sherer, 1984).

The elements of the political economy of accounting are, firstly, the acknowledgement of power and conflict as well as the acknowledgement of a political process in the area of accounting regulation. The second element is an explicit call to take account of the historical, environmental and institutional arrangements in accounting research. Thirdly, it is argued that accounting is capable of having an emancipatory role in society and can contribute to changes in society and to the distribution of wealth, because of its importance as a valuation technology (Tinker, 1985).

Similarly, the sociological theorists view accounting as a valuation technology that shapes and is shaped by the social environment in which it operates. However, while the Marxist school places greater emphasis on the role which economic and political factors play in determining the form and content of accounting regulation, the sociological approach rejects *a priori* determining factors and, instead, regards accounting as important in its own right and as one of a number of technologies. The basic position of the sociological approach is that accounting is a complex domain with a number of competing discourses (Hoskin, 1994). The dominant discourse in the regulatory bodies is the normative one, while the competing discourses in the academic literature may undermine the ideology of standard setters.

2.3 Public versus private regulation

This section begins with a discussion on the allocation of power in regulatory systems from a legal theory perspective and, in particular, makes reference to the delegation of rule-making to agencies and self-regulation by professional associations. Subsequently, the relevant literature refering to the institutional arrangements of accounting regulation, which is predominantly generated by UK authors, will be addressed.

Legal theory argumentation
According to Ogus (1994), there is a hierarchy of institutions on which relevant powers of policy formation, law-making, adjudication and enforcement can be conferred: the European Community, the national legislature, government departments, special (more or less independent of government) agencies and the courts. While under the Treaty of Rome, European law is to prevail over domestic law, nevertheless, the European norms may be very general in

character, leaving it to national institutions to determine the relevant rule intensity. Subject to European instruments, the primary source of regulatory law in member states is parliamentary legislation. The issue of interest to be addressed in this section is how and why rule-making powers are delegated to other institutions.

Powers can be conferred on ministers to directly promulgate rules in statutory instruments. Alternatively, parliament can confer power on an agency to issue a set of formally binding rules, although sometimes this may be subject to ministerial approval. Agencies may also be authorised to issue non-binding rules which serve as guides to the interpretation of legal provisions.

Although rule-making by agencies may create a problem of accountability, there are several arguments for delegating this function to them (Ogus, 1994). Firstly, expertise can be concentrated in a way which is not possible with government bureaucracies. In fact, legislature has neither the time nor the expertise to engage in detailed rule-making and when technical amendments are necessary, parliamentary scrutiny would impose heavy costs and serious delays. Secondly, maintaining a distance from government may reduce a risk of political interference, encourage a longer term perspective, and thus facilitate consultation and more open decision-making. Whether and to what extent the government should have a residual power to review agency rule-making is less clear. On the one hand, it is argued that such power is necessary to ensure that the agency's decisions in a specific regulatory context are compatible with the government's more general objectives (Baldwin and McCrudden, 1987). On the other hand, there is a danger that the government may interfere for short-term political purposes (Sunstein, 1987).

Views may differ on the degree to which regulatory agencies should be independent of government, but it would appear to be obvious that they should be independent of the interests that are being regulated. There are, nevertheless, many cases where the rules of conduct for professional occupations are determined by bodies drawn exclusively or predominantly from members of the profession and, which are also prevalent in the area of financial regulation (Page and Ferguson, 1992). The issue being debated is whether self-regulation can be reconciled with the argument for delegation in the public interest or whether it is a subversion of regulation to private interests (Ogus, 1994).

A private self-regulatory agency may be a cheaper and more effective rule-maker than a public agency (Cane, 1987). First, since a self-regulatory agency can normally command a greater degree of technical knowledge of the practices and innovatory possibilities within the relevant area than can a public agency, the information costs for the formulation and interpretation of standards are lower. Secondly, and for the same reasons, monitoring and enforcement costs are also reduced, as are the costs to practitioners of dealing with the regulators, given that such interaction may be fostered by mutual trust. Thirdly, to the extent that the processes of, and rules issued by, self-regulatory agencies are less formalised than those of public regulatory regimes, there are savings in the costs of amending standards.

In contrast, critics of self-regulation see it as an example of modern 'corporatism', the acquisition of power by groups which are not accountable (Lewis, 1990). Self-regulation may itself constitute an abuse if it lacks democratic legitimacy in relation to members of the association (Page, 1986), but the potential for abuse may become unacceptable if the rules affect third parties (Cane, 1987). Furthermore, if the self-regulatory agency's functions cover not only policy formulation, but also the interpretation of rules, adjudication and enforcement (including the imposition of sanctions), there appears to be a fundamental breach in the separation of powers doctrine. It follows that rent seeking behaviour and regulatory capture may characterise a self-regulatory agency which is free from external constraints (Kay, 1988).

However, self-regulation may actually not occur in its pure form. Baggott (1989) indicates that self-regulatory regimes differ according to several variables: notably, the degree of monopolistic power; the degree of formality, for example, whether or not they derive legitimacy from a legislative framework; their legal status, for example, whether or not the rules have binding force; and the degree to which outsiders participate in rule formulation and enforcement, or in other ways supervise the system.

Regulatory sources of accounting
The regulatory structures of accounting in Europe are currently undergoing considerable transformation subject to varied national and international processes, some of which began some twenty years ago but are only now reaching full development. The European Community attempted to harmonise company accounts, which commenced with a first draft to the Council in 1971 and are now embodied in a number of European Company Law Directives. However, the European Commission has admitted that its earlier approach of complete or very detailed harmonisation has not been successful and instead, has pursued the approach of 'minimum harmonisation and mutual recognition' (van Hulle, 1992). In contrast, the International Accounting Standards Committee (IASC), established in 1973, has played an intensifying and increasingly dominant role in the regulation of accounting (Flower, 1997;

Cairns, 1997). It is important to note that the IASC does not consist of representatives of national regulators, but is constituted from representatives of the local professions of its member countries (Cairns, 1995). Nevertheless, the IASC seems to have overcome these problems of 'legitimacy' (Freedman and Power, 1991) and International Accounting Standards (IAS) have become a significant focus for a new regulatory 'internationalism'. In 1995, a new strategy was announced by the European Commission which allowed European multinational companies to use IAS for consolidated financial statements, given their compatibility with the directives (van Hulle, 1997b). Furthermore, several European countries, namely, Italy, France, Belgium and Germany have recently approved legislation which allows national enterprises listed on international capital markets to use IAS for consolidated financial statements, if these policies are consistent with European accounting directives (Knorr, 1998).

In the accounting literature, similar arguments against and in favour of legislative policy making for financial reporting have been put forward by Bromwich and Hopwood (1992). The disadvantages of legislative accounting regulation are seen in the delay in dealing with urgent and emergent issues in financial reporting and furthermore, in the danger that technical accounting issues may be decided on the basis of the political views of the party in power. The principal benefits of accounting legislation are considered to be the legitimacy and social acceptance of such rules and also the procedure by which compliance with legislation may be enforced through the courts.

In the UK, the regulation of financial reporting has traditionally been in form of self-regulation, by accountants, auditors or other preparers of financial information (Whittington, 1993). However, following the recommendations of the Dearing report (1988), the setting of UK accounting standards is now supervised by a Financial Reporting Council (FRC) which represents a wide range of interests in addition to professional accountancy bodies. Furthermore, accounting standards have been given statutory support through the legal authority of the 1989 Companies Act (Turley, 1992).

The change in the regulatory strategy for financial reporting disclosure in the UK, in particular the 'legalisation' of accounting standards, has given rise to numerous research studies (special issue of The Modern Law Review, 1991; Bromwich and Hopwood, 1992; Laughlin and Broadbent, 1993; Sikka and Willmott, 1995a). The failure of the Accounting Standards Committee (ASC), the former self-regulated agency of the UK audit profession, to regulate accounting standardisation has been described by Hopwood (1992, p. 145) in these terms: "... the [ASC] was established by the audit industry to prevent more rigorous modes of State intervention in the accounting field. Once in existence, it tended to respond to crises which had the potential to destabilise the form of professional rather than State control over accounting that it represented. Rather than seriously trying to lay down a programme for the more effective regulation of corporate accounting, the [ASC] had a history that was more oriented to the preservation of the status quo and the legitimisation of the profession's model of self-regulation".

It seems, however, that following various defensive tactics, self-regulation and self interest of the professional accountancy bodies as well as their failure to take effective action against offending firms or their partners is pervasive in the UK (Robson, 1993; Mitchel and Sikka, 1993; Willmott *et al.*, 1993; Robson, *et al.*, 1994; Mitchel *et al.*, 1994; Sikka and Willmott, 1995b). But Hopwood (1992, p.145) suggests that, "[o]ften real effectiveness may not be one of the primary goals of a regulatory authority. Regulatory institutions, themselves reflecting the outcomes of compromises between the interested parties can sometimes be established in ways which constrain their ability to act in an effective manner and often are subject to regulatory capture."

2.4 Substance versus form

This section will discuss the literature on substance as opposed to form in policy formulation. Analogous to the previous section on institutional structures, the discussion starts by reviewing the arguments of legal theorists before going on to discuss relevant contributions in the accounting domain. As will be seen, only a few research studies exist on the subject of formalism in accounting policy formulation.

Legal theory argumentation
One of the central concerns of legal discussion is legal determinacy - the ability to formulate rules that yield certain or at least predictable outcomes. However, which regulatory form can achieve legal determinacy and, in particular, the optimal degree of formalism is open to controversy. While some believe that legal certainty will be improved if rigid, formalistic rules are abandoned in favour of general rules (Tushnet, 1984), others insist that the proliferation of detailed rules is fundamental to ensure predictable legal outcomes (Schauer, 1988).

At the heart of formalism lies the concept of 'decision making according to rule' (Schauer, 1988). The tasks performed according to rules take place for the most part through the language in which the rules are written. Formalism and language are conceptually intertwined. Arguments that law is indeterminate to the extent that legal questions lack a single correct answer and that hence all legal doctrine is bound to be unpredictable to some degree are rejected by the formalists (Kress, 1989). For the formalist the problem is not that all law is indeterminate, but rather that vague rules do not properly constrain legal decisionmakers (Weinrib, 1988).

There are suggestions, however, that neither regime actually exists in its pure form and a number of theoretical legal studies have analysed the optimal level of formalism in rules with regard to compliance costs for both the regulators and the regulated, by applying economic theory (Posner and Ehrlich, 1974; Diver, 1983; Johnston, 1991). The relationship between the level of formalism in rules and compliance behaviour will be discussed in Chapter Three.

Regulatory design of accounting policy
One of the few studies that assesses the advantages and disadvantages of formalism and 'anti-formalism' in the design of accounting regulation is that of McBarnet and Whelan (1991). Formalism is defined as a narrow approach to regulatory control, the emphasis being on the use of detailed rules and their literal interpretation, which leads to uniformity, consistency and predictability in the reporting of accounting transactions. Anti-formalism, on the other hand, emphasises a broad approach to regulatory control by the use of open-textured rules. In this case, the focus is on the spirit of a rule and, in accounting, on the reporting of the economic substance of a transaction instead of its regulatory form.

In the UK, the development of off-balance sheet schemes has motivated regulators to design broad standards in order to deal with the deeper issues which are common to a number of problems (Tweedy and Whittington, 1990, p.99). The authors state that "[d]etailed prescription is in many ways undesirable: it can lead to inflexibility and to incentives to conduct a standards avoidance game analogous to tax avoidance." However, the authors believe that some degree of detail in standards is necessary, and argue that the level of prescription required is a practical matter which is contingent on the strength of opposing forces: "[A] vague injunction to auditors to ensure that the accounts 'tell it the way it is' will be inadequate unless auditors have a remarkably similar set of thought processes (so that there is consistency of judgement) and considerable integrity and strength in resisting what is often (wrongly) described as 'client' (*i.e.* management not shareholder) pressure. One flexible way in which a standard-setting body can respond to the practical need for prescription is to have fairly broadly defined standards but to issue more detailed interpretations when required."

Only in the UK has the concern with off-balance sheet finance and creative accounting led to regulatory action and, in particular, to an explicit change in accounting rule formulation (FRS 5 'Reporting the Substance of Transactions', 1994). However, the lack of numerous arguments on this issue in the accounting literature (Macdonald, 1991), gives the impression that substance over form is seen as a peculiarly legal doctrine.

2.5 Creative compliance in financial reporting

As mentioned previously, in the UK, regulators of financial reporting are aware of the problems associated with creative compliance (Tweedie and Whittington, 1990; Whittington 1993). In 1985, the President of the Institute of Chartered Accountants of England and Wales (ICAEW) described the "potentially very serious problems of window dressing and off-balance sheet financing" (Accountancy, October, p.4). This was followed by the setting up of a working group (1985) and various Exposure Drafts ED 42 (1988), ED 49 (1990) before FRS 5 was drafted in 1994. Technical reports on current creative accounting schemes can be found in the commentaries contained in *Financial Reporting*, the survey of accounts published annually by the ICAEW (Skerrat and Tonkin, 1995).

The literature holds a pessimistic view of the struggle for control in financial regulation. It would seem that effective regulation of financial information disclosure is inevitably bound to fail as a result of the active manipulation of rules by the regulated themselves who wish to retain 'zones of discretion' and to preserve the control of interpretation (Power, 1993). In accounting, this stretching of rules is known as the problem of 'creative compliance'.

McBarnet and Whelan (1991, p.848) define creative compliance as "[the use of] law to escape legal control without actually violating legal rules." In assessing the effectiveness of different degrees of formalism in policy formulation with regard to the problem of creative compliance in accounting, the authors do not consider either formalism or 'anti-formalism' to be an effective form of regulatory control for accounting. Indeed, the dilemma seems to be that while detailed rules are easy to avoid by literal application which undermines the rule's intention, open-textured regulations allow room for judgement, which in turn requires interpretation in practice. Paradoxically, such interpretations will develop into working rules and hence will lead back to formalism and a continuation of creative compliance. The authors argue that attempts to combat creative compliance with general, anti-formalist rules - such as substance over form - run up against limits of control and almost inevitably generate a return to formalism. Power (1992) extends this argument, noting the implication that between general principles and detailed regulations there is an open 'interpretative space' in which creativity in the application of rules to a particular instance is always possible.

Generally, the issue has been explored in the context of 'creative accounting' rather than the more specific 'creative compliance'. Naser (1994), for instance, defines creative accounting as "(1) the process of manipulating accounting figures by taking advantage of the loopholes in accounting rules and the choices of measurement and disclosure practices in them to transform financial statements from what they should be, to what preparers would prefer to see reported, and (2) the process by which transactions are structured so as to produce the required accounting results rather than reporting transactions in a neutral and consistent way" (p. 59).

Like Naser (1994), Griffith (1986) and Smith (1992) explain and illustrate creative accounting with examples as diverse as leasing, fixed assets (including intangibles), quasi-subsidiaries, foreign currency reporting, goodwill and equity accounting. Peasnell and Yaansah, (1988) consider the general development of off-balance sheet financing schemes in the UK in the 1980s, whilst Power (1992) documents the brand accounting episode with regard to the active role of accounting practice in creating new mechanisms by stretching existing regulations. Shah (1996) presents further evidence of the manipulation of accounting rules in the case of convertible securities.

In summary, the research studies on creative compliance in accounting can be characterised as follows: firstly, the issue is treated by examining individual subject areas; secondly, the approach is descriptive; and, thirdly, the studies are limited to single countries. This thesis, however, introduces a research framework which is not only empirical, but also covers a number of accounting issues in an explicitly comparative context.

Research studies which deal with comparative aspects of accounting regulation tend to be of a descriptive nature (Bromwich and Hopwood, 1983; Wallace and Gernon, 1991; Flower and Lefebvre, 1997). Although the literature on international comparative accounting has demonstrated that the structures of accounting regulation vary considerably among nation-states, most of it has failed to develop a coherent explanation of how and why accounting systems differ from country to country.

A theoretical evaluation of the different types of accounting regulation has been carried out by Puxty *et al*. (1988) who compare the accounting regimes in four capitalist societies (Germany, United Kingdom, United States of America and Sweden). Associating different modes of accounting regulation with the distinctive histories and institutional specificities of different nations, the paper develops a rigorous framework for understanding the principles of accounting regulation. Exploring models of social order, the authors explain accounting regulation as an expression of the combination of the organising principles of Market, State and Community and theorise how the modes of accounting regulation are a function of how power is distributed. In a wider context, this paper also provides a framework for evaluating different authorities of accounting regulation, that is, the state on the one hand and the professional bodies on the other, expressing concern over the lack of accountability of professional bodies and questioning professional self regulation. Puxty *et al*. stress that "there will be no single matrix of Market, State and Community principles of organisation which will apply to all areas of regulation. Rather the extent to which each of these regulatory forms is prominent in its influence upon the arena under investigation (...) will vary from one issue to another" (p. 288). The present thesis builds on this theory and extends the explanation beyond the different regulatory modes to include the design of regulatory texts. Moreover, the theory is also subjected to extensive empirical analysis.

Looking at the internationalisation of accounting regulation it seems evident that the factors influencing accounting regulation vary through time. This thesis will demonstrate that such forces vary not only from country to country and through time but also from one accounting issue to another. In fact, this study is based on the belief that the categorising of national accounting systems on the basis of certain characteristics of their legal and business environment (Nair and Frank, 1980; Nobes 1983) is far too simplistic and superficial. Instead, international accounting differences are the result of an underlying process of competition and conflict between nations. While the exporting and importing of accounting regulations, through either international harmonisation or voluntary transplantation, are evident (Parker, 1989), the driving force of the remaining national distinctiveness may be attributed to the self-interest of national regulators. At any given time, accounting regulations are the product of an ongoing struggle between the forces of globalisation and the pursuit of autonomy by individual states (Ebbers and McLeay, 1997).

Finally, it should be noted that research on the measurement of international accounting harmonisation (van der Tas, 1988, 1992, Tay and Parker, 1990; Archer *et al.*, 1995, 1996) has been confined to the content of accounting regulations in different countries, rather than the design and the authority of the regulations themselves. The understanding of harmony in these studies is concerned exclusively with the influence of EC directives as a force which leads to harmonisation on a single accounting method, even though Archer *et al.* (1996, p.3) allow for 'different commercial circumstances' to explain the choice between different accounting methods. However, all the studies cited above assume that there is a choice between the different accounting method available, ignoring creative compliance and, furthermore, disregarding the possibility that the choices made might be influenced by the different regulatory forms to which European companies are subject. This thesis introduces these factors into the modelling of accounting policy choice and changes the focus of comparative research from harmonisation of accounting rules towards that of the manner in which institutional arrangements that differ from country to country influence compliance behaviour.

CHAPTER 3

REGULATORY STRATEGIES IN ACCOUNTING:

A REVIEW OF INSTITUTIONAL STRUCTURES AND

REGULATORY DESIGN IN EUROPE

3.1 Overview

European companies are governed by a variety of regulatory strategies, depending on their country of incorporation. In fact, the institutional structures of accounting regulation differ considerably from one European country to another. Furthermore the variety of laws, standards and recommendations issued by such institutions is intensified by the different approaches taken to the drafting of regulatory text, whereby a rule may either tend towards precision or be more open-textured.

The sources of accounting regulation include not only parliamentary legislation but also, depending on the jurisdiction, various types of delegated legislation such as decree law, ministerial orders and other promulgations having legislative powers. In the latter category are those rules issued in national accounting plans as well as judicial rulings and the regulations issued by capital market regulators. In addition, there are various types of standard setting bodies which have been set up either by the audit profession or by the government, or a mixture of the two. Finally, recommendations on specific aspects of accounting are issued by a variety of other associations and individuals involved in the regulatory framework of accounting. For instance, professional and industry associations may issue recommendations which provide guidance to their members, and authoritative interpretations of the regulations in force by individual experts may also carry considerable weight. Figure 3.1 provides a summary of the various sources of European accounting regulation.

Figure 3.1

THE SOURCES OF ACCOUNTING REGULATION

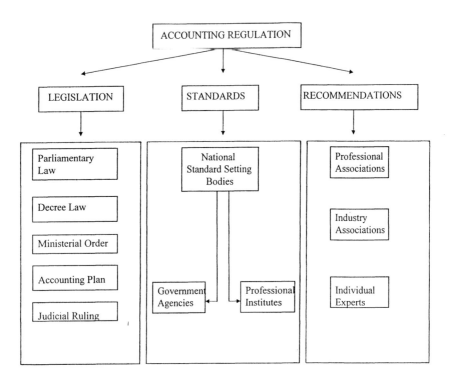

Accounting rules themselves may be either formulated in precise terms or drafted in general principles. On the one hand, detailed accounting regulation aims at a uniform reporting of transactions. On the other hand, a more open-textured approach to accounting regulation aims at reflecting the economic substance of transactions. Precise regulation eliminates discretion and uncertainty but because of its detail it is inflexible and cannot be accommodated to the variety of cases which might arise in practice. A more general rule, which can be interpreted to fit the special circumstances, requires judgement by the preparers of accounts and hence is open to abuse. Figure 3.2 illustrates the regulatory dilemma that appears to exist between the competing design of accounting rules with regard to compliance.

The second section of this chapter explores in further detail the components of the three main sources of accounting regulation: (i) legislation, (ii) standard and (iii) recommendation. The third section is concerned with the alternative design of policies: (i) precise regulations and (ii) general principles. The discussion focuses on the relationship between regulatory design and compliance and is based on an economic analysis of regulatory form and legal theory. Subsequently, the national approaches to the regulation of accounting in European countries are described and compared.

Figure 3.2

THE DESIGN OF ACCOUNTING REGULATION

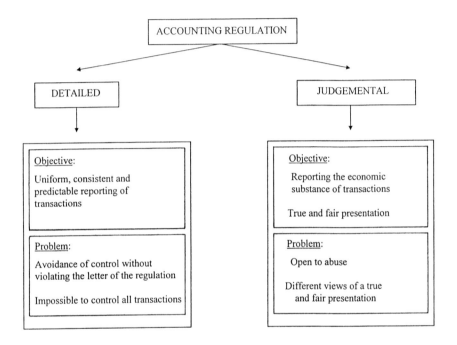

3.2 The sources of accounting regulation

3.2.1 Legislation

Law

Subject to the supremacy of EU law, the primary source of regulatory law in accounting, as in other areas of regulation, is parliamentary legislation. It is important to note that in many European countries accounting regulation became statutory as a consequence of the implementation of the Fourth and Seventh EC Directives. It is no secret, however, that the relevant European directives were very optional in character, leaving it to national institutions to determine the relative rule intensity. In general, a legal policy is formulated by the government, before the law incorporating the policy is passed by parliament.

Delegated legislation

Legal rule-making powers are often delegated to other institutions. Legislature may delegate the power to promulgate legislation within defined limits to government departments, such as ministries and separate government agencies. Indeed, within Europe the number of delegated legislative instruments is vast: decree law, ministerial order, circular, resolution and so on. However, while the rules contained in statutory instruments issued by ministers or public agencies play a major role in some countries, they are absent in others. In Spain and France, for example, power has been conferred by parliament on an agency operating under the auspices of a ministry, and this agency can issue legally binding rules, which are then implemented in the national chart of accounts, although this is subject to approval by decree. Decree law is a common feature of accounting legislation in Belgium, France, Spain and Italy and is approved by the government. In addition, in Italy and Spain, and also in Denmark and the Netherlands, ministers can directly promulgate legal rules in form of a decree or an order. In contrast, delegated legislation is not a regulatory instrument in either Germany or the UK. Table 3.1 summarises the legislative instruments used in the context of accounting in the countries under study.

Table 3.1

Legislative Instruments of European Accounting Regulation[1]

Belgium	Denmark	France
Law (*Loi/Wet*) Royal Decree (*Arrêté Royal/Koninklijk Besluit*)	Financial Statements Act (*Årsregnskabsloven*) Financial Statements Order (*Årsregnskabsbekendtgørelsen*) Ministerial Guidelines	Commercial Code (*Code de Commerce*) Law (*Loi*) Decree (*Décret*) Accounting Plan (*Plan Comptable Général*)
Germany	**Ireland**	**Italy**
Commercial Code (*Handelsgesetzbuch*)	Companies Act Group Accounts Order	Civil Code (*Codice Civile*) Law (*Legga*) Legislative Decree (*Decreto Legislativo*) Law Decree (*Decreto Leggo*) Ministerial Decree (*Decreto Ministerialo*) Circulars (*Circolare*)
The Netherlands	**Spain**	**United Kingdom**
Civil Code (*Burgerlijk Wetboek*) Administrative Decree (*Besluit*)	Commercial Code (*Codigo de Commercio*) Law (*Ley*) Royal Decree (*Real Decreto*) Accounting Plan (*Plan General de Contabilidad*) Ministerial Order (*Orden Ministerial*) Resolution (*Resolución*) Circulars (*Circulars*)	Companies Act Statutory Order

---

[1] Note. Instruments on related tax legislation, securities market law and legislation for special industries and financial institutions have been excluded.

The role of the courts
The adjudication of disputes is a mechanism for securing compliance with the provisions of the law and judicial interpretation thus contributes to legal development in each jurisdiction. However, judicial rulings have a relatively small impact on the development of accounting regulation in Europe, even though some countries have explicitly integrated the courts into the institutional structures of financial reporting regulation. For instance, in the Netherlands a special court has been instituted to deal with judicial disputes on financial reporting, while in the United Kingdom a review panel may seek an order from the courts requiring the directors of a company to prepare revised accounts in case that company's accounts do not comply with the requirements of the law. But although the independence and autonomy of the judicial regulatory process favours a decision making process insulated from political pressures, the limitation of the judicial source of accounting regulation may be seen in the fact that the courts act only on matters which have been drawn to their attention.

The Role of the Stock Exchange
Stock market regulators can suspend share trading if a company contravenes extant regulations, and this represents a strong intervention into the activities of a firm. The requirement by stock market surveillance commissions to comply with existing accounting regulation or with rules issued by the stock market regulator itself may thus constitute a very powerful status for compliance. However, across Europe, the stock market regulators vary in their power over financial reporting regulation. In France and Italy, securities commissions have been empowered by law to issue regulations relevant to the financial reporting of listed companies, but in other countries, including the Netherlands and Germany, the stock market regulations do not have a direct impact on accounting matters. Yet, even where legal authority has been granted, stock market regulators usually confine intervention to demanding compliance with existing accounting legislation and standards and do not issue regulations themselves.

3.2.2 Standards

As can be seen in Table 3.2, the rules issued by standard setting bodies procure their status from very different authorities. As noted earlier, a standard setting body is established either by the government in a special law, or as a self-regulated body of the audit or accounting profession, or, in the case of the UK's ASB, as a professional body with the government appointing the chairmen. A second characteristic is whether the rules issued by standard setting bodies have been granted more or less statutory support, whether they are endorsed by the stock exchange or, finally, whether they are not backed by a public institution and only respected by the audit profession itself. If backed by statute, the standards may either have full legal force, or the law requires companies to disclose compliance with the standards.

It is important to note that the term standard is only used for the rules issued by the UK's ASB. In this study, however we use the term for those rules which are issued by an official accounting standard setting body which has been assigned with this responsibility, either by itself as a self-regulatory body of the profession or by the government as a public accounting standards commission.

The authority of each accounting body is peculiar to individual nation states, especially in terms of its importance in relation to legislative accounting regulation as well as in terms of its private or public status, its way of funding and its membership structure. Within Europe, at one extreme of the spectrum, a body may be set up as part of a government ministry, while, at the other end, the body will be established and entirely funded by the auditing profession. The official recognition of a standard setting body may be through a law passed by the government, or in a ruling by the courts of law, or by the Stock Market regulators which themselves have been empowered to regulate. Other bodies have an exclusively private status. However, even though the rules they issue are not officially recognised, they may be followed for moral reasons of conduct and may serve as a safeguard for the auditor in a judicial dispute. Standard setting bodies either interpret the law, supplement the law or deal with new accounting issues which have not yet been dealt with in the law.

3.2.3 Recommendations

Recommendations are considered here as rules issued by all 'non-official' bodies involved in accounting regulation, that is non-legal bodies and non-standard setting bodies. These comprise a large set of rule-makers, in particular professional association of auditors or accountants, industrial associations and individual experts. As with standards, the terminology used for this type of rule may be very different across European countries. Also, the importance of such recommendations, which are often derived by convention and custom varies from one country to another. For instance, recommendations take on more authority in countries where a standard setting body is non-existent, such as in Germany, but may be less important in a country with a great number of legislative instruments, such as Spain. Recommendations are primarily interpretations of existing regulations. They serve to assist companies where the law is ambiguous, or where an emergent issue has not been dealt with by the law.

Table 3.2

The status of rules issued by standard setting bodies

	Public Body: set up by government law	Private Body: set up by the profession	Hybrid Body: set up by the profession, government appoints chairmen
Following approval by government, the standards have legal status	**French CNC** (*Conseil National de la Comptabilité*) **Spanish ICAC** (*Instituto de Contabilidad y Auditoria de Cuentas*)		
Company law requires to disclose compliance with standards			**British ASB** (Accounting Standards Board)
Without granting legal recognition, the government supports the standards informally		**Dutch RJ** (*Raad voor de Jaarverslaggeving*)	
Stock Exchange requires listed companies to comply with standards		**Italian CSPC** (*Commissione per la Statuizione dei Principi Contabili*) **Danish Accounting Panel** (*Regnskabspanelet*)	
The audit profession respects the standards, but they are not endorsed by a public institution.	**Belgian CBN** (*Commission des Normes Comptables/Commissie voor Boekhoudkundige Normen*)	**Spanish AECA** (*Asociación Española de Contabilidad y Administración de Empresas*)	

3.3 Regulatory design and compliance

At the heart of the substance versus form debate in accounting regulation is the concern with effective control in financial reporting. This section addresses the alternative strategies in rule formulation and considers the relationship between regulatory design and compliance. The discussion is based on legal theory and, in particular, on an economic analysis of law.

Regulation may be either formulated in general principles or drafted in precise and detailed terms. Ogus (1994) argues that there is a spectrum representing different degrees of formalism in rule formulation:

"At one end of the spectrum, a standard setter may create a highly precise, perhaps quantitative, rule (*e.g.* vehicles must be driven at a speed not exceeding 30 m.p.h. in a given area); at the other end, a general rule (*e.g.* vehicles must be driven at a 'reasonable' speed in urban areas), requiring interpretation by both the actor and the enforcement agency. Because a precise rule eliminates discretion and uncertainty, it reduces the agency's administrative cost and the regulated firm's information cost. On the other hand, its specificity means that it is inflexible and cannot be accommodated to the variety of circumstances to which it must be applied. It is likely to be over-inclusive (deterring more than is optimal in the circumstances) or under-inclusive (deterring less than is optimal in the circumstances). Thus the 30 m.p.h. limit will unduly deter faster driving during times when few pedestrians will be present and when the optimal speed might be 40 m.p.h.; and will insufficiently deter slower driving in icy conditions, when the optimal speed might be 15 m.p.h. A more general rule, which can be interpreted to fit the special circumstances, will avoid these costs arising from mismatch, but is more expensive to administer" (p.169).

A number of theoretical legal studies have attempted to analyse the optimal level of formalism in rules with regard to compliance costs for both the regulators and the regulated, by applying economic theory (Diver, 1983; Johnston, 1991; Posner and Ehrlich, 1974).

Distinguishing three dimensions of regulatory precision, transparency, accessibility, and congruence, Diver (1983) develops an efficiency criterion of rule precision for a utility-maximising rulemaker who would estimate the social costs and benefits arising from different scenarios. It is argued that the degree of precision can have an impact on compliance behaviour and the transactions costs associated with administering a rule. Increased precision may increase compliance and decrease evasion costs. However, while increased transparency may be easier to enforce and may discourage violators from making costly efforts to avoid compliance, it may increase the variance between intended and actual outcomes, as the rulemaker may be unable to foresee all of the circumstances to which the rule may apply. While he can change the rule after learning of its incongruence, the process of amendment will be costly and will result in social losses in the interim. A more general rule, though facially congruent, may be over- or under-inclusive in application, because its vagueness will invite misinterpretation. Furthermore, the cost to both the regulated and the regulator of applying a rule tends to increase as the vagueness and inaccessibility of the rule increases.

Johnston (1991) analyses the effect of legal uncertainty on legal decisionmaking and suggests a pattern of dynamic legal change from detailed rules to broad rules and back again. Under the premise that private actors act on their *ex ante* beliefs about how the legal decisionmaker will answer the *ex post* questions that determine their legal liability, both the world of *ex ante* private choice and the world of *ex-post* legal decision will be inherently uncertain. The declaration that liability will be avoided if a certain action is taken provides an artificial incentive for actors to comply with the rule. If legal decisionmakers apply detailed rules with rigidity these are likely to be over- or under-inclusive. On the one hand, there is no incentive for the actor to do more than the rule requires, because he is completely insulated from liability by just barely complying. On the other hand, the actor may comply even though the circumstances are such that compliance with a detailed rule would generate high compliance costs, which is not socially optimal.

Johnson theorises that a rigid rule may well dictate behaviour which is optimal under typical or average circumstances, but when the circumstances are far from typical the actor incurs 'atypical' costs and benefits and will rationally disobey the rigid rule, as it may be better to bear the cost of liability than the cost of avoiding liability. Thus, when compliance with rigid rules is too costly, rational actors will make the socially correct choice and undercomply. But by undercomplying rational actors incur liability even though they have behaved optimally. However, the uncertainty of the legal process (judges may create exceptions when the rule seems at odds with economic reality) cuts the incentive to comply with a rigid rule, because compliance may lead to liability and non-compliance to non-liability.

In the case of a general rule, compliance is defined precisely as optimal conduct in a particular situation. In the perfect scenario, where the legal decisionmaker does not err, there is no incentive do do more than is really optimal, because the probability of liability can be lowered to zero simply by doing the optimal thing. There is a strong incentive not to do less, because this would entail liability. However, the legal process is not perfect and legal decisionmakers differ in how they interpret a vague standard, such as 'reasonable'. Uncertainty of this sort can cause a general rule to be either too weak or too strong a signal. Actors may cut their own costs and do less than is 'reasonable' under the circumstances, because they know that they may be found not liable even though they failed to behave reasonably. They may do the opposite, however, and behave too carefully in an attempt to lower the probability that the legal decisionmaker will incorrectly find that they have failed to behave reasonably. Both factual evidence and opinion as to what is 'reasonable' may be most obvious in extreme situations, and most ambiguous under typical circumstances.

Johnson concludes from his theoretical analysis that general rules should induce optimal care under extreme circumstances when there is little uncertainty over what was and what should have been done, but they may induce too much care under normal circumstances, when there is reasonable disagreement about what constitutes optimal behaviour. Uncertainty, if not too great, improves incentives under rigid rules, by blurring artificial incentives to comply. In contrast, in average circumstances uncertainty causes a broad rule to deter excessively. In most frequently occurring situations (uncertainty and normal situation), broad rules result in overdeterrence while rigid rules cause neither systematical overdeterrence nor underdeterrence.

Finally, Posner and Ehrlich (1974) examine the optimal level of specificity in a legal rule under the desire to minimise cost. They theorise that there is an optimal specificity for any given regulation where the administrative costs are approximately equal to the costs of any potential mismatch. They suggest that a perfectly detailed and comprehensive set of rules brings society nearer to its desired allocation of resources. The analysis is based on a model that integrates the social loss (from activities that society wants to prevent and from the deterrence of socially desirable activities) and the cost of producing and enforcing rules, including litigation costs. Efficiency is maximised by minimising the social loss function.

The authors argue that the more homogeneous the conduct which detailed rules affect is, the lower the costs of those rules. However, several different costs are associated with greater precision of rules. Some of these arise from the fact that making law more precise involves making it more detailed in order to minimise the cost of overinclusion and underinclusion. The more specific a rule, and the more heterogeneous the world it regulates, the greater the costs of overinclusion and underinclusion. A general rule will involve underinclusion and overinclusion when the legal process is imperfect. Thus, Posner and Ehrlich conclude that even a perfect rule is necessarily overinclusive and underinclusive.

3.4 National approaches to accounting regulation

This section describes the financial reporting regimes in France, Germany, Belgium, Spain, Italy, Denmark, the UK, Ireland and the Netherlands. The analysis addresses the relevant national institutions and their interaction in the rule-making process and describes the sources of authority and design of policy of the regulations issued by the various parties involved.

France

In France, accounting regulation is primarily legalistic. A statutory public agency, the *Conseil National de la Comptabilité* (CNC), has the central responsibility for financial reporting regulation. Government ministries contribute to the regulatory process by approving a law or decree drafted by the CNC. Other institutions involved in the accounting rule making process are the French Stock Exchange Commission (*Commission des Opérations de Bourse*, COB) and the two professional accounting organisations: the Association of Accountants (*Ordre des Experts Comptables*, OEC) and the National Association of Auditors (*Compagnie Nationale des Commissaires aux Comptes*, CNCC). Table 3.3 summarises the sources of accounting regulation in France.

Accounting legislation is contained in the commercial code (*Code de Commerce*) and in the national accounting plan (*Plan Comptable General*, PCG). The law (83-353) of 30 April 1983 together with the decree (83-1020) of 29 November 1983 modified the commercial code in accordance with the Fourth European Directive thereby introducing statutory legislation for accounting in France. A further law (85-11) of 3 January 1985 and decree of 17 February 1986, incorporated the Seventh Directive and modified the law of 24 July 1966 on commercial companies (*Loi sur les Sociétés Commerciales*) with regard to consolidation requirements.

The CNC [2] operates under the auspices of the Ministry of Finance. The essential role of the CNC is to advise the government on accounting regulation, to develop detailed rules of accounting to be enacted in the PCG and to promote their uniform application (de Kerviler and Standish, 1992). The CNC's

---

[2] The power to make proposals for amending the PCG has been delegated to the CNC in France by a government decree in 1957, albeit legal modifications have to be promulgated by ministers.

involvement in the legal texts on accounting and their application is twofold. Firstly, it initiates accounting regulations which usually lead to proposals to the Ministry of Finance. Secondly, it publishes opinions on technical issues and interprets legal texts when consulted by public or private organisations. Some institutions adapt the PCG to individual circumstances, which are then examined by the CNC.

Because of its legal power to regulate the operations of the securities market, the COB has considerable authority to investigate the disclosure of financial information by listed companies and also to impose sanctions on non-compliant companies[3]. However, even though the COB has issued a number of recommendations in the *Bulletin Mensuel de la Commission des Opérations de Bourse,* it has not imposed authoritative rulings (*instructions*) on accounting matters for companies quoted on the stock exchange. Nevertheless, the COB exercises indirect influence on accounting regulation through its representation in the CNC.

In addition to the law, the regulation of accounting in France is influenced by the 'accounting doctrine'; that is, the non-binding opinions published by the CNC referred to above, and also the interpretation of the regulations in force by the professions: the accountants and the auditors.

The OEC, representing the association of accountants, is mainly responsible for setting the rules of the profession and for regulating its members. While it participates indirectly in the accounting standard setting process of the CNC through elected representatives, the OEC directly provides its members with its interpretation of extant accounting regulation. The OEC statements on accounting issues are defined as opinions (*avis*) and are part of the French accounting doctrine, while the rules on professional conduct, defined as *normes,* are mandatory. In addition the OEC publishes a journal, *Revue française de la comptabilité,* and a general handbook for the use of its members.

Albeit a member of the CNC, the CNCC, in comparison to the OEC, is less active in the interpretation of accounting issues. Its main task is to define standards of professional practice and to provide interpretations on technical issues. The association publishes numerous journals, such as the *Guide des Commissaires aux Comptes,* the *Telex Commissaires* and the *Bulletin du Conseil National des Commissaires aux Comptes,* which are concerned with the regulation of the auditors.

---

[3] The statutory power of the COB was increased in Law of 2 August 1989, which permitted the COB to sanction practices which contravene its regulations.

The French accounting regime is currently subject to major reforms. Recently, an important legal amendment to the composition and the authority of the CNC has reformed it, by reducing membership from 103 to 58, thus making it a more flexible body. In fact, the law of 26 April 1996 modified the institutional structure of the CNC with a view to giving direct legal authority to issue accounting regulation to the CNC through the new *Comité de Règlementation Comptable* (CRC). A White Paper launched by the French accountancy profession in May 1997 has been relatively critical on the degree of detail of current French accounting principles (Accountancy, March 1998). Furthermore, recent legislation of March 1998 gives companies whose shares are listed on a regulated EU or other foreign stock exchange the option to prepare their consolidated accounts by applying IAS, provided that the relevant IAS has been translated into French and that it has been adopted by the CRC.

Table 3.3

The sources of accounting regulation in France

Legislation	Standard	Recommendation
Law	Accounting standardisation	Accounting Doctrine
Commercial Code Art. 8-17 *(Code de Commerce)*	*Conseil National de la Comptabilité*	*Conseil National de la Comptabilité* Opinions
Law of 24 July 1966 on Commercial Companies *(Loi sur les Sociétés Commerciales)*		*Ordre des Experts Comptables* -*Avis* -*Revue française de la Comptabilité*
Law (83-353) of 30 April 1983		*Compagnie Nationale des Commissaires aux Comptes*
Law (85-11) of 3 January 1985		-*Guide des Commissaires aux Comptes*
Decree		-*Telex Commissaires*
Decree (83-1020) of 29 November 1983		-*Bulletin du Conseil National des commissaires aux comptes*
Decree of 17 February 1986		
National Accounting Plan *(Plan Comptable Général)*		
COB Instructions *(Instructions)*		

Germany

In Germany, accounting regulation is currently undergoing similar substantial institutional changes. Traditionally, accounting regulation has been enacted by the legislature and, accordingly, has been approved by parliament. As can be seen in Table 3.4, in contrast to all the other countries under investigation, until the present time there has been no other type of regulation in Germany, either in the form of delegated legislation through government departments or in the form of a governmental or professional accounting standard agency.[4] The current reforms aim to establish a *Bilanzrat*, set up by representatives of industry, the audit profession and academia, as a private accounting standardisation council with the task of reforming the existing German consolidation regulations and of representing Germany at the IASC (Frankfurter Allgemeine Zeitung, 14 February 1998). Furthermore, a bill passed through the lower house of parliament on 27 March 1998 which exempted German companies which use either IAS or US GAAP from presenting their consolidated financial statements in accordance with German consolidation regulation.

This is a break with the traditionally legalistic character of German accounting, which is instituted as part[5] of the Commercial Code (*Handelsgesetzbuch*, HGB). Of considerable importance in Germany are the legally codified principles of *Grundsätze ordnungsmäßiger Buchführung* (GoB) which fill a legal vacuum in the case of loopholes and ambiguities in the law. In the absence of a standard setting body, legal interpretations of the GoB, the general principles of 'proper bookkeeping', close to a considerable extent remaining gaps in accounting regulation. GoB are often the basis for an intensive exchange of arguments between academics and practitioners (Busse von Colbe, 1992) who contribute to the development of a body of very detailed rules by deductive reasoning (Leffson, 1987). There is in Germany a vast literature of legal interpretations, published in journals on accounting and collected as law commentaries[6] and financial accounting handbooks[7]. In addition, the *Institut der Wirtschaftsprüfer* (IdW), which represents the audit profession, publishes position statements (*Stellungnahmen*), based on interpretations of GoB. These are recommendations on specific accounting questions which, although not binding in a contractual sense for its members, may be regarded as authoritative in the event of a judicial dispute (Ballwieser, 1995). The statements of the Schmalenbach Society for Business Economics (*Schmalenbachgesellschaft für Betriebswirtschaft*) on

---

[4] Albeit 'informal' consultations between government and interest groups, such as industry associations, the *Institut der Wirtschaftsprüfer* (IdW), trade unions, academics, etc. are common during the legislative process (Ordelheide, 1997a).
[5] Third Book §§238-341 of the HGB
[6] Adler/Düring/Schmalz; Küting/Weber
[7] Castan/Heymann/Müller/Ordelheide/Scheffler 1987

specific accounting problems may also be taken into consideration by reporting companies. Finally, firm-specific rules based on the interpretation of existing accounting regulations are developed by large corporations and distributed to subsidiaries in form of accounting manuals, with the aim of consolidation under a uniform set of rules.

In addition, a system of detailed tax legislation and court decisions on tax related accounting issues by the Federal Fiscal Court (*Bundesfinanzhof*) are of practical importance for accounting purposes. This follows directly from the unified income approach to commercial and tax accounting, the so-called authoritativeness principle (Maßgeblichkeitsprinzip) laid down in §5(1) of the Income Tax Law (*Einkommensteuergesetz*). This requires that, in the absence of specific tax rules, the determination of taxable profit must be in accordance with the principles of proper bookkeeping (GoB) codified in the HGB. In turn, Income Tax Implementing Orders (*Einkommensteuerdurchführungs-verordnungen*), judicial interpretations by tax courts of GoB and specific tax legislation are of practical relevance for company accounts.

The German system of accounting rules has been described by Ordelheide (1998) as a hierarchical system in which rules become more detailed when descending through the levels of the hierarchy, with the incomplete and unclear rules established at one level being further elaborated at one or other of the following levels.

However, the sub-levels of the text of law, which are described as 'interpretations' and 'elaborations' of the law, possess a different degree of authority. In fact, only court decisions derive their authority from the commercial code, while the rules issued at subsequent levels, such as statements of private organisations, legal commentaries and interpretative articles have 'expert authority' only and are not legally binding.

Table 3.4

The sources of accounting regulation in Germany

LEGISLATION	RECOMMENDATIONS
Parliament	Institute of Auditors
	Institut der Wirtschaftsprüfer
§§ 238-341 Third Book Commercial Code	
Handelsgesetzbuch	
Grundsätze ordnungsmäßiger Buchführung	*Stellungnahmen*
	Schmalenbach Society for Business Economics
Federal Supreme Court	*Schmalenbach Gesellschaft für Betriebswirtschaft*
Court decisions on financial reporting	*Stellungnahmen*
	Individual Experts, lawyers, auditors, academics
Ministry of Finance	
	Law commentaries
	Bilanzkommentare
Tax specific legislation	
Einkommensteuergesetz	
Einkommensteuerdurchführungsverordnungen	
Einkommensteuerrichtlinien	
Federal Fiscal Court	
Court decisions on tax law with practical relevance for financial reporting	

Belgium

In Belgium, the codified tradition of law has also dominated the regulation of accounting. In this case, however, accounting legislation is usually issued in the form of a decree (*besluit/arrêté*) which does not pass through parliament but is instead approved by members of the government. Albeit set up by the government for the development of accounting regulation, the activity of the Belgian standard setting commission has been confined to the interpretation of existing legislation. Table 3.5 summarises the Belgian sources of accounting regulation.

The Central Economic Council plays a special role in the establishment of Belgian accounting law, advising the government and parliament on accounting matters. The Council, which is composed of employer and employee representatives, provides policy recommendations, either upon request or voluntarily. The Council's advice thereby has a direct influence on the draft laws, even though the responsibility for the enactment of the various laws and decrees rests with the legislature and the executive (Lefebvre and van Nuffel, 1998). The Accounting Law of 17 July 1975[8] provides only the framework of financial reporting and the Royal Decree of 8 October 1976[9] sets out valuation rules and the format and content of the annual accounts. The Royal Decree of 6 March 1990[10] deals with consolidated accounts implementing the Seventh Directive.

Belgian accounting legislation appears to be very detailed. According to Jorissen and Block (1995, p. 391), the preparers of financial statements in Belgium "prefer detailed rules to general legal principles which have to be applied in different situations. This is partly due to the fact that they are used to working under a codified law system. Further given the importance of taxation in accounting and the concept of *dirigisme* in Belgium, both demanding conformity, the exercise of individual judgements has been unfamiliar to accountants and preparers of financial statements. There is no tradition among practicioners of applying general accounting principles to specific cases".

The degree of detail of extant decrees in accounting regulation may explain the relative unimportance of the Belgian Accounting Standards Commission (*Commissie voor Boekhoudkundige Normen / Commission des Normes*

---

[8] *Loi du 17 juillet 1975 relative à la comptabilité et aux comptes annuels des entreprises Wet van 17 juli 1975 op de boekhouding en de jaarrekening van de ondernemingen.*
[9] *Arrêté royal du 8 octobre 1976 relatives aux comptes annuels des entreprises/Koninklijk Besluit van 8 oktober 1976 met betrekking tot de jaarrekening van de ondernemingen.*
[10] *Arrêté royal du 6 mars 1990 relatif aux comptes consolidés des entreprises/Konijklijk besluit van 6 maart 1990 op de geconsolideerde jaarrekening van de ondernemingen.*

Comptables, CNC). In fact, even though this public body[11] was established with the purpose of advising the government and parliament and of formulating accounting rules by way of opinions, most of the *bulletins* issued by the CNC have been limited to the interpretation of existing accounting legislation (Jorisson and Block, 1995). The members of the CNC are representatives of the government, the Banking and Finance Commission, the professional institutes of auditors and of accountants and the small business organisations as well as individual experts selected by the Central Economic Council. By March 1995, the CNC had published 34 *bulletins* (Bollen and van Nuffel, 1997). The rules contained therein are considered to be authoritative pronouncements to help companies interpret the law, even though these do not have the force of law.

Apart from their membership in the CNC, the professional bodies in the field of auditing and accounting remain passive with regard to the regulation of financial reporting in Belgium. However, in accordance with their individual capacity, each of the three institutes exercises an indirect impact: the Institute of Auditors (*Instituut der Bedrijfsrevisoren/Institut des Reviseurs d'Entreprises*) by being responsible for the formulation of auditing standards; the Institute of Accountants (*Instituut van Accountants/Institut des Experts Comptables*), by imposing sanctions in cases where the rules of conduct are contravened; and the Institute of Bookkeepers (*Instituut van Boekhouders/Institut Professionel des Comptables*), by advising the accountants not represented by the two other institutes. The opinions on accounting problems issued by the professional organisations are not published but only communicated to their members.

It should be noted that in order to allow Belgian companies to use IAS or US GAAP for consolidation, the Minister of Economics has been empowered to exempt, on request, such enterprises from Belgian rules for consolidated financial statements. However, the conditions for exemption have not yet been published (IASC Insight, March 1998).

---

[11] Instituted under Law of 17 July 1975.

Table 3.5

The sources of accounting regulation in Belgium

1. Legislative Sources of Accounting Regulation enacted by Parliament and Government under the advise of the Central Economic Council

(i) Law

Law of 17 July 1975 *(Loi du 17 juillet 1975 relative à la comptabilité et aux comptes annuels des entreprises Wet van 17 juli 1975 op de boekhouding en de jaarrekening van de ondernemingen)* This law was amended by the laws of 30 March 1976, 24 March 1978, 1 July 1983 and 30 December 1991 and by the Royal Decrees of 15 December 1878 and 12 September 1983.

(ii) Royal Decree

Royal Decree of 8 October 1976 *(Arrêté royal du 8 octobre 1976 relatives aux comptes annuels des entreprises/Koninklijk Besluit van 8 oktober 1976 met betrekking tot de jaarrekening van de ondernemingen)* This Royal Decree was amended several times by the Royal Decree of 12 December 1977, 7 March 1978, 14 February 1979, 12 September 1983, 5 March 1985, 6 November 1987, 30 December 1991 and 3 December 1993.

The Royal Decree of 6 March 1990 *(Arrêté royal du 6 mars 1990 relatif aux comptes consolidés des entreprises/Koninklijk besluit van 6 maart 1990 op de geconsolideerde jaarrekening van de ondernemingen)*

2. Rules issued by the Accounting Standards Commission (*Commissie voor Boekhoudkundige Normen / Commission des Normes Comptables*, CBN).

The 34 CBN Bulletins published in 1995 interpreted articles of the

Law of 17 July 1975
Royal Decree of 8 October 1976
Royal Decree of 12 September 1983
Royal Decree of 6 March 1990

3. Rules issued by non-authoritative bodies

The Institute of Auditors (*Instituut der Bedrijfsrevisoren/Institut des Reviseurs d'Entreprises*) Publication of auditing standards

The Institute of Accountants (*Instituut van Accountants/Institut des Experts Comptables*) Rules of conduct

Institute of Bookkeepers (*Instituut van Boekhouders/Institut Professionel des Comptables*) Advise other accountants

Spain

In Spain, accounting regulation has become legalistic following the country's entry into in the European Union and in particular following the enactment of Law No. 19 of 1989 which reformed Spanish corporate law in line with the European Company Law Directives. This development has been enforced by the establishment of the Accounting and Audit Institute (*Instituto de Contabilidad y Auditoria de Cuentas,* ICAC) which, as an autonomous government agency under the Ministry of Economics and Financial Affairs, has undertaken responsibility for developing regulation on accounting and auditing since 1989. In addition, the Bank of Spain (*Banco de España*), the Commission surveying the stock market (*Comisión National del Mercado de Valores*), the State Audit Agency (*Intervención General de la Administración del Estado*) and the Directorate General of Insurance (*Dirección General de Seguros*), oversee accounting regulation in their respective sectors of the economy in association with ICAC. Nonetheless, as can be seen in Table 3.6, private standard setting which, prior to the legal reforms, promoted the development of Spanish accounting regulation, continues to be influential.

The legislative instruments governing accounting are detailed and vary in status. They include law (*ley*), royal decree (*real decreto*), ministerial order (*orden ministerial*), resolution (*resolución*) and circular (*circular*). The parliament and the council of ministers formally approve laws and royal decrees which have been prepared by ICAC and the Ministry of Economic and Financial Affairs. ICAC makes proposals for updating the National Chart of Accounts (*Plan General de Contabilidad*, PGC) and its sectorial adaptations and for implementing other legal accounting rules. For instance, ICAC prepared the 1990 version of the PGC, which was approved by Royal Decree 1643/1990 as well as the regulations for the preparation of consolidated annual accounts, approved by Royal Decree 1815/1991 (*Normas para la formulacíon de las cuentas anuales consolidadas*). Royal Decree 1643/1990 empowered the Ministry of Economic and Financial Affairs and ICAC to issue mandatory accounting regulations. Both ICAC and the Ministry have made use of these extended delegated legislative powers: ICAC has issued rules in the form of resolutions, most of which concern the valuation rules in the PGC; the Ministry of Economic and Financial Affairs has issued a number of Ministerial Orders, following the recommendations of ICAC (López and Rivero, 1995). The ICAC is advised by a Consultative Committee which has two technical subcommittees: the Accounting Committee and the Auditing Committee.

In its function of controlling the activities of banks and other financial institutions, the Central Bank of Spain has legal power to enact accounting rules for banks. These are issued in the form of circulars in conformity with the

European Directive on accounting for banks. Similarly, the Directorate General of Insurance, as an agency of the Ministry of Economic and Financial Affairs, has the legal power to regulate the preparation of financial statements by insurance companies, while the State Audit Agency performs the same function for public sector companies. Finally, the National Securities Market Commission issues mandatory accounting regulation for investment firms and intermediaries; that is, agencies that settle and clear stock market transactions. These regulatory powers do however not extend to listed companies themselves (Gonzalo and Gallizo, 1992).

Tax legislation, which has traditionally been a deterministic source of accounting legislation in Spain, continues to be of practical importance even though the link between accounting and taxation has been abolished by law with the implementation of EC directives. A remaining link concerns the revaluation of certain fixed assets for both tax and accounting purposes in accordance with inflation indices published by the government[12]. In 1996 a new tax revaluation law permitted companies the restatement of fixed assets based on defined price-level indexation and allowed deviation from the accounting legislation which prescribes the historic cost principle in financial statements.

Standard setting by the accounting profession is inextricably linked with the Spanish Accounting and Business Administration Association (*Asociación Española de Contabilidad y Administración de Empresas*, AECA) which was established in 1979. Its four instituted commissions cover the areas of (i) accounting principles and standards, (ii) company valuation, (iii) management accounting and (iv) organisation and methods and have to date issued 18 documents on accounting principles and standards (*Principios y normas de contabilidad en España*). The AECA documents cover all the main components of financial statements and in its first statement AECA defined a conceptual framework for financial reporting. The standards published by AECA are considered to be of great practical importance. According to Canibano and Cea (1998) a substantial part of the 1990 PCG was based on accounting regulations formerly issued by AECA. The audit profession considers AECA documents to be valid supplements to legislative accounting regulation, particularly those concerning aspects which have not been dealt with by law.

None of the three professional auditing bodies in Spain - the Institute of Chartered Accountants (*Instituto de Auditores-Censores Juados de Cuentas de España*), the Register of Economist-Auditors (*Registro de Economistas Auditores*) and the Register of Commerce Graduate-Auditors (*Registro de Titulares Mercantiles Auditores*) are directly involved in the regulation of

---

[12] Such revaluation laws were passed in the period between 1961 and 1983.

accounting. However, by issuing technical standards and rules of conduct to their members these bodies inevitably deal with the content and presentation of financial statements and provide opinions. Moreover, by translating IAS into Spanish, the Institute of Chartered Accountants has greatly aided the influence of international standards on Spanish accounting.

A further source of accounting regulation in Spain comes from university researchers, academics who not only have an influence through the publication of books and journal articles, but who also give their expert opinion to the committees which prepare draft statements on accounting regulation.

Table 3.6

The sources of accounting regulation in Spain

Legislation	Standard	Recommendations
Law enacted by Parliament	Accounting standardisation by ICAC	Issued by the auditing bodies
Commercial Code		Institute of Chartered Accountants *Instituto de Auditores-Censores Jurados*
Law 19 of 25 July 1989	Accounting principles and standards by AECA	
Royal Decree approved by the Spanish Council of Ministers and the Parliament		Register of Economist-Auditors *Registro de Economistas Auditores*
1643 of 20 December 1990		Register of Commerce Graduates-Auditors *Registro de Titulares Mercantiles Auditores de Cuentas de Espana*
1815 of 20 December 1991		
Other legislative accounting regulation		Comments by individual academics
Plan General de Contabilidad prepared by ICAC, approved through royal decree		
Ministerial Orders issued by the Ministry of Economy and Finance		
Resolutions published by ICAC Circulars issued by the Bank of Spain		
Insurance regulation issued the Directorate General of Insurance		
Security Market Law issued by Commission surveying the stock market		
State Industry Regulation by the the State Audit Agency		

Italy

Accounting regulation in Italy derives its authority solely from the state, not only through the provisions of the Civil Code (*Codice Civile*) but also in form of detailed legislative decrees, law decrees and presidential decrees. In addition, fiscal law is influential, as are clarifying orders from government ministries and rulings in the Italian courts. The stock market regulator (*Commissione Nazionale per le Società e la Borsa*, CONSOB) is empowered by law and in turn requires that listed companies follow the accounting principles of the *Commissione per la Statuizione dei Principi Contabili* (CSPC). In spite of the variety of legal instruments, a number of institutions assist companies in interpreting accounting law. The Italian regulatory regime is summarised in Table 3.7.

Accounting legislation is contained in a number of legal instruments. The basic regulatory framework is codified in Articles 2423 to 2435 bis of the Civil Code. Parliamentary law (*legge*) is enacted by parliament after a law proposal has been prepared by a special parliamentary committee and the bill has been discussed in parliament. The parliament may also empower the government to enact legislative decrees (*decreti legislativi*) through a delegating law (legge delega). For instance, for the revision of the Civil Code in order to implement the Fourth and Seventh European Directives, a proposal was prepared by the D'Alessandro Commission of the Ministry of Justice on 14 April 1986. Bill No. 1519 of 6 January 1989 by the Council of Ministers proposed that the implementation of the EC directives be delegated to the government. Law No. 69 of 26 March 1990[13] delegated to the government the responsibility for the incorporation of the Fourth and Seventh Directive into Italian law, and this was eventually enacted through Legislative Decree No. 127 of 9 April 1991.

Law decrees (*decreti legge*) must be submitted to parliament for enactment on the day that they are issued and then confirmed in law within 60 days. As they become immediately effective, such law decrees are reserved for urgent cases only, but the practicality of this accelerated mode of legislating has made it a frequently used instrument (Riccaboni, 1998). A further element of the structure of legislative accounting regulation in Italy are the presidential decrees which are issued as adjuncts to legislation. For instance, while Law No. 216 of 7 July 1974 gave CONSOB the power of surveillance of the information disclosed by companies listed on the Italian stock exchange, this law also enabled the government to enact rules on accounting and auditing, which were subsequently implemented by presidential decrees. Further legislative powers may be exercised autonomously by ministers. However, so called ministerial decrees

---

[13] According to Riccaboni and Ghirri (1994), this law added only very few innovations to the 1986 draft made by the D'Alessandro Commission.

(*decreti ministeriali*) and circulars (*circolari*) are issued with the aim of providing legal clarification and have less authority than the law itself. The responsibility for accounting legislation concerning banks and financial institutions has been delegated through a legislative decree[14] and a ministerial decree[15] to the Bank of Italy.

A strong influence of tax legislation on financial reporting is evident in a number of accounting areas, even though contradictions within the Consolidated Law on Income Tax (*Testo Unico delle Imposte sul Reddito*, TUIR) mean that the dependence of corporate profit on tax rules is not straightforward. An example of the use of tax legislation in financial statements is the revaluation of assets which are issued at irregular intervals by the government with certain fiscal objectives.

As noted earlier, CONSOB was given legal power to issue regulation with respect to the financial reporting of listed companies. In particular, it required the preparation of consolidated accounts long before the Seventh Directive was enacted. In 1982, CONSOB granted official recognition to the regulations issued by the CSPC through Resolution No. 1079. In cases where these principles were insufficient, CONSOB recommended the application of IAS, provided that these were not conflict with Italian law.

With respect to professional self-regulation, the main contributors to the development of accounting rules are the national associations of auditors (*Consiglio nazionale dei dottori commercialisti,* CNDC) and of accountants (*Consiglio nazionale dei ragionieri,* CNR). The Commission for the Establishment of Accounting Principles (*Commissione per la statuizione dei principi contabili,* CSPC) is composed of equal representations of both the CNDC and the CNR. The CSPC is supported by a large number of working committees, in which not only the profession, but also academics and representatives of CONSOB participate. Apart from the official endorsement by CONSOB, referred to above, the CSPC has never been given formal acknowledgement in law. However, the CSPC is perceived as a standard setting body in Italy (Riccaboni, 1998).

Interpretations of extant accounting legislation are provided by a number of institutions, in addition to those mentioned above. Another association representing auditors (*Associazione Italiana Revisori Contabili,* ASSIREVI) has published research documents (*documento di ricerca*) dealing for instance with differences between the Civil Code and the CSPC regulations. The

---

[14] Decreto legislativo 87 of 27 January 1992
[15] Decreto ministerialo of 24 June 1992

association representing the interests of Italian limited liability companies (*Associazione fra le Società Italiane per Azioni*, ASSONIME) assists such companies in interpreting the law, particularly through its circulars (*circolari*).

Table 3.7

The sources of accounting regulation in Italy

Legislation	Standards	Recommendations
Parliament	Commissione per la Statuizione dei Principi Contabili (CSPC)	Assonime Circulars Circolare
Parliamentary law *Legge*	Documents *Principi Contabili*	Assirevi Research Documents *Documento di ricerca*
Civil Code, Art.2423-2435 *Codice Civile*		ADC
Government Ministry of Finance		Rules of conduct

Legislation (continued)

Government
Ministry of Finance

    Decreti Legislativi
    e.g. Legislative Decree 127 of 1991

    e.g. Legislative Decree 216 of 1974

    Law Decree
    Decreti legge

    Ministerial Decree
    Decreti Ministeriali

    Circulars
    Circolare

Courts

    Judicial rulings

Ministry of Finance

    Related tax regulation
    Testo Unico delle Imposte
    sul Reddito
    (Art. 52, 75)
    Revaluation laws:
    Law 576 of 02.12.1975
    Law 72 of 19.03.1983
    Law 408 of 29.12.1990
    Law 413 of 30.12. 1991

CONSOB

    Circulars *(Circolare)*
    Resolution No. 1079 of 1989

Denmark

In Denmark, a combination of public and private institutions contributes to the development of accounting regulation, there being a history of explicit arrangements to avoid parliamentary involvement in highly technical matters concerning the regulation in accounting (Christiansen, 1998). It is noteworthy that accounting legislation for individual accounts and group accounts has been promulgated by different institutional powers. While the group accounting rules were incorporated in a special Financial Statements Order published by the Ministry of Industry, the accounting rules for individual accounts were enacted in the Financial Statements Act approved by Parliament. It is also worth noting that, on a number of occasions, structural reforms of the financial reporting regime followed cases of non-compliance and fraud in Denmark.

The implementation of the EC directives considerably increased the degree of legislative accounting regulation in Denmark. The Financial Statements Act (*Årsregnskabsloven*) implemented the Fourth Directive in 1981 and was accompanied by a Financial Statements Order (*Årsregnskabsbekendtgørelsen*). The Bookkeeping Act (*Bogføringsloven,* Statutory Order No. 60) of 19 February 1986 contains general rules concerning the keeping of books for all Danish businesses but no rules on the preparation of annual accounts which are dealt with in the Bookkeeping Order (*Bogføringsbekendtgørelsen,* Order No. 598) of 21 August 1990. In 1991, the Financial Statements Act was revised for the implementation of the Seventh Directive. However, the basic provisions relating to the format and content of group accounts were adopted in a Financial Statements Order (*Årsregnskabsbekendtgørelsen)* and an accompanying Ministerial Guideline. According to Christiansen (1995), even though the implementation of the Fourth and Seventh Directive brought significant changes in Danish accounting practice, Danish accounting regulation has remained fairly flexible.

Denmark has two official accounting standard setting bodies: the Accounting Panel (*Regnskabspanelet*), which was set up as a professional standard setting body and the Accounting Council (*Regnskabsrådet)* which has only recently been instituted[16] by the Government. The Institute of State-Authorized Public Accountants (*Foreningen af Statsautoriserede Revisorer,* FSR*)* after initially endorsing IAS, started to issue accounting standards (*Regnskabsvejledninger*) in 1988. By 1995, it had published nine accounting standards and two exposure drafts. Until 1992, the FSR Accounting Committee (*Regnskabsteknisk Udvalg*) drafted the standards which were, after a period of discussion, eventually adopted by the FSR. The *Regnskabspanelet* was set up by the FSR in 1992 in order to increase the involvement in standard setting to other parties with an

---

[16] Under Investigation Act 1994

interest in financial reporting, such as the Copenhagen Stock Exchange, which endorses standards set by the Accounting Panel. In particular, Information Obligations for Issuers of Listed Securities (*Oplysningsforpligtelser for udstedere of børsnoterede værdipapirer*, OUBV) require that the annual accounts of companies quoted on the stock exchange be prepared in compliance with Danish accounting standards (OUBV, section 15).

In addition to standard setting, the Danish accounting profession (FSR) publishes opinions in two professional journals: the *Revision & Regnkabsvæsen* and in the *Revisorbladet*. In addition, law commentaries (*Årsregnskaber - Kommentarer til regnskabs*-lovgivningen) by individual experts, assist companies in interpreting the legal provisions. The Danish regulatory regime is summarised in Table 3.8.

Table 3.8

The sources of accounting regulation in Denmark

1. Legislative accounting regulation

(I) Laws enacted by Parliament

Bookkeeping Act
Bogføringsloven

Financial Statements Act
Årsregnskabsloven

(ii) Ministerial Orders promulgated by the Ministry of Business and Industry

Bookkeeping Order
Bogføringsbekendtgørelsen

Financial Statement Order
Årsregnskabsbekendtgørelsen

(iii) Ministerial guidelines issued by the Ministry of Business and Industry

Ministerial Guideline concerning Bookkeeping

Ministerial Guideline concerning Group Accounts

(iv) Information Obligation for Issuers of Listed Securities (*Oplysningsforpligtelser for udstedere of børsnoterede værdipapirer)* published by the Copenhagen Stock Exchange

2. Rules issued by Institute of State-Authorized Public Accountants
Foreningen af Statsautoriserede Revisorer, FSR

Danish Accounting Standards issued by the Accounting Panel (*Regnskabspanelet)*
Regnskabsvejledninger

3. Rules issued by non-authoritative bodies

(i) Commentaries on accounting regulation

Årsregnskaber - Kommentarer til regnskabs-lovgivningen

(ii) Professional Journals

Revision & Regnskabsvæsen

Revisorbladet

United Kingdom

The legislation of accounting has traditionally been rather unimportant in the UK. Instead, accounting regulation has been largely developed by the audit profession and issued as statements of 'best accounting practice'. However, in recent years accounting standards and legislation have become increasingly 'intertwined' in the UK (Bromwich and Hopwood, 1992). The Companies Act of 1985 provided for a much more complete codification of accounting regulation by introducing the EC Fourth Directive. It was, however, the Dearing report, published in 1988, which introduced the radical reforms to the UK accounting regulatory system in 1990, when the Accounting Standards Board (ASB) together with a set of constituted bodies took over responsibility for the preparation of accounting standards from the Accounting Standards Committee (ASC). The present regulatory arrangements are described below.

The Companies Act 1981 implemented the EC Fourth Directive which introduced legal requirements in company law concerning the form and content of accounts, as well as basic accounting principles such as accruals, consistency and prudence. Hence, a substantial part of accounting regulation that had previously been delegated to the accounting profession was now regulated by company law (Gordon and Gray, 1994). Like the Fourth Directive, the Seventh Directive, implemented by the Companies Act 1989, extended the scope of company law into areas which had previously been the preserve of accounting standards. Also, it incorporated the legislative changes that the Dearing Report recommended and this resulted in an enhanced position for accounting standards. In particular, the 1989 Companies Act introduced a requirement for the directors of large companies to state whether the annual accounts are in accordance with applicable accounting standards and to indicate details and reasons for any material departures. Nevertheless, it is important to note that the British government, in implementing the legal reforms to the status of accounting standards, explicitly avoided giving statutory force to accounting standards and instead endorsed the view that standard setting should remain a private sector activity in the UK[17].

As shown in Figure 3.3, the present regulatory structure is placed under the umbrella of a Financial Reporting Council (FRC) which is responsible for the general guidance of the ASB with regard to policies and work programme and for securing sufficient financing for the regulatory system[18]. The Chairman and

---

[17] The Dearing recommendations on presumption of support for standards in the courts, and that the burden of proof should be on those justifying departure from standard accounting practice were also rejected by the Government because, similarly, they were considered too close to giving standards statutory authority (Turley, 1992).

[18] The FRC's finances are provided to one third from the Department of Trade and Industry, to one third from the Consultative Committee of Accountancy Bodies (CCAB), with the balance provided by the London Stock Exchange and the banking community.

the three deputy chairmen are representatives from the profession, the Stock Exchange and the industry and are all appointed by the Secretary of State for Trade and Industry and the Governor of the Bank of England. It is important to note, that formally the FRC has no say in the development of specific policies for inclusion in any individual standard (Turley, 1992). The actual responsibility for setting standards goes to the members of the Accounting Standards Board (ASB), appointed by the FRC. The Board publishes standards on its own authority and these are not subject to formal approval by the FRC or other groups. The ASB is supported by a full-time Chairman and a technical Director as well as by ten part-time members.

The element which is concerned with the enforcement aspects of the system, is the Financial Reporting Review Panel (FRRP). This Panel is independent of the ASB and was established by the FRC to examine the non-compliance of accounting standards by large companies. The Panel is headed by a lawyer and has 20 members appointed by the FRC. The actions of the Review Panel have so far been confined to obtaining the agreement of the companies concerned that they will amend non-compliance in subsequent years (Cooke and Wallace, 1995). However, the Panel also might ask that accounts be reissued, and if necessary, might even institute court proceedings to require the company concerned to do so. By 1996 no such court action had been taken, although preliminary steps had been initiated (Hopwood and Vieten, 1998).

A further element in the regulatory structure for financial reporting in the UK, is the Urgent Issues Task Force (UITF) which was created in 1991 as a committee of the ASB. Its duty is to respond to urgent issues not covered satisfactorily by existing company law and accounting standards, either in the case of new and emergent areas of accounting or where controversial interpretations of extant regulations are developing. Albeit subject to acceptance by the ASB, the conclusions of the Task Force are published in abstract form. These abstracts are not mandatory, but are expected to be observed, as they form the basis for what determines a 'true and fair view'(Gordon and Gray, 1994).

Since FRS 5, 'Reporting the Substance of Transactions', was issued in April 1994, accountants have been required to assess and report the 'economic reality' of the reporting entity. The perceived need for a standard to regulate the reporting of the substance of transactions has followed the growth of multidivisional firms and off balance sheet financing schemes. Rather than formalising innovations *ex post*, the ASB attempts to shape accounting in the name of a wider set of principles (Tweedy and Whittington, 1990). However, even though the economic impact of new accounting rules has been explicitly integrated as an argument in the rule-making process by the ASB, it would be incorrect to generalise that economic substance prevails in the totality of UK accounting rules. In fact, only recent rules have been issued by the ASB, while the majority of standards are those issued by the old ASC.

Figure 3.3

The framework of accounting regulation in the United Kingdom

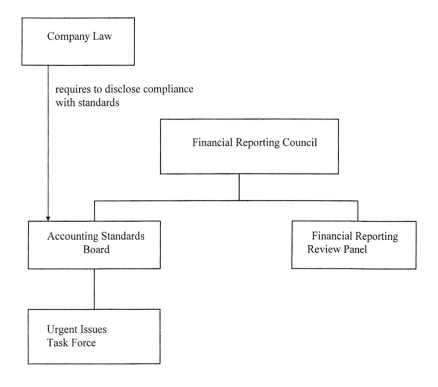

Ireland

Traditionally, Ireland has closely linked the regulation of accounting to the UK regulatory framework and this dependence was maintained to a large extent after the recent reforms of the UK accounting system and the establishment of the ASB in London.

In fact, Ireland is represented via both the Government and the accountancy profession in the UK's FRC, although it is not a member of the ASB. However, there appears to be substantial informal contact between the ASB and the Irish accountancy profession - particularly the Institute of Chartered Accountants in Ireland (ICAI) which promulgates the ASB's standards in Ireland with the approval of the Irish Government (Cahill, 1998).

It should be noted, however, that there are important differences in the regulatory frameworks of accounting between Ireland and the UK, and these have implications for the monitoring and enforcement of accounting standards in Ireland. Firstly, unlike the Companies Acts in the UK, Irish Company Law does not legally endorse the standards issued by the ASB. In fact, in Ireland, even though the standards issued by the ASB are applicable, there is no equivalent statutory support. The authority of ASB standards is based only on the legal requirement that accounts must give a true and fair view as provisioned in the Irish Company Act of 1986 (Quinn and Sørensen, 1997). Secondly, the UK's Review Panel does not monitor Irish companies and as there is no corresponding Irish Review Panel, the function of enforcing standards remains with the auditor.

It is worth mentioning, however, that Irish listing rules require public companies to comply not only with national company law but also with UK accounting standards, as well as US GAAP and IAS. Figure 3.4 summarises the framework of accounting regulation in Ireland.

Figure 3.4

The framework of accounting regulation in Ireland

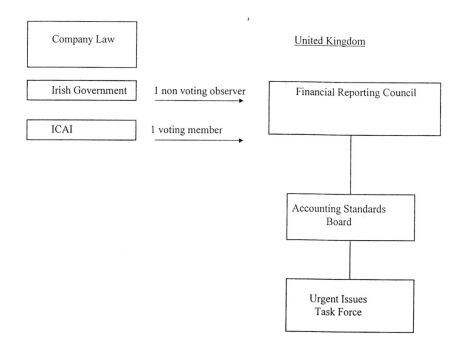

The Netherlands
In the Netherlands, accounting regulation is based on two principal sources: Parliamentary legislation and the Guidelines (*Richtlijnen*) published by the Council on Annual Reporting (*Raad voor de Jaarverslaggeving*). The Enterprise Chamber (*Ondernehmingskamer*) has contributed jurisprudence to a number of financial reporting cases. Also, the theoretical works of individual accountants have played an influential role in reporting practice, while other regulatory bodies such as the stock exchange are relatively unimportant. Table 3.9 summarises the Dutch financial reporting regime.

The legislative source of financial reporting regulation is the Dutch parliament which enacts, upon the initiative of the Ministry of Justice, relevant legislation in Title 9, Book 2 of the Civil Code (*Burgerlijk Wetboek*). The Social and Economic Council (*Sociaal-Economische Raad*, SER), which represents employers and employees as well as individual experts, has the function of providing advice on draft legislation. In parliament, draft law passes through the second chamber (*Tweede Kamer*) before the first chamber (*Eerste Kamer*) decides upon the final approval of the proposed legislation. Large sections of the Civil Code relating to financial reporting are, however, restricted to disclosure requirements, while the code contains only some general clauses concerning the valuation of assets and liabilities (Klaassen and Heekers, 1995). In order to comply with European Company Law Directives, the Ministry of Justice has issued a number of administrative orders containing more detailed rules with regard to the layout of the financial statements[19] and the application of current value accounting[20].

With regard to the financial sector, sections of company law dealing with the financial reporting of banks and insurance companies were included in Title 9 of Book 2 of the Civil Code in 1993. In the same year, an administrative order implemented further detailed regulations concerning the financial statements of banks[21].

Compliance with the law is enforced by a special court, the Enterprise Chamber (*Ondernehmingskamer*, OK), which is a chamber of the Court of Justice in Amsterdam, and specialises in disputes between companies and other parties with an interest in financial reporting. Since it was instituted in 1977, the Chamber has given its verdict in approximately fifty complaints. However, in

---

[19] *Besluit tot vaststelling van model schema's voor de inrichting van jaarrekening*, Staatsblad, 30.12.1983, no.666.
[20] *Besluit houdende regels voor de inhoud, de grenzen en de wijze van toepassing in de jaarrekening van waardering van activa tegen actuele waarde*, Staatsblad , 30.12.1983, no. 665.

[21] *Besluit houdende bepalingen voor de balans, de winst-en verliesrekening en de toelichtingen daarop van banken*, Staatsblad, 27 May 1993, no. 259.

recent years the number of new cases has declined. In fact, most of the complaints had been put forward by the Foundation to Investigate Company Reporting (*Stichting Onderzoek Bedrijfs-Informatie*, SOBI), a public interest group concerned with the quality of financial reporting, but which has withdrawn from this activity in the last few years[22]. The judicial rulings of the OK, especially when they enjoy general application, have the status of law in the Netherlands (Zeff *et al.* 1992).

The lack of comprehensive and detailed accounting legislation in the Netherlands, has provided the initiative for the Council on Annual Reporting (*Raad voor de Jaarverslaggeving*, RJ) and its predecessor, the Tripartite Accounting Study Group (*Tripartite Overleg*, TO) to define accounting regulations that are 'acceptable in the economic and social climate'[23]. Without granting legal recognition to the RJ, this view was confirmed by the Minister of Justice in the Explanatory Memorandum which accompanied the draft law on the implementation of the Fourth Directive[24]. However, even though self-regulation has been stimulated by the Ministry of Justice in the Netherlands and, moreover, the SER still provides two-thirds of the RJ's financial support, neither the government nor the SER have become involved itself in the RJ's policies or monitored its operations.

Formally, the RJ was instituted in 1981 by the Foundation on Annual Reporting (*Stichting voor de Jaarverslaggeving*) and in particular by industry organisations, employer's federations, trade unions and the Dutch Institute of Registered Accountants (NivRA), to issue pronouncements and recommendations on financial reporting (Buijink and Eken, 1998). Before final guidelines are issued, exposure drafts are published to permit comments by all interested parties. The Guidelines may have either the status of affirmative pronouncements (if printed in bold type-face) which companies should not depart from, or that of advisory statements, which are less authoritative. However, it is worth mentioning that if a company does not comply with an affirmative pronouncement, it is not obliged to mention or justify this departure in the notes to the accounts. Even though it is the policy of the Council on Annual Reporting to include relevant decisions of the Enterprise Chamber as part of its Guidelines, the Chamber itself does not acknowledge the Guidelines in its verdicts. Finally NIvRA, although contributing to the set up of the RJ and representing the Dutch audit profession in negotiations on the drafting of the

---

[22] Of the 45 cases dealing with financial reporting that were adjudicated by the Enterprise Chamber in 1991, 21 had been brought by SOBI (Zeff et al. 1992).

[23] The Ministry of Justice suggested in 1968 that "organised business" and the organisation of auditors take an "inventory of valuation principles that are considered to be acceptable in the economic and social climate" and judge their acceptability (Zeff et al. 1992, p. 366).

[24] *Bijlagen Handelingen Tweede Kamer*, Zitting 1979-1980, 16326, No.3.

Richtlijnen, has never required its members to follow the Guidelines. But it encourages the use of them in a more informal way[25]. In summary, no authority enforces the compliance with the Guidelines issued by the RJ and the status of the Guidelines is a contentious question[26].

Although the Royal Netherlands Institute for Registered Accountants (*Koninklijk Nederlands Instituut van Registeraccountants,* NIvRA) is member of the RJ, the influence of the Netherlands Order of Accountants and Administrative Consultants (*Nederlandse Orde van Account-Administratie consulenten,* NOVAA) on accounting regulation has not been established, as it is only since 1993, when the Dutch parliament passed a law implementing the Eighth EC Directive, that accountants who are represented by NOVAA have been able to carry out the statutory audit of large and medium-sized companies (Buijink and Eken, 1998).

Theodor Limperg Jr. (1879-1961), professor of business economics (*bedrijfseconomie)* and auditing, had a profound influence on auditors and accountants with his theory of replacement value. In fact, replacement value accounting had been established in reporting practice (Muis, 1975) long before the Dutch legislature made it a statute when implementing the Fourth Directive in 1983.

The Stock Exchange Association (*Vereniging voor de Effectenhandel*) has issued a number of rules for financial reporting of companies quoted on the Amsterdam Stock exchange, which are not referred to in Company Law. These regulations are, however, limited to the publication of an interim financial statement and a prospectus as well as the obligation to reveal significant information which could impact on share prices. But the Association does not impose additional rules on the layout and the content of the annual financial statements.

---

[25] NIvRA's Consultative Committee on Published Auditors' Reports has sought to use quiet persuasion with auditors concerning apparent departures.
[26] See Zeff et al. (1992) pp. 335-337.

Table 3.9

The sources of accounting regulation in the Netherlands

Legislation	Standard	Recommendation
Parliament Social and Economic Council Ministry of Justice	Council for Annual Reporting (*Raad voor de Jaarverslaggeving*)	Royal Netherlands Institute for Registered Accountants Netherlands Order of Accountants and Administrative Consultants
Civil Code, Title 9, Book 2 (*Burgerlijk Wetboek*)	Guidelines for Annual Reporting (*Richtlijnen voor de Jaarverslaggeving*)	Individual contributions
Administrative Order on the formats for financial statements (*Besluit tot vaststelling van modelschema's voor de inrichting van jaarrekening*) Staatsblad, 30.12.1983, no.666		
Administrative Order on the valuation of assets (*Besluit houdende regels voor de inhoud, de grenzen en de wijze van toepassing in de jaarrekening van waardering van activa tegen actuele waarde*) Staatsblad , 30.12.1983, no. 665		
Enterprise Chamber Court Rulings		

3.5 Summary

Across Europe, there are vast differences in the regulatory regimes of accounting. Even though all the countries make use of law for the regulation of accounting, the intensity of legal rules and their relative importance in comparison to the influence of the standard setting agencies varies from country to country. Within Europe, there are countries where accounting legislation is confined to a single source; that is, legislation enacted by parliament, while other countries employ a hierarchy of laws and delegated legal instruments. With regard to standard setting bodies, the spectrum ranges from agencies of the government, whose rules are accepted as part of the law, to private bodies set up by the profession whose standards have no legal status. However, such standards may have been granted formal authority by other institutions including the stock exchange. In addition, the scope and relevance of recommendations varies from country to country and fill a regulatory vacuum, particularly in countries where the standard setting body is either unimportant or absent. Despite attempts to harmonise the accounting rules between countries, firstly, in the form of EC Company Law and currently in the form of International Accounting Standards, the institutional structures and forms of accounting regulation continue to differ from one nation state to another.

PART II

ACCOUNTING DIVERSITY IN EUROPE: THREE REPRESENTATIVE AREAS OF ACCOUNTING POLICY

CHAPTER 4

REGULATORY STRATEGIES IN INDIVIDUAL ACCOUNTING AREAS

Notwithstanding national differences in the institutional arrangements of accounting regulation, the diversity of regulatory strategies in accounting can be more completely understood when specific areas of rule-making are compared.

Each instance of accounting policy emerges from a different constellation of actors, theories and external economic and political factors, all of which affect the rule-making process. Moreover, the regulatory structures of accounting are subject to transformation over time, which results in the involvement of different institutions and alterations in the allocation of power. This has implications not only on the authority of a rule but also on its design.

In this study, three representative accounting areas have been chosen to describe the diversity of institutional structure and regulatory design of European accounting regulation: asset revaluation, accounting for foreign currency translation and the definition of a subsidiary for consolidation. Through examination of these areas, it can be seen how the regulatory instruments governing a specific issue can vary from law to standards and recommendations and, in addition, how their design may differ from one jurisdiction to another. From the comparison of different accounting policies rather than different national accounting regimes, it can be concluded that regulatory strategies vary not only between countries, but also between different instances of accounting policy within the same country.

These three instances of accounting policy have been chosen because they represent considerable differences in regulatory form when regulating similar accounting problems between European countries. They comprise both individual and consolidated financial statements and affect measurement and recognition in the financial statement. All three areas have been described as potentially falling into the devices of 'window dressing' and off-balance sheet financing (Naser, 1994). They also have been subject to harmonisation efforts through the EC company law's Fourth Directive (revaluation of fixed assets) and Seventh Directive (definition of a subsidiary). In contrast, foreign currency reporting was not dealt with in EC company law, but, instead was dealt with in the harmonisation programme of the IASC (IAS 21).

Furthermore, these three areas are fundamental to accounting research and academic theorisation. Firstly, asset valuation has been central to accounting theory throughout the 20th century as evidenced in the debate on the 'correct' method to account for inflation (Schmalenbach, 1921; Schmidt, 1921; Limperg, 1937; Edwards and Bell, 1961; Watts and Zimmermann, 1978). Secondly, and related to the issue of valuation, the effects of currency fluctuations on financial statements have generated extensive theoretical and empirical studies on the consequences of different translation methods with regard to both foreign subsidiaries and foreign transactions (Busse van Colbe, 1972; Nobes, 1980; Gebhardt 1987; Rezaee, 1990; Soo and Soo, 1994; Flower, 1995). Finally, the scope of consolidated accounts, and hence the definition of a subsidiary has been subject to theorisation and discussion in the accounting literature (Petite, 1984; Odenwald, 1992; Hadden, 1992).

Most importantly, all three areas of accounting policy have been subject to controversial regulatory debates, both within and among nations. Asset valuation has a long history of regulatory debate centring on prescriptive (price-level-adjustment) as opposed to more judgemental methods (current value, replacement value) of asset valuation which took place for instance in the UK (PSSAP7, SSAP16, SSAP19, ED 51, FRS 5, FRED 17) but also, as will be seen, in other European countries. In the Fourth Directive, the issue of revaluation remained optional and open to definition by individual member states.

The degree of contention on foreign currency reporting rules in Europe can be demonstrated by the fact that the issue was not included in the EC company law harmonisation programme (Accounting Advisory Forum, 1995). In particular, the accounting for foreign currency transactions remains unresolved among European member states (Accountancy, April 1998, p.71). As will be seen, translation rules are a particularly good example of the different authoritative sources of accounting regulation to which reporting companies are subject in Europe.

The third area of accounting, the definition of a subsidiary company for consolidation, is a prime example of regulatory disagreement with regard to legal (formal) group control as opposed to actual economic (judgemental) group control. Indeed, the topic was described as one of the most controversial during the negotiations leading to the adoption of the Seventh Directive (van Hulle and van der Tas, 1995). It was not possible for the national regulators to reach a satisfactory solution but only a compromise in which consolidation was made compulsory under legal control, while economic control was retained as a member state option.

Part Two of this thesis is concerned with the different regulatory approaches in Europe for these three areas of accounting policy. The preceding historical perspective on the origins of rule development serves to explain the current diverse strategies between nations. Furthermore, for each area, the different regulatory forms are related to observed European reporting practices.

CHAPTER 5

FIXED ASSET REVALUATION

5.1 Introduction

This chapter reviews the development of different revaluation strategies and compares, across European countries, the current regulatory framework with respect to both the sources and the design of fixed asset revaluation rules. It then considers how the different regulatory forms are interpreted and consequently affect the content of accounting practices in the policy notes published in the annual reports of European companies.

5.2 A historical perspective

An early instance of asset revaluation in Europe is to be found in Denmark where the assessment of land and buildings for tax purposes, which dates back to the 1840s, led to the introduction of such values into the annual accounts of Danish companies (Christiansen, 1995). However, throughout Europe, the factor which brought about proposals for an alternative to historic cost accounting was the incidence of inflation itself. In fact, the theoretical foundations as well as the practical application of accounting for the effect of changing prices both evolved in Germany during the period of hyperinflation after the first world war. In these circumstances the inadequacies of financial statements based on historic cost were already self evident by the beginning of the 1920's. The experience of exceptionally high price increases led to not one but two solutions in Germany: purchasing power accounting on the one hand and current cost accounting on the other. That is, while the German accounting theorists Schmalenbach (1921) and Mahlberg (1923) were the proponents of indexing, based respectively on a price index and the gold standard, it was another German (Schmidt, 1921) who advocated current values in the form of replacement cost.

These two fundamentally different approaches to revaluation were taken up and further developed by accountants in other countries. The German experiments with purchasing power indexation based on the gold standard influenced French accounting thought, as the work of Delavelle (1924) and Faure (1926) shows. It is now known that Schmidt's replacement cost accounting ideas were taken up in the Netherlands some time before 1925 (Camfferman and Zeff, 1994) and they were provided with a rigorous analytical framework by the Dutch accountant Limperg whose theory of current value was published in the 1930s as part of his broader treatise on *bedrijfseconomie* (Limperg, 1937).

Under the conditions of hyperinflation that persisted during the 1920s, contemporaneous accounting practices in Germany and in France were such that the conversion of the currencies into gold as a standard value was usually confined to balance sheets. The German *Goldmarkbilanzgesetz* of 1924 was the first legal attempt to 'stabilise' the balance sheet (Sweeney, 1927), in this instance with respect to the value of gold. A similar regulatory approach was taken by the fiscal authorities in France in 1930 when the *Direction des Contributions* accepted the practice of revaluing depreciable fixed assets on the basis of the relation between the franc and the dollar price of gold (*franc-or*) for each year from 1914 to 1928. It may be noted that this decision was reversed by the *Conseil d' Etat* in a Decree dated 14 November 1938 which required that depreciation should be calculated only on the basis of historic cost (Collins, 1994).

In the Netherlands, the legislation of 1928/29, although not prescribing a valuation method, acknowledged the existence of alternatives in practice by requiring companies to disclose the method used (Zeff et al., 1992).

In Denmark during this period, a different approach to accounting for the effect of changing prices was adopted in law, based on the longstanding practice, which had developed beyond the law, of using taxable values for revaluation in the accounts. The *Aktieselskabslov* (Companies Act) of 1930 contained the first Danish authorization to revalue fixed assets that had experienced a permanent increase in value (Christiansen and Elling, 1993). However, as the valuation basis was not defined in the law, the outcome was to legitimate the use by companies of tax assessments as a basis for asset valuation in annual accounts (Christiansen, 1995).

The aftermath of the Second World War

Accounting for changing prices soon reemerged as an important issue throughout Europe following the Second World War. Germany experienced yet another currency collapse which led to the introduction of the Deutsche Mark on 20 June 1948. A new law, the *Deutsche Mark Eröffnungsbilanzgesetz,* was ratified on 21 August 1949, and required all balances to be restated in the new currency for both financial reporting and tax purposes. Companies were given the right to use current values as at the end of August 1949 or alternatively one year earlier as at August, 31, 1948 (Most, 1977). Following this, the German legislator returned to historical cost accounting and has not authorized any departure since then.

In France, following the Second World War, revaluation based on purchasing power accounting continued and was now promoted by the Government as well as official accounting bodies such as the *Ordre des Experts Comptables* and the *Conseil National de la Comptabilité* (CNC). In fact, if a company did not revalue, it had to pay a tax penalty of 2% on turnover (Collins, 1994). An Ordonnance issued on 15 August 1945 and a Law dated 14 May 1948, gave companies the right to revalue their assets. This right was eventually cancelled by the Law of 28 December 1959, but companies were given the possibility to carry out further revaluations up until 31 December 1962. The revaluation of each specific category of depreciating fixed asset as well as its accumulated depreciation was based on the application of published indices.

In the Netherlands during this period, although there were no changes to the regulations, Limperg's system of *vervangingswaarde* (replacement value) accounting was adopted in practice by some of the larger Dutch companies, notably Phillips from the period 1945-46 onwards (Brink, 1992).

The effect of inflation on accounts was also considered in the UK at this time by the Institute of Chartered Accountants in England and Wales (ICAEW) which put forward two proposals, N12 'Rising price levels in relation to accounts' in 1949 and N15 'Accounting in relation to the purchasing power of money' in 1952. However, the proposals rejected any form of inflation accounting, whether by replacement cost or by general index methods, and recommended that historical cost should continue to be the basis of published accounts. Instead, the ICAEW advocated appropriations of profits to reserves, rather than charges against profits, as a means of recognising in the accounts the excess of reported profits over inflation-adjusted profits. However, by the time the proposals were made public, the rate of inflation and interest in the subject had both fallen. Nevertheless, the ICAEW continued to discuss the problem of accounting under inflationary conditions and, in 1968, published its report entitled 'Accounting for Stewardship in a Period of Inflation'. The report argued in favour of the current purchasing power method and strongly influenced subsequent developments on this issue in the UK (Westwick, 1980).

Elsewhere in Europe, the impact of inflation on accounting was invariably regulated by the national tax authorities using price-level adjustments to accounts. In this context, fiscal revaluation laws were enacted in Italy and

Spain, Greece and in each case the treatment required or permitted for tax purposes was also made mandatory in the annual accounts. In Italy several price-level adjustment laws were adopted (RD No. 2325 in 1936, DL No. 436 in 1946, DL No.49 in 1948, Law No. 91 in 1949 and Law No. 74 in 1952) which authorized the revaluation of different categories of fixed assets. In Spain, the Ministry of Finance enacted Law 76 in 1961 which permitted the restatement of fixed assets, but this had little effect on accounting practice due to a possible increase in tax liability (Fernandez Peña, 1992). In 1964, a new revaluation law No. 41 was issued which provided, that there would be no tax penalty for companies which complied, thus finding widespread acceptance in practice.

Inflation in the 1970s

The third wave of inflation to hit Europe was during the early 1970s and, as noted by Mumford (1979), this brought about a revival of the debate concerning the appropriate method of accounting for price changes. This took place in the Netherlands and in the UK, and there was a radical change in policy in the UK from the purchasing power approach, which was originally favoured, to current cost accounting (Tweedie and Whittington, 1984).

In the Netherlands, current cost accounting in the form of replacement value accounting had been favoured by the Rijkens Committee and its follow-up committee, the Hamburger Committee, which was established by the employers' organisation in order to study the annual financial reporting of listed companies. The Committees proposed a valuation of fixed assets according to current values, if it was anticipated that the relevant assets would be replaced in future. Furthermore, the Committees recommended that depreciation on the basis of current value was necessary in order to calculate profits accurately. However, the Verdam Committee, which was appointed by the Government to make proposals for a revision of company law did not share the view that current value accounting was superior to historic cost accounting but, instead, recommended both valuation concepts. But although there was recognition of the need to account for increasing asset values, Dutch legislation in the 1970s continued to be imprecise with respect to the valuation method to be used in annual accounts. In fact, the laws on annual accounts of both 1970 and 1976, only required the minimum of disclosure regarding the valuation of assets and the measurement of profit. The law was centred on the notion of a 'true and fair view' of income and capital based on principles satisfying criteria considered to be "acceptable in the economic and social life" (van Hoepen, 1984, p.69). Muis (1975) reports that by 1972/73, 4 out of a sample of 50 large companies published current value financial statements, 8 applied a mixture of current value and historic cost and 38 reported on a historic cost basis with occasional supplementary current value information.

In the UK, rising price levels had caused the newly-formed Accounting Standards Steering Committee (ASSC) to consider inflation accounting as one of the first priorities of its programme. Indeed, it was in 1971 that the ASSC Plenary Committee published its discussion paper entitled 'Inflation and Accounts' which advocated the current purchasing power method, although only as supplementary to historic cost accounting. This report eventually formed the basis for the 1973 exposure draft ED 8 'Accounting for changes in the purchasing power of money' which again suggested current purchasing power. However, the apparent consensus on the use of a price index system in preference to current cost accounting was overturned by the British Government. Just before the discussion period for ED 8 was due to expire, it was announced that an independent committee of enquiry (the Sandilands Committee) would be set up. Nevertheless, the accelerating inflation rate prompted the ASSC to issue in 1974 a provisional accounting standard PSSAP No.7 'Accounting for changes in the purchasing power of money' based on ED 8, although this standard was itself abandoned in 1975 in favour of the Sandilands recommendations which had Government backing. The Sandilands Report rejected the use of general purchasing power indices in favour of current cost accounting as the best form of accounting in a period of inflation. Furthermore, the report proposed the use of current cost accounting as the basis for the main published accounts, and not merely for supplementary statements, thus expressing outright opposition to the approach seemingly favoured by the profession at the time. On the basis of the Sandilands Report, the professional standard-setters were given the task of producing an inflation accounting standard. ED 18 'Current Cost Accounting' was issued by the Inflation Accounting Steering Group in 1976. However, this exposure draft was rejected soon afterwards by a resolution of a special meeting of the ICAEW in July 1977 when its members were opposed to the compulsory character of current cost statements as well as to their complexity and, finally, their application to all companies irrespective of size. In response, the ASC issued interim recommendations on inflation accounting known as the 'Hyde Guidelines' in November 1977, before producing its next exposure draft ED 24 in 1979. This eventually became the first British current cost accounting standard, SSAP 16 'Current Cost Accounting', in 1980. The essential features of the compromise in the Hyde Guidelines, such as the gearing adjustment and the minimum requirement of current cost accounts as supplementary financial statements for leading companies only, were retained in SSAP 16. However the accounting standard was short-lived and was eventually suspended in 1985, due to widespread non-compliance and also as a result of the decreasing rate of inflation.

In Germany, in 1975 in the light of renewed discussions brought about by the oil price rise and the world-wide inflationary shock, the *Hauptfachausschuss* of the *Institut der Wirtschaftsprüfer* (the Main Technical Committee of the *IdW*) issued a recommendation '*Zur Berücksichtigung der Substanzerhaltung bei der Ermittlung des Jahresergebnisses*' (Accounting for capital maintenance in the measurement of company profits) for companies to provide supplementary information restricted to certain adjustments to reported income. These adjustments were limited to those assets which were equity-financed (Coenenberg and Macharzina, 1976). The opinion was influenced by a number of voluntary disclosures at the time (Portland Zement Heidelberg AG, Siemens AG and Mannesmann AG etc.) and followed Schmidt's *organische Tageswertbilanz* (organic current value balance sheet) approach (Coenenberg, 1991).

In France, interestingly, some companies carried out asset revaluations even when these were not initiated by a specific Government law. It seems that these were tolerated by the authorities even though the Commercial Code did not permit revaluation except under explicit authorization. However, since these *réévaluations libres* (free revaluations) incurred a tax penalty on the unrealized gain, they were usually applied only by loss-making companies, as profitable companies were reluctant to revalue assets unless under fiscally-neutral Government action (Scheid and Walton, 1992). The CNC became involved in 1974, when it disallowed the practice of offsetting losses against the revaluation reserve, and expressed the view that the Government should bring to an end the legal uncertainty with respect to revaluation. In response, the Government initiated a new revaluation in 1977, again using a price-level adjustment approach. The effect on company accounts was spread over two years by the Finance Acts of 1977/1978 which, although permitting companies some discretion in revaluing all their fixed assets (tangible, intangible and financial) at "utility value", specified that the revalued amounts could not exceed the ceilings obtained by applying the appropriate published indices (Collins, 1994).

Elsewhere, in both Italy and Spain, the inflation of the 1970s resulted in further price-level adjustments, which were regulated as before by the national tax authorities. While Italy saw only one further price-level adjustment, Law No. 576 in 1975, in Spain there were several revaluation laws during this period (Law 12 in 1973, Law 50 in 1977, Law 1 in 1979, Law 74 in 1980 and Law 9 in 1983) which adjusted tangible and other fixed assets in accordance with the general price level. It is interesting to note that the Spanish company Telefónica revalued its tangible fixed assets virtually each year from 1967 to 1987 based on specific rights given by the State and had also done so before in 1946. However, a change in the contractual arrangements between Telefónica and the State has prevented such revaluations since 1988 (Fernandez Peña, 1992).

The impact of the 4th Directive

The implementation of the Fourth Directive in the European Community had the effect of forcing national legislators to re-consider their position with respect to the method of valuation to be used in annual accounts. Article 33 of the Directive authorized countries to allow or to require 'alternative valuation methods' and therefore to depart from historic cost accounting. However, the Directive did not specify the method to be used to account for the effect of either general or specific price increases, clearly a result of the variety of approaches existing in Member States at the time (van Hulle and van der Tas, 1995). Instead, in those cases where the option of 'alternative valuation methods' was to be allowed or required by local law, the text of Article 33 delegates the definition of revaluation methods and their mode of application to each country.

In the final version of the Directive, enacted in 1978, Article 33(1) makes reference to alternative valuation methods as follows,

- (a) the replacement value method for tangible fixed assets with limited useful economic lives and stocks
- (b) valuation methods other than that provided for in (a) which are designed to take account of inflation for the items shown in the annual accounts, including capital and reserves
- (c) revaluation of tangible fixed assets and financial fixed assets.

According to van Hulle and van der Tas (1995, p.999-p.1003), the replacement value method mentioned in (a) above was specified in the Directive at the request of the Netherlands in 1968 as it was applied by a number of Dutch companies at this time. With respect to (b), the option to allow "valuation by methods other than the replacement value method, which take into account current values" was included in the draft Directive in 1974, notably at the request of the UK. Finally, in the case of (c), it was the Belgian delegation which proposed the option for companies to "revalue tangible fixed assets at fair values". In fact, during the discussions leading to the final text of the Directive, the scope of application of the 'alternative valuation methods' was considerably narrowed, but opposed only by Germany.

In Belgium, the Law of 17 July 1975 with its associated Royal Decree of 8 October 1976 was the first national accounting law to be based on the Fourth Directive, in this case a draft of the Directive (Lefebvre, 1984). Previously, Belgium had little accounting legislation (the principal exception was the 1973 Royal Decree on financial and economic information for industrial relations councils). The Royal Decree of 1976 authorized companies "to revalue in the case of certain and permanent surplus values, fixed assets, intangible assets and fixed financial assets (Art. 34)" and "to use replacement values for recording tangible fixed assets and inventories (Art. 35)"; however, the adjustment of accounts for inflation was prohibited (Lefebvre, 1984, p.17). The reason for not adopting inflation accounting was given in the Report to the King as "having regard to the general practice both in this country and abroad, as well as to the fiscal provisions, the decree retains acquisition cost as the principal valuation rule. In the absence of accepted opinion or tried and tested methods of inflation accounting, the government does not intend to permit, still less enforce, their adoption before practical experience, particularly abroad makes a proper appreciation of the advantages, disadvantages and risks possible." (Lefebvre and Flower, 1994, p.100).

Belgian companies were only able to use replacement cost for a few years because the Royal Decree of 12 September 1983 removed this option, as it appeared that few enterprises were using replacement cost and "Belgium felt incapable" of defining the replacement cost method, "given the lack of a consensus at the international level to which reference could be made in determining the principles and the means of applying this method". Lefebvre and Flower (1994, p.101) indicate that companies that wanted to use the replacement cost method could submit a request for derogation to the official Commission for Accounting Standards. In fact, as replacement cost accounting was not accepted by the tax authorities for the purpose of determining taxable income, Belgian companies generally opted generally for a valuation at acquisition cost, which was also accepted for tax purposes (Jorissen and Block, 1995). Thus, after initially allowing replacement cost accounting, the Belgian lawmakers eventually adopted the general notion of Art. 33.1 (c) of the Directive without specifying a 'revaluation method'.

Denmark was the first country to base its company law on the final version of the Fourth Directive in 1981 and, like Belgium, exercised the option contained in Art. 33.1 (c); that is, the revaluation of tangible and financial fixed assets. Similarly, the Danish legislature did not specify the revaluation method in law. The revaluation of assets had been allowed in Denmark since the 1930 Companies Act, but now depreciation had to be based on the revalued amount. This was not a general practice at the time (Elling and Hansen, 1984). In 1994, a draft accounting standard ED 11 (Sec. 69) mentioned that assets may be revalued if their utility value is significantly higher than their book value (Christiansen and Hansen, 1995, p. 817).

The UK, by including the provisions of the 4th Directive in the 1981 amended Companies Act, for the first time gave statutory support to current cost accounting which had previously been a matter of professional standards (Nobes and Parker, 1984). As a result of this legislation, companies could prepare pure historic cost accounts or alternatively incorporate certain assets at revaluation, or they could prepare pure current cost accounts. With respect to fixed assets, the Companies Act permits the valuation of intangible fixed assets (other than goodwill) at current cost, tangible fixed assets either at market value or current cost and fixed investments at either market value or on a basis which appears to the directors to be appropriate (Gordon and Gray, 1994). Companies are not required to value on a regular basis and may revalue individual assets only. As a result of "lobbying" by the property industry (Gordon and Gray, 1994, p.127), SSAP 19 "Accounting for Investment Properties" was issued in 1981 which requires revaluation of such assets at open market value and specifically exempts investment property from depreciation. In May 1990, the ASC issued ED 51 "Accounting for Fixed Assets and Revaluations" which suggests that management should decide whether to apply historic cost or current value for each class of asset. In the case where current value is used, it should be kept up to date and no valuation more than five years old should be used. With respect to the valuation basis, the exposure draft proposes the open market value except where it cannot practically be determined, in which case the depreciated net replacement cost should be used. ED 52 is limited to intangible fixed assets and proposes that these assets may be carried at depreciated replacement cost if they satisfy certain recognition criteria (see Ernst and Young, 1994, p.516).

Similarly, the Netherlands put current value accounting onto the legal statute upon implementing the Fourth Directive in 1983. In fact, even though replacement cost accounting is traditionally assumed to have developed in the Netherlands, no reference to it existed in law until the 1983 revision of the Dutch Civil Code (van Hoepen, 1984). The legislators' original intention was to give preference under certain circumstances to current value accounting either in the financial statements or in the notes, but this was rejected by the Dutch parliament (Klaassen and Hekers, 1995). The final legal provision (Art. 384 (1)) allows the application of current values only for tangible and financial fixed assets and stocks in the annual accounts. Different definitions of current value were included in a separate general Administrative Order with a legal authority, issued by the Ministry of Justice on 22 December 1983. These regulations distinguish between three types of current value; namely, (i) replacement value, which must be used if it is assumed that the asset will be replaced in due course, (ii) economic value, which ought to be applied if replacement of the asset is unlikely and, finally, (iii) net realizable value which should be used if the business will not continue in future. However, according to Klaassen and Hekers (1995, p. 2132), the administrative order does not specify how to determine the replacement value.

In France, since the implementation of the 4th Directive in 1984, Article 12 (4) of the Commercial Code authorizes the revaluation of tangible and financial fixed assets. The Government has thereby legitimised the previously 'tolerated' *réévaluations libres* (free revaluations) which some companies carried out beyond the scope of revaluation laws. By adopting Art. 33 (c) of the Directive, France seems to have changed from price-level accounting (enacted in 1945, 1959 and 1977/78) to a form of current value accounting. However, French law does not specify the revaluation method although guidance on valuation has been issued by the COB and the CNC in line with the earlier regulations issued in 1977; that is, 'the amount which any prudent manager of a business would be prepared to pay for such an asset with regard to its usefulness to the business'. The utility value (*valeur d'utilité*) may be the "current value in an appropriate market or the restatement of the purchase price by either a general or a specific price index" (Griziaux, 1995, p.1246).

In contrast to the above, Germany remained resolute in support of historic cost, when the Fourth Directive was implemented in 1985. Indeed, in the minutes of the Council meeting at which the Fourth Directive was adopted in 1978, the German delegation explained that: "for reasons of monetary and economic policy, the Federal Government cannot accept valuation methods designed to take account of inflation as authorized by the Fourth Directive Art. 33 by way of derogation from the purchase price principle laid down in Art. 32. It will therefore not permit such valuation methods in the Federal Republic of Germany" (Council Declaration No.10 entered in minutes of EC Council meeting 25 July 1978; see van Hulle and van der Tas, 1995, p.999).

When Spain implemented the Fourth Directive in 1989, the legislator's position did not change with respect to asset revaluation, as the new accounting regulations and the amendments to the PGC indicated that a company may revalue only if there is authorisation under a special revaluation law (López Díaz and Rivero Torre, 1995). A further asset revaluation law in Spain was implemented in 1983 pursuant to the General State Budget law 9/1983. In June 1996 the Spanish Government issued again a fiscal revaluation law which authorises companies to revalue fixed assets according to inflation levels and involves a tax liability of 3% on the revaluation surplus. It is worth mentioning that before 1996 several asset revaluations have taken place in the Basque country where companies are subject to regional tax regimes. Indeed, even though these independent revaluations have been questioned in court by the Spanish Government, the legal decision was in favour of the regions.

Italy, the last EU country to implement the Fourth Directive, had seen further price level adjustment laws in 1983 (Law No.72), in 1990 (Law No.408) and 1991 (Law No. 413). Upon implementation of the Directive in 1991, the opportunity for companies to revalue was restricted by the *Codice Civile* to special revaluation laws for years after 1992.

In summary, the implementation of the 4th Directive had different effects on Member State company laws. It resulted in statutory reference to current values in a number of countries where there had been no mention beforehand in the law, in spite of its use in practice, and led to the adoption of current value accounting in some countries where previously only price indexing had been used. Other jurisdictions stipulated on implementing the Directive that revaluation is restricted to inflation indexing and authorisation by a special tax law. In only one case was Art. 33 not implemented in national law. The situation is summarised in Figure 5.1.

5.3 The revaluation rules in Europe

Although there are similarities in the ways rules have developed to account for changing prices, the current regulatory structures of revaluation rules differ with respect to both their design and sources.

With regard to regulatory design, European countries are divided on the degree of formalism in revaluation rules. In Italy and Spain price-level-index laws authorise the revaluation of defined assets, during a limited time, in line with prescribed inflation indices, while in the UK, Ireland, the Netherlands, France, Belgium and Denmark, regulations permit current value accounting or revaluation at the discretion of companies, which are allowed to judge the basis and timing of the revaluation of individual fixed assets.

Figure 5.1

Fixed asset revaluation in Europe

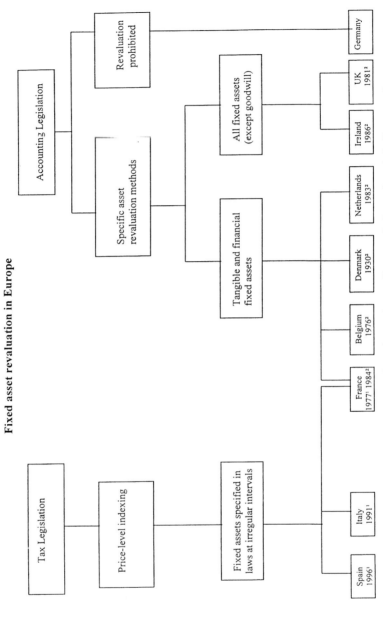

Key: [1] indicates the year where the last fiscal revaluation law was enacted ; [2] indicates the year where specific asset revaluation was first authorized by company law

This diversity with respect to the revaluation of fixed assets can be explained in two ways. First, in those countries adopting price-level indexing, such revaluations have depended to a great extent on national fiscal policies. Second, in the remaining countries (except Germany where revaluation is not allowed), national legislators did not follow Art. 33 of the Directive in defining the "content and limits" of valuation methods nor the "rules for their application". Indeed, the 4th Directive gave countries considerable flexibility in determining revaluation methods, and commercial law typically only contains broad reference either to *current cost* or to *revaluation*. For instance, while the Companies Acts in the UK and Ireland refer to the three revaluation concepts of *market value*, *current cost* and *directors' valuation*, the approach adopted by the Dutch Civil Code is that of *current value (actuele waarde)* only. Even less precise on the issue is accounting legislation in Denmark, Belgium and France, where the laws refer only to revaluation, *opskrivning* in Denmark and *réévaluation* in Belgium and France.

Not only the policy design but also the authoritative sources of revaluation rules differ among European countries. In addition to parliamentary law, interpretative documents that have been issued in some of these countries have led to further conceptual conflict: particularly, statements by the accounting profession in the UK and Ireland (SSAP 19, ED 51, ED 52) and in Denmark (ED 11), the ministerial order in the Netherlands and, in France, the guidelines issued by the accountancy bodies OEC and CNCC. In contrast, the source of revaluation rules in Belgium is confined to government decree and in Spain and Italy to fiscal law issued by the Ministry of Finance.

The co-existence of different regulatory sources does not necessarily affect the regulatory detail of revaluation rules. For example, in the UK, the accounting profession does not define the revaluation concept contained in the Companies Act. Instead, the ASB requires the valuation of land and buildings by external valuers and proposes in ED 51 the *open market value,* except in circumstances in which this cannot be determined (in which case the *depreciated replacement cost* should be used). The Danish exposure draft ED 11, which is limited to the valuation of tangible fixed assets, defines revaluation with respect to their *utility value*. The Dutch ministerial order defines three types of current value: *replacement value, economic value* and *net realizable value,* where *current value* is generally interpreted as *replacement value* unless the firm will discontinue operations in future. In France, the CNCC and OEC issued further rules with respect to specific categories of assets, which include market price (*prix du marché*) or replacement value (*valeur de reconstitution*) for tangible fixed assets. According to Raffegeau *et al.* (1989) the legal interpretation suggests that revaluation should be based on the concept of utility value (*valeur d'utilité)* as applied on the occasion of the last legal revaluation in 1977. In order to determine this value, the enterprise may use the most appropriate of the following: (i) a market price, (ii) a specific price index or (iii) a general price index. In Belgium, revaluation remains obscure. In fact, the Government has objected not only to inflation accounting (*comptabilite d'inflation*), as evident in the Report to the King introducing the Royal Decree of 1976, but also to replacement value (*valeur de remplacement*), which was officially repealed in 1983. Therefore, the only remaining definition to guide revaluation is contained in Art. 34 of the 1976 Decree; that is, 'usefulness to the enterprise' (Flower and Lefebvre, 1994, p. 264).

The interaction between revaluation and taxation

Although it is clear that high inflation in Europe stimulated a debate concerning accounting for changing prices which still continues, the current situation regarding the rules of revaluation is also strongly influenced by national fiscal policies which directly affect accounting practices. Indeed, the view that the interrelation between accounting and taxation may be the principal explanatory factor that divides Europe on the issue of asset revaluation appears to be largely confirmed, as shown in Figure 5.2. That is, in all countries where published earnings do not serve as the basis for corporate taxation (the UK, Ireland, the Netherlands and Denmark), revaluation is dealt with by specific asset revaluation methods, while in two of the countries (Spain and Italy) where the financial accounts do form the basis for taxation, general price-level indexing is authorised by the tax authorities through specific revaluation laws. However, in three further countries (Belgium, France and Germany), the relationship is not so clear, and it is worthwhile reexamining each of these in turn:

In Belgium, where the published annual accounts serve as the basis for corporate taxation and yet general price-level indexing has never been applied, the government has in fact authorised individual asset revaluation. However, a special tax law exempts the surplus on revaluation from taxation, with depreciation for tax purposes being limited to acquisition cost (Lefebvre and Flower, 1994, p. 102).

In France, the policy has changed from one of price-level indexing towards individual asset revaluation, whereby the use of mandatory indexing revaluation as an instrument of fiscal policy has progressively been abandoned. While the first attempt to limit the strong fiscal influence dates back to the creation of the PCG in 1947, it was in 1960 that the French government took the first steps to abolish fiscal revaluation by authorizing companies to use accelerated depreciation of assets for tax purposes (Scheid and Walton, 1992, p. 208). This was followed in 1977 by a fiscally-neutral revaluation law and, finally, specific asset revaluation was introduced in commercial law upon the implementation of the 4th Directive in 1984. Today, in contrast to Belgium, the French fiscal authorities tax the revaluation surpluses as income but permit companies to charge increased tax depreciation on revalued assets against profit (Griziaux, 1995, p.1247).

In Germany, the legislature has always avoided the link between fiscal policy and revaluation, as departures from historic cost are prohibited. It is generally assumed that the reluctance to adopt revaluation accounting results from the historical experience of severe inflation in Germany, but it is also influenced by the earlier legislation on asset revaluation. In fact, the upper valuation limit of acquisition cost for fixed assets was enshrined in German accounting legislation in the *Aktiengesetz* amendment of 1884. The preceding legislation, the *Allgemeines Deutsches Handelsgesetzbuch* of 1861 (General Commercial Code), required all assets and liabilities to be stated at their 'attributable value' (*beizulegender Wert*) which was interpreted as the current value at the balance sheet date (Ballwieser, 1995). However, this quickly led to abuses which became apparent in a number of frauds and bankruptcies, and which brought about the return to historic cost in 1884. The current situation in Germany is one in which historic cost accounting is seen as reducing uncertainty both with respect to balance sheet values and corporate taxation.

The analysis of Belgium, France and Germany suggests that the separation on the basis of tax accounting is too simplistic. While the Belgian and French decision to introduce revaluation in commercial law has relaxed the link between accounting and taxation, the Germans have remained resolute supporters of historic cost accounting.

The interaction between revaluation and corporate taxation

Figure 5.2

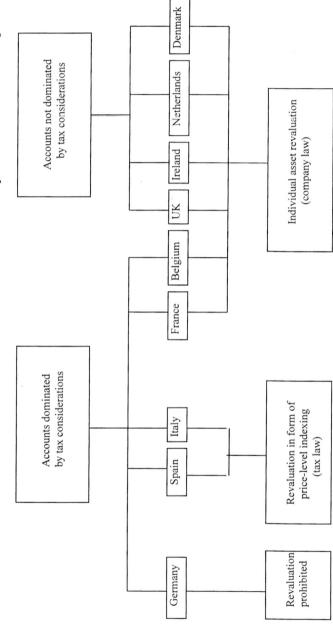

The interaction between revaluation and accounting practice

A final explanation of the current diversity in the regulatory structures of asset revaluation in Europe is the effect on rulemaking of accounting practice itself. Indeed, the revaluation of assets is a good example of an area of accounting regulation where the rules implied by accounting practices go beyond the text of company legislation. In fact, in some jurisdictions, the regulation of asset revaluation has followed the 'rules in action' rather than anticipating them. In particular, in countries which allow individual asset revaluation, the development of the regulatory framework was able to take account of generally accepted reporting practices. In the Netherlands and the UK, for instance, current cost revaluation had occurred in practice and had been considered by the accounting profession, but was not acknowledged in the letter of the company law until the implementation of the Fourth Directive.

The relationship between practice and the development of accounting rules in law can also be seen in other circumstances. In some cases, revaluation practices which occurred beyond regulatory legitimisation, have been tolerated and have then become the law. For instance, in Denmark, the Company Law of 1930 legalised revaluation accounting but the practice of using public assessment valuations for accounting purposes was established long before this law. In France, the Government's regulatory action in this area emanated on several occasions from the effective use of revaluation in accounting practice, and these illegal revaluations were eventually legitimised when the Fourth Directive was implemented.

A further example of the influence of the rules in action on the law itself is to be found in Belgium where the abandonment of replacement cost valuation by the 1983 Royal Decree was a consequence of its rare application in practice.

In summary, the current rules with respect to the revaluation of fixed assets vary considerably across European countries. This diversity emanated from (i) the lack of rigorous regulation by both the EC and national legislators, (ii) the international variations with respect to the degree of connection between accounting and taxation for profit measurement in this area and, finally, (iii) the individual accounting practices interpreting the discretionary rules beyond the letter of the law. Table 5.1 provides a detailed analysis of the regulatory framework with respect to the form and content of revaluation rules for fixed assets in European countries.

The revaluation of fixed assets: The regulatory framework in EU countries

Table 5.1

Country	Accounting and Tax Law	Fixed assets concerned	Condition for revaluation	Revaluation basis	Revaluation reserve	Amortization
EU	Fourth Directive: Article 33.1 (a),(b),(c)	Tangible fixed assets with limited useful economic lives; items shown in the annual accounts; tangible fixed assets and financial fixed assets	Pending authorization and implementation in legal provisions by Member States	Art.33.1: Replacement value for tangible fixed assets with limited useful economic lives; other valuation methods designed to take account of inflation for the items shown in the annual accounts, including capital and reserves; revaluation of tangible and financial fixed assets	Art.33.2: The revaluation surplus must be entered in a revaluation reserve and recorded under liabilities. Subsequently the revaluation differences may be capitalized or transferred otherwise. The revaluation surplus may not be distributed unless it represents a gain actually realized.	Art.33.3: Value adjustments shall be calculated each year on the basis of the value adopted for the financial year in question. Member states may permit or require that only the amount of the value adjustment arising as a result of the application of the general rule laid down in Art. 32 (cost) be shown under the relevant items and the difference arising as a result of the valuation method adopted under Art.33 be shown separately in the layouts. Furthermore Art.34 to 42 shall apply mutatis mutandis
Belgium	Royal Decree 8th October 1976, amended by Royal Decree 1983, Chapter II, Section III, Article 34	Tangible fixed assets, participating interest and shares under financial fixed assets or specific categories of such assets	When considered that value of asset by reference to usefulness to the enterprise clearly and permanently exceeds its carrying value. The revaluation must be justified by reference to profitability	Value is determined "by reference to the usefulness and profitability to the enterprise"	Revaluation surplus, recorded on the liability side of the balance sheet, should be maintained as long as the assets to which it relates have not been disposed of. However, these surpluses may be transferred to a reserve to the extent of the depreciation charged against the surplus; incorporated into capital or reversed in case of a future diminution in value to the extent that the surplus has not yet been depreciated	Surplus arising on revaluation shall be depreciated following a plan

Country	Accounting and Tax Law	Fixed assets concerned	Condition for revaluation	Revaluation basis	Revaluation reserve	Amortization
Denmark	Financial Statements Act 1981 (revised), chapter 5 section 30, 40	Tangible and financial fixed assets	If value is materially and permanently higher than the book value	Revaluation to a "higher" value	As long as asset is in the balance sheet the surplus may be transferred to share capital, if asset falls in value the reserve must be adjusted. On sale choice to transfer surplus as realized gain to P+L or to other distribuable reserves	Depreciation must be valued on the new revalued amount and charged to the P+L account
France	1984 Commercial Code Art. 12 authorizes revaluation ; PCG refers to the revaluation in consolidated accounts Fiscal revaluations in: 1945, 1959 and 1977/78	Tangible and financial fixed assets in accordance with Commercial Code requirements; Fiscal revaluation referred to all fixed assets	If a company decides to revalue assets, it must comprise all tangible and financial fixed assets	The Commercial Code does not provide a revaluation basis; inflation coefficient in case of fiscal revaluation	The revaluation surplus must be included in a separate reserve in the balance sheet; subsequently the reserve may be transferred to capital, or to other reserves. The revaluation reserve may not be distributed and may not directly be offset against losses	Depreciation is based on revalued book values. During the 1978 revaluation, depreciation was based on revalued amounts but subsequently adjusted to cost.
Germany	Art.253 sec. 1 and 2 HGB	Valuation of fixed assets is limited to acquisition or production cost reduced by depreciation				
Ireland	Companies Act 1986 (idem UK)					
Italy	Tax Legislation: R.D. No 2325 of 05/10/1936 D.L. No 436 of 27/05 1946 D.L. No. 49 of 14/02/1948 Law Nos. -91 of 01/04/1949 -74 of 11/02/1952 -576 of 02/12/1975 -72 of 19/03/1983 -408 of 29/12/1990 -413, 30/12/1991	Fixed assets are specified in the relevant fiscal law.	The revaluation of fixed assets has been restricted to explicit permission by tax law	Inflation coefficients based on the year of acquisition for fiscal revaluation	Revaluation reserve can be transferred to share capital after offsetting accumulated losses	Accumulated depreciation is revalued with the coefficient applicable to the corresponding asset
Netherlands	Title 9 Book 2 Civil Code Art.384 1, Art.390; General Administrative Order of 22 December 1983	Tangible and financial fixed assets	Alternative to historic cost	Replacement cost, net realizable value, economic value	Revaluation surplus must be carried in the balance sheet, the revaluation reserve may be converted into capital, it must be reduced by any decrease in value, but may not be reduced further than the sum of the revaluations of assets included in the balance sheet	The valuation basis for depreciation is not necessarily the same as for asset valuation

Country	Accounting and Tax Law	Fixed assets concerned	Condition for revaluation	Revaluation basis	Revaluation reserve	Amortization
Spain	Fiscal legislations in the years: Laws:76 in 1961; 41 in 1964; 12 in 1973; 50 in 1977; 1 in 1979; 74 in 1980; 9 in 1983: in 1996 Further laws in the Basque Country	Fixed assets are specified in the relevant fiscal law	Revaluation is prohibited unless authorized by fiscal law	Published inflation coefficients based on the year of acquisition	Can be used to offset recorded losses and/or be transferred share capital, other reserves	The previous depreciation charge is revalued with corresponding coefficient for each year separately
U.K.	Paragraphs 29-34 of Schedule 4 Companies Acts SSAP 19 "Investment Properties" ED 51 "Accounting for Fixed Assets and Revaluations" ED 52 "Accounting for intangible fixed assets"	Tangible, intangible and financial fixed assets	Alternative to historic cost	Current cost for intangibles and tangible fixed assets; market value for tangible and financial fixed assets; Directors' valuation for financial fixed assets	The revaluation surplus must be included in a revaluation reserve, any surplus or deficit that arises must be transferred to it. A capitalization of the reserve is permitted in paying up unissued shares, a transfer to the profit and loss account is allowed when the gain is realized	Depreciation is based on the revalued amount and must be charged in its entirety to the profit and loss account (Exception: Investment properties are not subject to depreciation)

5.4 Asset revaluation in practice

The foregoing discussion indicates the varying degree of discretion a European company might have when interpreting the rules to revalue fixed assets. In fact, in countries where individual asset revaluation is allowed, a company decides *whether*, *when* and *how* to revalue *which* fixed assets. On the other hand, in countries where price-level indexation is authorized, companies may decide *whether* to revalue but, in doing so, have to follow the law which indicates the revaluation basis in terms of price indices as well as the assets subject to revaluation. In order to investigate the exercise of this varying degree of discretion in reporting practice, in this study annual reports of multinational European companies have been analysed with respect to their valuation policies adopted for fixed assets.

The following analysis of reporting practice attempts to illustrate the different valuation approaches that have been reported under the different authoritative sources and the alternative rule design of revaluation regulations to which European companies are subject.

Based on an earlier investigation (Ebbers, 1997a) for the years 1987 and 1993, Table 5.2 indicates the frequency of asset revaluations of the companies included in the sample of this thesis which have multiple listings in Europe. For the years 1987 and 1993, 118 and 191 companies respectively, disclosed that the valuation of tangible fixed assets was based on either (i) historic cost, (ii) individual asset revaluation or (iii) a book value which could include past fiscal revaluations. For many companies, revaluation was limited to land and buildings only and, accordingly, a distinction is made in the table between the revaluation of land and buildings and the revaluation of other tangible fixed assets.

With respect to land and buildings, in 1987, 53% of the companies used historic cost, 35% applied revaluation and 12% made a price-level adjustment to the book value. In 1993, 43% of the reporting companies valued land and buildings at historic cost, 34% at a revalued amount and 23% indexed the book value of land and building to a general price level.

With respect to other tangible fixed assets, the proportion of companies which used historic cost valuation was higher for both years. In 1987, 74% of companies valued other tangibles at historic cost and 17% at revaluation, while 9% revalued on the basis of a price level index in accordance with a fiscal law. In 1993, 67% of companies valued other tangibles at historic cost, 13% revalued under commercial law and 20% under a fiscal revaluation law.

The table presents evidence that some of the Italian companies revalued in addition to fiscal price-level indexation laws, and did so seemingly without the specific authorization of the national legislator. In France, the second country where reporting practice applied both forms of revaluation, the reference in some instances to the last fiscal revaluation law in 1977 can be regarded as an element from the past.

The following examples have been selected to illustrate the different interpretation of revaluation rules in each country, indicating the consequences of different regulatory strategies with regard to both source and design of rules to which European companies are subject.

In Denmark, companies frequently apply the public value assessment of land and buildings as a guide for revaluation. This policy is illustrated by the company ISS:

ISS (1993):
"Fixed assets are recorded at historical cost prices except for certain land and buildings in Denmark, which were revalued to market value in accordance with public valuation."

In France, the valuation at the time of the last government-initiated price-level adjustment (in 1977) was still being reported by some companies. A feature of French practice is that a company might value at historic cost in the individual accounts, while fixed assets might be subject to revaluation in the group accounts. This policy which is illustrated by the company Pernod Ricard, is in accordance with French law and is a result of the tax implications with respect to individual accounts.

Pernod Ricard (1993):
In the notes to the individual accounts the company reported:
"Property, plant and equipment are valued at acquisition cost (purchase price plus ancillary expenses, excluding acquisition expenses on fixed assets), with the exception of fixed assets acquired prior to December 31, 1976, which have been revalued."
In the notes to the consolidated financial statements the valuation policy was described as follows:
"Property, plant and equipment are valued at cost, or when applicable, at a revalued cost in compliance with legal requirements."

In Italy, fixed assets have been subject to several price-level accounting laws in recent years, the revalued amount generally being included in the book value of balances in Italian annual accounts. Some companies such as Tamoil used to revalue beyond the scope of the fiscal revaluation laws. This was seemingly in accordance with the Commercial Code and was allowed until the 4th Directive was implemented in 1991.

Tamoil (1993):

"Fixed assets are stated at their purchase price including directly attributable ancillary costs, and have been increased in line with monetary revaluation pursuant to law no. 72 of March 19, 1983 and law no. 413 of December 30, 1991, and adjusted by any accumulated depreciation. In accordance with art. 10 of law no. 72/1983, we confirm that revaluations other than those mentioned above have been carried out, in accordance with art. 2425, paragraph 3 of the Civil Code, which article was no longer applicable after December 31, 1992. (...) Capital surpluses arising from revaluations were utilised prior to 1986 to cover losses with the exception of the reserve deriving from Law No. 413/91."

In the Netherlands, revaluation may take the form of the use of current cost valuation in the balance sheet, generally in the form of replacement value, as in the case of Océ van Grinten, or alternatively through the disclosure of supplementary current cost information in the notes, as in the case of Akzo:

Océ van Grinten (1993):

"Land, buildings, plant, etc. are valued on a current cost basis. Normally this is the same as the replacement value. In a few cases the current cost is taken to be the lower of the value to the business or the net realizable value. In determining the current cost, allowance is made for the nature and location of the assets involved. The valuation also takes technological considerations into account. Price-index figures are used to determine the replacement value; the revaluations are verified periodically by experts. Adjustments to current cost are credited or debited to the revaluation reserve after deduction of deferred taxation."

Akzo (1993):

"The principles of valuation and determination of income used in the consolidated financial statements are based on historical cost. Due to the low level of inflation in key industrial countries, the disclosure of supplementary current value information has lost much of its significance and will therefore be discontinued effective this fiscal year. (...) Property plant and equipment are valued at cost less depreciation."

In Spain, all companies made reference to assets which had been subject to the last fiscal revaluation law in 1983, as illustrated by Repsol:

Repsol (1993):
"Property, plant and equipment acquired prior to December 31, 1983, are carried at cost restated pursuant to the applicable enabling legislation in order to reflect the inflationary conditions prevailing in those years. Subsequent additions are carried at cost."

In the UK and Ireland, companies may value in annual accounts either under the historic cost convention, or alternatively under historic cost as modified by the revaluation of certain fixed assets, as illustrated here by GKN, or alternatively under the current cost convention, as illustrated by British Gas. The revaluation of specific items refers usually to land and properties and is carried out by independent surveyors.

GKN (1993):
"Major freehold land and long leasehold properties were revalued at 31st December 1990 by chartered surveyors in the employment of the Group on the basis of open market value assuming existing use or, for specialist properties, at depreciated replacement cost. The original cost of land and buildings at 31st December 1993 was £180.9m; the notional net book value on that basis would have been £126.1m."

British Gas (1987):
"The accounts have been prepared under the current cost accounting convention. Under this convention provision is made in the accounts for the effects of specific price changes on the resources necessary to maintain the operating capability of the business."

Table 5.2

Valuation of tangible fixed assets in European reporting practice

Countries	Belgium		Denmark		France		Germany		Ireland		Italy		Netherlands		Spain		U.K.		Totals	Totals
Year	1987	1993	1987	1993	1987	1993	1987	1993	1987	1993	1987	1993	1987	1993	1987	1993	1987	1993	1987 (%)	1993 (%)
Number of reporting companies	9	10	4	6	15	26	28	29	7	9	7	24	18	22	4	18	26	47	118 (100)	191 (100)
Land and buildings																				
Historic cost less depreciation	3	3	2	2	6	14	28	29	1	1			12	16			11	17	63 (53)	82 (43)
Individual asset revaluation	6	7	2	4	4	4			6	8	2	6	6	6			15	30	41 (35)	65 (34)
Fiscal revaluation					5	8					5	18			4	18			14 (12)	44 (23)
Other tangibles																				
Historic cost, less depreciation	3	3	3	3	9	19	28	29	7	9	2	6	13	20			22	39	87 (74)	128 (67)
Individual asset revaluation	6	7	1	3	4	4							5	2			4	8	20 (17)	24 (13)
Fiscal revaluation					2	3					5	18			4	18			11 (9)	39 (20)

101

5.5 Concluding remarks

This chapter has been concerned with the diversity that now exists under different European accounting regimes with respect to the revaluation of fixed assets in company accounts. Although some common features of accounting for price changes can be identified, the situation at the present time is that the regulatory approaches concerning fixed asset revaluation vary considerably among European countries.

The development of regulatory strategies with respect to accounting for the effect of changing prices have been influenced (i) by the existence of inflation itself, (ii) by accounting theorists, who formulated accounting solutions to the problems of changing purchasing power, (iii) by governments which linked accounting revaluations to fiscal policies and finally (iv) by innovations in accounting practice which tended to precede legal change. Indeed, the regulation of asset revaluation has had a long history of following the 'rules in action' in some countries rather than anticipating them. For instance, illegal practices have been tolerated and then have become the law. While in some countries there has been a tendency to legislate in broad terms, other jurisdictions have varied the detailed prescriptive rules from time to time as part of general fiscal policy.

CHAPTER 6

FOREIGN CURRENCY REPORTING

6.1 Introduction

In accounting, whether regulation is by legislation, professional standard, or by recommendation, and whether these are drafted in precise terms or in general principles, there appears to a borderline between regulation that is facilitative and regulation that is onerous, and those affected will be motivated to determine the regime which best meets their aims.

The widespread acceptance in Europe of the rules on the consolidation of foreign financial statements, in FAS 52 and IAS 21, which favour the 'cheap and easy' closing rate method, illustrates one approach to the construction of international accounting law, that of transplanting rules into jurisdictions with or without prior regulations in this area in a manner which seems to be cost-effective for both the regulators and the regulated.

In contrast, with regard to accounting for foreign currency transactions, a less harmonious regulatory process can be observed which is characterised by instances in which the regulations are ignored in practice (as seems to be the case with respect to the treatment of unrealised exchange gains) or circumvented through reinterpretations of the rules within the scope of legality (in the choice of translation rates, for example, and in the distinction between the long term and short term), by partial regulation (of utilities in this case, which could undermine the notion of equal treatment of all enterprises), and by the creation of legal voids (regarding currency hedging).

As as result of fluctuations in exchange rates, the translation of assets and liabilities denominated in a foreign currency can have a significant effect on a company's financial statements. Nevertheless, the only mention of this issue in the EC directives is the requirement that a company should disclose the basis of any such translation (Fourth Directive Art. 41, para.1(1); Seventh Directive Art. 34, para.1).

This chapter compares the development of rules in a number of European countries relating, firstly, to accounting for foreign currency transactions and, secondly, to the translation of foreign financial statements. It then considers the current regulation for both aspects of foreign currency reporting, not only with regard to the content of such rules but also with regard to the regulatory strategies adopted in nation-states. The diversity of policies found in individual accounts regarding the treatment of foreign currency transactions and the consensus found in consolidated accounts regarding the translation of foreign financial statements are illustrated by examples from the published accounts of European companies.

6.2 The historical development of foreign currency reporting rules

Although it is widely recognised that the development of accounting regulations for foreign currency reporting in Europe has to a great extent followed IAS 21, which itself was based on FAS 52, it appears nevertheless that in several countries (France, Spain, Belgium, Germany and Italy) the rules regarding the two aspects involved, namely accounting for foreign currency transactions and the translation of foreign financial statements, have developed along different paths.

In France, for example, the regulations governing foreign currency transactions were already established in the first *Plan Comptable Général* (PCG) of 1947, re-affirmed in the PCG of 1957 and extended in the PCG of 1982 (PCG, p.II.12). However, until 1986, no accounting plan had referred to the translation of foreign financial statements. In fact, it was not until the requirement for consolidation was incorporated in the 1986 amendment of the PCG that rules for the translation of foreign company accounts were introduced in France (PCG, p. II.155-157).

In Spain, on the other hand, the first *Plan General de Contabilidad* (PGC) of 1973 and the tax regulations in force at that time required companies to adjust foreign balances in their accounts using exchange rates established by Government decree (Gonzalo and Gallizo, 1992). This continued until 1977 when the Government ended its policy of fixing the rate of exchange of the Peseta. A few years later, in 1983, the *Associación Española de Contabilidad y Administración de Empresas* (AECA) statement No. 4 on 'Exchange Differences' was published. The rules contained in that statement are now in the current PGC of 1990 (part V, 14a). Subsequently, in 1991, rules for translating foreign financial statements were issued together with the legal requirement to consolidate (Real Decreto 1816 of 20 December 1991, Art.54-59).

In Belgium, accounting for foreign currency transactions was first dealt with in 1987 in Opinion No.20 issued by the Belgian Accounting Standards

Commission *(Commissie voor Boekhoudkundige Normen / Commission des Normes Comptables)*, but there is no provision in law. On the other hand, the translation of foreign financial statements was codified in 1990 as part of the Decree on Consolidated Accounts (Art. 42-43).

In Germany, accounting for foreign currency transactions has developed solely on the basis of the German *Grundsätze ordnungsmäßiger Buchführung* (GoB; the general principles in the Articles 264(2), 252(1) No.2-4, 253(1) and (2), 279(1) of the *Handelsgesetzbuch* of 1985 (HGB)), but there is no accepted convention with respect to group accounts (Ordelheide and Pfaff, 1994). The main technical committee of the IdW *(Hauptfachausschuß des Instituts der Wirtschaftsprüfer)* published a proposal with respect to foreign currency reporting in 1977 (revised in 1986) in which the IdW confirmed the principle of accounting for foreign currency transactions, but without giving specific guidance on the issue of translation of foreign financial statements. The HGB regulates neither the reporting of foreign currency transactions, nor the translation of foreign financial statements, the only legal provision being the EC disclosure requirements which are codified in Art. 284(2) No.2 and Art. 313(1) S.2 No.2, respectively.

In Italy, accounting for foreign currency transactions was first dealt with under tax regulations in 1973 (Presidential Decree No. 597) and later in 1986 (Art. 72 of Income Law 917/1986). In 1988 the *Commissione per la Statuizione dei Principi Contabili del Consiglio Nazionale dei Dottori Commercialisti e Ragionieri* (CSPC), issued Document No.9 *'Conversione in Moneta Nazionale delle Operazioni et delle Partite in Moneta Estera'* which deals with accounting for transactions in a foreign currency in the individual accounts. However, the CSPC is currently discussing a draft document concerning the translation of foreign financial statements. The *Codice Civile* does not deal in any detail with either accounting for foreign transactions or the translation of foreign financial statements except for the minimum disclosure requirements enforced under the EC Directives.

In contrast to the above, in the UK, Ireland, the Netherlands and Denmark, foreign currency reporting with respect to translation both of transactions *and* of financial statements has coincided not only in content but also in time with the accounting principles established in the USA (FAS 52, 1981) and mirrored by the IASC (IAS 21, 1983). FAS 52 "Foreign currency translation" replaced FAS 8 which had been published in 1975 and, in so doing, introduced the 'functional currency concept' for the translation of foreign currency statements (para. 5-14) and laid down rules for foreign currency transactions (para. 15-21). It has remained the effective standard since its introduction in 1981. On the other hand, IAS 21 was revised in 1993 to narrow some of its options.

In the UK, even though the Accounting Standards Committee (ASC) had issued several exposure drafts on the topic (ED 16, 1975; ED 21, 1977; ED 27, 1980), accounting standard, SSAP 20, was not published until 1983 when it followed closely the American position in FAS 52 (Taylor, 1995). It should be noted, that SSAP 20 applied in Ireland from the same date as in the UK.

In the Netherlands, apart from a brief treatment of the provisions for exchange rate losses in 1979 (Zeff et al.,1992), no regulation or guideline existed until October 1983, when the *Raad voor de Jaarverslaggeving* (RJ; Council on Annual Reporting) issued its first draft statement on accounting for foreign currencies, which followed the FASB approach (Dijksma and Hoogendorn, 1993). The definitive guideline was issued in April 1986 (RJ 1.03.906-12 and RJ 1.03.913-936).

In Denmark, no rules existed for foreign currency translation until 1994 when the issue of Accounting Standard No.9, which reflects the revised IAS 21, was made mandatory for listed companies starting from 1 July 1995 (Christiansen and Hansen, 1995). However, since 1983, the *Foreningen af Statsautoriserede Revisorer* (FSR; Institute of State-Authorized Public Accountants) had recommended the original IAS 21, together with a Danish translation, which could be deviated from if necessary to give a true and fair view.

6.3 The current regulations

Foreign currency transactions
Generally, foreign currency transactions are recorded at the date the foreign transaction is recognised and, at the end of each accounting period, foreign payables and receivables which increase or decrease with a change in exchange rates may be restated, whereupon transaction differences will arise. Comparing the relevant regulatory positions across European countries, it is clear that, while there is relatively little controversy concerning the exchange rate to be used to translate unsettled foreign currency accounts at the balance sheet date, disagreement centres on whether and to what extent unrealised exchange gains and losses arising from such restatements should be included in income. As shown below, differences in the accounting treatment of these gains and losses are based to a great extent on principles of accruals and prudence which differ in interpretation across countries.

I The transaction date

A foreign currency transaction may be recorded initially by applying the exchange rate ruling at the date of the transaction (the so-called 'actual rate'). However, the actual rate is rarely well-defined and it may be the rate operating on the date of negotiation, the date when the contract was agreed, the date of delivery, the date when the invoice was recorded or the date of payment. Depending on the length of period between negotiations, contracting, delivery, invoicing and payment and the volatility of exchange rates, this choice may have significant impact. Already, there exist differences between FAS 52, IAS 21 and SSAP 20 on this point: Whilst FAS 52 refers to the rate at the "date when the transaction is recognised", IAS 21 considers the rate at the "date of the transaction" and, finally, SSAP 20 refers to the rate on the "date on which the transaction occurred". Given the differences in contract law across Europe, this is an area where detailed specification in accounting rules may lead to a conflict of laws.

II The exchange rate used to translate foreign payables and receivables

Foreign currency payables and receivables at the balance sheet date might be translated at either the closing rate (the rate prevailing at the balance sheet date), the historic rate, or a combination of both. The general rule of using the closing rate is followed in most countries, but not in Germany and, in some circumstances, not in Italy, as indicated in Table 6.1

The exchange rate used to translate unsettled foreign receivables and payables   Table 6.1

Countries	Translation at closing rate	Translation at historic rate or closing rate
Belgium	X	
Denmark	X	
France	X	
Germany		X
Ireland	X	
Italy		X
Netherlands	X	
Spain	X	
UK	X	

In Germany, even though the HGB does not regulate the translation of foreign transactions but contains only a disclosure requirement in Art. 284 (2) No.2, a generally accepted accounting principle has been established which applies the same valuation rules (GoB) to foreign currency assets and liabilities as to balances that are valued in national currency. In particular, the historic cost principle (HGB Art. 253 (1)), the realization principle (HGB Art. 252, (4)) and the prudence principle (HGB Art. 252, (1) No. 4) require the use of the closing rate for the accrual of unrealised losses but forbid the recognition of unrealised gains. Hence, assets denominated in a foreign currency are valued at the lower of the historic rate and the closing rate, while liabilities are valued at the higher of the historic and closing rate.

The situation is less clear in Italy. While Art. 72 of the Income Tax Law refers to foreign currency monetary items translated at the official closing rate published by the Minister of Finance, the CSPC considers alternative procedures for translating monetary items. In fact, even though the CSPC recommends the use of the closing rate to translate all foreign payables and receivables at the balance sheet date, it allows companies to value long term monetary items at the historic rate, if they wish.

III Exchange gains and losses on foreign payables and receivables

There is consensus within the Community that losses arising from the restatement of foreign debtors and creditors at the balance sheet date should be taken to income. In contrast, unrealised gains are not accounted for in the same way across countries. In fact, as shown in Table 6.2, three different approaches to the recognition of gains on unsettled foreign balances exist in Europe. Those countries that require the recognition of unrealised currency gains as a profit in the income statement are Denmark, Ireland, the Netherlands, and the UK. Conversely, those countries which require companies to defer unrealised translation gains in the balance sheet are Belgium, France, Italy and Spain. Finally, in Germany, unrealised foreign currency gains are not recognised at all; that is, are not taken into account, as the receivables (payables) continue to be valued at the lower (higher) historical exchange rate.

The recognition of translation gain on unsettled foreign receivables and payables   Table 6.2

Countries	Gain taken to income	Gain deferred in balance sheet	Gain not recognised
Belgium		X	
Denmark	X		
France		X	
Germany			X
Ireland	X		
Italy		X	
Netherlands	X		
Spain		X	
UK	X		

Within the above categories, some differences appear to exist with respect (i) to the distinction between short term and long term monetary items, (ii) to the setting-off of positive and negative translation differences and (iii) to the treatment of hedged foreign currency positions, as shown in Table 6.3.

(i) Short term versus long term gains and losses

The IASC has changed its position on the issue of distinguishing between short term and long term transactions. While the original IAS 21 (1983, para 28) authorised the optional deferral not only of exchange gains but also of losses on long term transactions, in the revised standard (1993) neither losses nor gains on long term foreign transactions may be deferred.

In the UK, Ireland and Denmark, the requirement to take unrealised gains to income applies to all such exchange gains. However, in the Netherlands it is restricted to short term gains. Dijksma and Hoogendorn (1993, p.169) report that the Dutch Council on Annual Reporting (RJ 1.03.908/10) allows companies to defer unrealised exchange gains on long term transactions to maturity, while unrealised gains on short term transactions should be taken to income.

Subsequent exchange losses on long term transactions in the same currency should then be deducted from the deferred gain.

Exchange differences on short term and long term transactions may also be treated differently in jurisdictions in which positive translation differences are generally deferred while exchange losses are generally taken to income. For instance, in France, the PCG (p.II.13) indicates that for foreign currency transactions covering more than one accounting period (*opérations affectant plusieurs exercises*), unrealised exchange losses may be amortised to maturity (Raffegeau et al., 1989, p.545). In Italy, the CSPC allows companies not to restate long term monetary items at the close of the balance sheet, in which case neither gains nor losses on such unsettled balances are recognised (Accounting Advisory Forum, 1995, p. 55). In contrast, rules in Spain, Belgium and Germany do not distinguish between short term and long term monetary items for the recognition of translation differences.

(ii) Setting-off positive and negative translation differences

The setting-off of positive and negative translation differences is an indirect way of recognising gains in income in countries where gains are not, as a general rule, taken to the profit and loss account. However, the rules with regard to the set-off of gains and losses on unsettled foreign transactions are not always unambigous and appear to vary within the Community. While some countries allow a full set-off between all positive and negative translation differences, other countries require separate set-offs between short term items and between long term items, or other jurisdictions require a separate set-off between gains and losses in individual currencies. An alternative point of view is that a set-off should be restricted to short term transactions only. Indeed, the Accounting Advisory Forum (1995, para 12) considers it appropriate to set-off all translation differences on short term items, irrespective of the currency in which they are expressed.

In the UK and Ireland, SSAP 20 (para 60) suggests that all positive translation differences should be fully set-off against negative translation differences. A similar approach has been adopted in Denmark in the DRV 9 (Christiansen and Hansen, 1995, p. 815).

In the Netherlands positive and negative exchange differences are set-off against each other for each foreign currency, with a further distinction being made between those exchange differences arising from short term and those arising from long term transactions. Where long term gains have been deferred, which is optional (Dijksma and Hoogendoorn, 1993, p.169), future exchange losses on long term transactions should be deducted from deferred unrealised gains in the same currency.

In Belgium, on the other hand, the set-off of unrealised gains and losses by currency is permitted, but no separation between short term and long term translation differences is made (Jorissen and Block, 1995, p. 473). The Spanish rules go one step further and require that the maturities of the assets and liabilities involved must coincide exactly. According to Lopez Diaz and Rivero Torre (1995, p. 2283) exchange differences must be classified by maturity and currency and unrealised gains may be credited to profit up to the amount of the losses within each homogeneous group. Furthermore, unrealised gains may be credited to profit up to an amount of unrealised exchange losses which have been charged to previous years' profits, and gains deferred in prior years may be credited to income up to an amount of the current year's exchange losses. In France, the setting-off of positive and negative translation differences may be carried out with the remaining balance being shown in the balance sheet as a provision (Griziaux, 1995, p.1242). In Germany, even though the set-off between positive and negative translation differences is accepted under certain circumstances, there remains controversy with respect to the extent to which the item by item valuation may be departed from (Ordelheide and Pfaff, 1994, p.148). According to the IdW's revised proposal (1986) netting between positive and negative differences is allowed as long as hedged positions exist (von Wysocki, 1987).

(iii) Hedged positions

The contrast in points of view on the issue of foreign currency transactions is also reflected in the area of hedged foreign currency positions. It may be noted however, that the issue of accounting for financial instruments used to hedge balances in a foreign currency is currently under international discussion.

The relevant rule adopted in the original IAS 21 (1983, para 26) suggested that "for short term transactions, the forward rates specified in the related foreign exchange contracts *may* be used as the basis for measuring and reporting the transactions." However, the revised IAS 21 (1993, para 14) now states that it does not deal with hedge accounting other than the hedge of a net investment in a foreign entity. Instead the standard indicates that "other aspects of hedge accounting, including the criteria for the use of hedge accounting and the requirement for the recognition of exchange differences and the discontinuance of hedge accounting, will be dealt with in an IAS on financial instruments". The

Accounting Advisory Forum considers it "common practice to use the exchange rate specified in the hedging instrument as the basis for translation and to defer any resulting translation difference until the expiry of the position." (1995, para 23).

At present, the degree of discretion with respect to the use of the forward rate varies across countries. In the UK, for instance, SSAP 20 (1983, para 6) suggests that "where there are related or matching forward contracts in respect of trading transactions, the rates of exchange specified in those contracts *may* be used". For the Netherlands, Dijksma and Hoogendoorn (1993, p.168) indicate that the RJ's position (RJ 1.03.907) is that, in cases where the foreign exchange rate risk is hedged, "it is *preferable* to value those receivables or payables at the relevant forward rate". In France, the PCG (p.II.13) provides in the circumstance of hedging an exception from the general requirement to record a provision for exchange differences (Griziaux, 1995, p. 1241). In Germany, the IdW's opinion is that the use of the forward rate or the closing rate is optional under the specific circumstance of a hedge (von Wysocki, 1987, p. 225).

In Belgium, on the other hand, the regulations are less flexible. The recommendation issued in 1987 by the Commission on Accounting Standards indicates that "when a forward contract was entered into as a hedge the commercial transaction *will* be recorded at the exchange rate stipulated in the forward contract and no exchange results are recognised under this treatment. If however, the company takes out a forward contract for trading purposes, the accounting treatment is the same as for an unhedged transaction" (Jorissen and Block, 1995, p.473). Similarly, in Denmark, the DRV 9 (sections 74-78) deals explicitly with forward cover. Exchange rates relating to a hedged transaction *must* be adjusted, if adjustments for the corresponding receivables and payables were made. "Both exchange rate adjustments *must* be entered in the profit and loss account" (Christiansen and Hansen, 1995, p.815).

Finally, it may be noted that the reporting on hedged positions has not been dealt with at all in Italy.

A further aspect on the issue of reporting foreign exchange differences concerns partial regulation in response to special economic conditions. In Spain, companies in regulated industries have been the subject of a number of ministerial orders concerning the treatment of translation differences on foreign receivables and payables as a result of the substantial devaluation of the peseta against the ECU in 1992 and 1993 which affected companies with high foreign currency debt. Whilst the regulators refused to authorize price increases to absorb the exchange losses, they introduced new accounting rules which allowed the amortization of exchange losses over the life of the foreign payable or receivable.

A final point of difference is related to the specific topic of foreign debt. Where a loan has been raised in a foreign currency in order to finance a fixed asset, there are specific regulations concerning the accounting treatment of the effects of exchange rate movements in Spain (PGC Art. 14) and France (PCG, p.II.13). In Spain the unrealised gain or loss on foreign loans may be capitalised and included in the cost of the assets financed, while French law allows the capitalization and amortization of unrealised losses arising from loans in a foreign currency.

Table 6.3 demonstrates that even though countries may be divided into three principal groups with respect to the 'general' treatment of the recognition of translation differences, at a detailed level the regulatory positions appear to be quite diverse.

Translation of foreign financial statements

I Principal methods of translating foreign financial statements

Various methods of translating foreign financial statements for incorporation into the consolidated accounts have been developed, of which the principal will be briefly characterised. Under the *closing rate method* all balance sheet items are translated at the rate prevailing at the balance sheet date (the 'closing rate'). No agreement exists with respect to the translation of items in the income statement, which may be either translated at the closing rate, or alternatively the rate ruling when revenues and expenses are recognised (the 'actual rate') which might be approximated by an average rate. Translation gains and losses under the closing rate method are transferred to the balance sheet and included under reserves.

The *monetary/non-monetary method* translates monetary assets and liabilities at the closing rate, and all other balance sheet items at the historic rate. Income and charges are translated at their date of recognition ('historic rate'), for which the average rate for the financial year is often used as an approximation. The translation of depreciation, however, always follows the treatment of the corresponding assets. The translation differences are recognised in the profit and loss account.

The recognition of translation differences on unsettled foreign currency receivables and payables

Table 6.3

Countries	Gains recognised in income					Gains deferred to balance sheet			Gains not recognised
	UK	Ireland	Denmark	Netherlands	France	Spain	Belgium	Italy	Germany
Legal requirement	No	No	No	No	Yes	Yes	No	No	No
Location of rule	ASB SSAP 20 (1983)	ASB SSAP 20 (1983)	FSR Standard No. 9 (1994)	RJ Standard 1.03.906-12 (1986)	PCG p.II.12-13 (1982)	PGC V part, 14a (1983)	Commission des Normes Comptables Bulletin No.20 (1987)	CSPC Document No.9 (1983)	General Accounting Principles Art. 252.253 HGB (1985)
Distinction between long term (LT) and short term (ST) monetary items	*	*	*	Option to defer gain on LT items	Option to amortize losses on LT items	*	*	Option to not recognize gain or loss on LT items	*
Set-off between positive and negative translation differences	Full set-off	Full set-off	Full set-off	Separate set-off between ST and LT differences in the same currency	Set-off under the condition of a provision in the balance sheet	Separate set-off between homogeneous currency groups (by maturity and currency)	Separate set-off between identical currencies	*	Set-off under the condition of hedging
Treatment of gain or loss on foreign loans for purchase of fixed assets	*	*	*	*	Loss capitalized and amortised	Gain or loss capitalized	*	*	*
Use of forward rate in case of specific hedging	Optional	Optional	Required	Optional	Optional	Required	Required	*	Optional

* = No reference made to the specific issue in the local regulations

Under the *temporal method* the relevant translation rates depend on the measurement basis of the assets and liabilities. Balances valued at historic cost are translated at the relevant historic rate, balances carried at present value (i.e. replacement cost or net realisable value) or future value (i.e. value of future receipts) are translated at the closing rate or appropriate future rate. The translation of the income statement and the reporting of the translation difference corresponds to the monetary/non-monetary method.

Under a system of historic cost accounting, the monetary/non-monetary method is almost identical to the temporal method, since balances which are measured at historic cost (generally non-monetary items) are translated at the historic rates, while balances which are valued on a current basis (generally monetary items) are translated at the closing rate, with the exception of inventory measured at net realisable value. Under a system of current cost accounting, the temporal method is identical to the closing rate method.

The *current/non-current method* uses the closing rate for current balances, and the historic rate for all other assets and liabilities. The translation of the income statement and the reporting of the translation difference corresponds to the monetary/non-monetary or temporal method.

A combination of the closing rate method and the temporal method is prescribed in FAS 52, the choice of method being determined by the 'functional currency' in which the foreign subsidiary ('foreign entity') operates. The functional currency is "the currency of the primary economic environment in which that entity operates" (para 5). FAS 52 defines the local currency as the functional currency if the subsidiary's operations are "relatively self-contained and integrated within a particular country" and for these entities the use of the closing rate method is prescribed. If a foreign subsidiary ('foreign operation') is a "direct and integral component or extension of the parent company's operations", the functional currency is the parent's currency and in this case the use of the temporal method is required. It might be noted, that FAS 52 does not use the term temporal method, but refers to it as 'remeasurement' and provides in its appendix guidance for remeasurement into the parent's functional currency. IAS 21, which followed FAS 52 in time and in content, similarly divides subsidiaries into the 'two categories' and prescribes the closing rate method for 'foreign entities' and the temporal method or monetary/non-monetary method for 'foreign operations that are an integral part of the operations of the parent'.

With the exception of Germany, the regulatory position in all Member States, has been greatly influenced by IAS 21 and thus by FAS 52 in this area, as a similar choice is generally allowed between the closing rate method for independent subsidiaries and the monetary/non-monetary method or the temporal method for subsidiaries which are integrated into the parent company's operations.

It may be noted that, in advising the European Commission on this matter, the Accounting Advisory Forum (1995, para 34) suggests a similar distinction between integrated operations and non-integrated operations and the translation of financial statements of non-integrated foreign operations using the closing rate method and integrated foreign operations using the temporal method.

In some countries, the rules on translating the accounts of foreign subsidiaries have been given the force of law. In Belgium, for instance, the Royal Decree of 1990 refers (in Art. 42-43) to the closing rate method and the monetary/non-monetary method to translate foreign subsidiaries into consolidated statements - without specifying the conditions of their use - although another method may be applied if it is more likely to provide a true and fair view. However, the Report to the King (included as an appendix to the law) suggests the use of the monetary/non-monetary method in particular for foreign subsidiaries which constitute an integrated part of the parent company and the closing rate method for economically and financially independent subsidiaries (Aerts and Theunisse, 1995). It should be noted that in Belgium, the translation gain under the monetary/non-monetary method have to be recorded in the profit and loss account but can alternatively be treated in the same way as unrealised exchange differences in the accounts of individual companies; that is, by deferral to the balance sheet. Interestingly, the same option is provided to companies in Spain, where the Real Decreto of 1991 prescribes the closing rate method except when the activities of the foreign company are so closely linked to those of a Spanish group company that it can be considered as an extension of its activities, in which case the monetary/non-monetary method is applied (López Díaz and Rivero Torre, 1995). In France, the *Conseil National de la Comptabilité* (CNC) formulated the relevant regulations in the revised PCG (1986), which, although not mandatory, proposed the use of the closing rate method for independent subsidiaries and the monetary/non-monetary method, referred to as "historic rate method" (Scheid and Walton, 1992, p.247), for subsidiaries which are integrated into the parent operations. An alternative treatment for translation differences under the monetary/non-monetary method exists, as profit and loss on long term monetary items may be amortized, similarly to the treatment in the individual accounts.

In Italy, the CSPC has drafted a document in which it recommends rules similar to IAS 21. In the UK, Ireland, the Netherlands, and Denmark where standards of accounting practice have been issued by professional bodies in this area, these also closely reflect the suggestions in IAS 21.

It appears that only in Germany has there been no regulatory solution with respect to the translation of foreign financial statements and, in contrast to the accounting for foreign transactions, there is no accepted convention. The guidelines issued by the IdW and the Schmalenbach Gesellschaft differ and do not represent a binding or accepted standard. The IdW suggests in its revised proposal (1986) the use of the closing rate method and the temporal method, without however linking their use to the degree of integration of the foreign subsidiary into the parent undertaking. Furthermore all of the methods described earlier are permitted and prominent in practice. Ordelheide (1995, p. 1596) comments that "the variety of methods used in practice impairs fundamentally the comparison between groups on the basis of their annual accounts, notably for quoted undertakings".

The following diagram (Figure 6.1) demonstrates the dominant influence of IAS 21 / FAS 52 with respect to the translation of foreign financial statements through the different regulatory modes - law, standard or recommendation - in Europe, and contrasts the German position to the regulatory consensus.

A final point to note is that, in spite of the near unanimiy on this issue, it is superficial. At the detailed level, there are differences with respect to the translation of profit and loss items, as is shown in Table 6.4 below. In fact, the Accounting Advisory Forum (para. 33) allows the alternative of using either the closing rate, or the rate existing at the time of the transaction (which might be approximated by an average rate) to translate the income statement under the closing rate method. A similar approach has been adopted in France, the UK, Ireland, Germany and the Netherlands. It may be noted that IAS 21 has changed its position on this particular issue, as in 1993 it limited the translation of profit and loss items under the closing rate method to the use of the exchange rate at the date of the transaction which may be for practical purposes an average rate (para. 30). This position is now consistent with FAS 52 (para. 12).

Figure 6.1

The translation of foreign financial statements in Europe

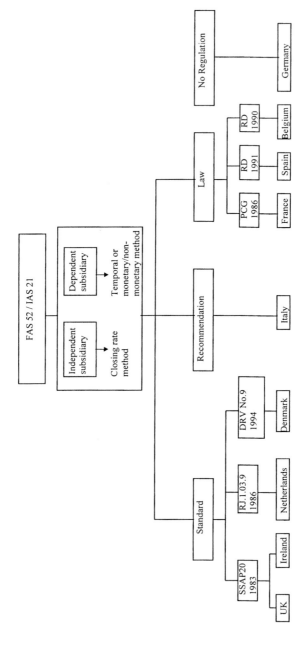

The translation of foreign financial statements in the EU

Table 6.4

Country	SOURCE		RULES		PRESCRIBED				METHOD		
	Law	Binding standard	Non-binding recommendation		Closing rate method				Temporal or monetary/non-monetary method		
					BS	IS	TD		BS	IS	TD
		FAS 52 (1981)			CR	AR	E		CR/HR	HR/AR	IS
		IAS 21 (1983)			CR	AR or CR	E		CR/HR	HR/AR	IS
		IAS 21 (1993)			CR	AR	E		CR/HR	HR/AR	IS
Belgium	Art.42,43 Royal Decree (1990)				CR	AR	E		CR/HR	HR/AR	IS*
Denmark		FSR Standard No.9 (1994)			CR	AR	E		CR/HR	HR/AR	IS
France	P.II 155-157 PCG (1986)				CR	AR or CR	E		CR/HR	HR/AR	IS*
Germany			IdW Proposal (1986)		CR	AR or CR	E		CR/HR	HR/AR	IS
Ireland		SSAP 20 (1983)			CR	AR or CR	E		CR/HR	HR/AR	IS
Italy			Draft Document of CSPC (1995)		CR	AR	E		CR/HR	HR/AR	IS
Netherlands		R.J. 1.03.913-36 (1986)			CR	AR or CR	E		CR/HR	HR/AR	IS
Spain	Art.54-59 Real Decreto (1991)				CR	AR	E		CR/HR	HR/AR	IS*
U.K.		SSAP 20 (1983)			CR	AR or CR	E		CR/HR	HR/AR	IS

Legend: AR = Average rate; BS = Balance sheet; CR = Closing rate; E = Equity (Reserves); HR = Historic rate; IS = Income statement; TD = Translation difference; * = alternatively recognition of translation difference corresponds to the rule in individual accounts.

119

6.4 Foreign currency accounting in practice

In order to investigate the effect, if any, of the different regulatory strategies of European countries with regard to the sources of authority and the degree of formalism in rules on the foreign currency accounting policies adopted in practice, the annual reports of European companies were analysed. The results presented are based on an earlier investigation (Ebbers, 1997b) for the financial years 1987 (120 companies) and 1993 (182 companies) of the thesis sample which comprises European multinational companies.

Foreign currency transactions

Table 6.5 shows (i) the different exchange rates reported by companies to translate foreign payables and receivables at the balance sheet date and (ii) the treatment of exchange gains and losses in the annual accounts.

(i) The exchange rate

The closing rate was the dominant rate used to adjust foreign currency receivables and payables in the sample, with the exception of German companies which applied a combination of the historic rate and the closing rate. 87 (73%) out of 120 companies in 1987, and 146 (80%) out of 182 companies in 1993 disclosed the use of the closing rate to translate foreign receivables and payables, while 25 German companies in 1987 and 24 in 1993 applied the closing rate only if this led to the recognition of an exchange loss. Companies reported the use of the forward rate to measure foreign transactions which were effectively hedged by forward contracts. These results are in line with a study carried out by the *Fédération des Experts Comptables* (see FEE, 1991, p.242) for the year 1989, where in 198 (71%) out of 278 cases the closing rate was reported. The results indicate a high level of uniformity with respect to the valuation basis of foreign transactions among Member States, the exception being Germany.

(ii) Reporting exchange differences

All exchange differences (both unrealised losses and unrealised gains) were taken to income by about half the sample companies in both years, namely 87 (48%) companies in 1993 and 62 (52%) companies in 1987, a similar finding to the study by FEE for the year 1989 (FEE, 1991, p.243). The use of separate methods for gain and loss (unrealised gain deferred in the balance sheet and unrealised loss taken to income) was found in the accounting policies of 63

(34%) companies in 1993 and 40 (33%) companies in 1987. In line with national regulations, other treatments of exchange rate differences were observed, such as the deferral of unrealised exchange losses in the case of Spanish utility companies and the separate treatment of translation differences for long term transactions and short term transactions in the case of Dutch companies. However, in several instances, the reported treatment of the translation difference was not in conformity with national regulations. These departures from the local rules will be illustrated next.

The use of the closing rate to adjust foreign receivables and payables at the balance sheet date is, with the exception of Germany, uniform across Europe both in terms of regulations and practices. Moreover, the use of a forward rate in those cases where a foreign transaction is specifically hedged appears to be standard accounting practice, even though its use has an optional character in some Member States' regulations.

German reporting is in line with the strict interpretation of the *GoB (Grundsätze ordnungsmäßiger Buchführung)*, referred to earlier, in particular the prudence principle and the historic cost principle, and thus inducing an understatement of receivables and an overstatement of payables. The accounting policies of Daimler Benz and Henkel illustrate this principle, whereby Henkel indicates its policy in the case of hedged or closed positions.

Daimler Benz (1993):
"Foreign currency receivables are translated in the individual financial statements at the bid price on the day they are recorded or at the spot rate on the balance sheet date if lower. Foreign currency payables are translated at the asked price on the day they are recorded or at the spot rate on the balance sheet date if higher."

Henkel (1993):
"Accounts receivable and payable in foreign currency are translated in the financial statements of individual companies at the rates of exchange in force when they first originated. If, however, translation of foreign currency items at the rate in force on the balance sheet date produces a lower amount for receivables or a higher amount for liabilities, then foreign currency items are translated at the rates in force on the balance sheet date, unless amounts receivable and payable in a particular currency balance each other out or the amounts involved are covered by forward exchange transactions."

Table 6.5

Reporting practice of foreign receivables and payables in the annual accounts

	Belgium		Denmark		France		Germany		Ireland		Italy		Netherlands		Spain		U.K.		Total	
Year	1987	1993	1987	1993	1987	1993	1987	1993	1987	1993	1987	1993	1987	1993	1987	1993	1987	1993	1987	1993
Number of reporting companies	9	10	4	5	15	24	28	27	7	9	7	24	18	24	7	17	25	42	120	182
Translation of monetary items																				
Closing rate	9	10	4	5	12	20			7	9	6	21	18	24	6	15	25	42	87	146
Lower (higher) of CR/HR							25	24											25	24
Unspecified					3	4	3	3			1	3			1	2			8	12
Recognition of unrealised translation difference in income																				
Gain and loss	2	2	3	4	6	7			6	7	3	7	16	18	3	3	23	39	62	87
Only loss	5	6	1	1	4	11	25	24			2	10	1	2	2	9			40	63
Other	2	2			5	6	3	3	1	2	2	7	1	4	2	5	2	3	18	32

As it is indicated in Table 6.5, the treatment of exchange differences observed in the sample was diverse. This observance concerned not only discrepancies between European regulations as explored above, but also between national regulations and corresponding reporting practices.

Even though the Belgian *Commission des Normes Comptables* recommends the deferral of unrealised exchange gains, 2 Belgian companies included unrealised exchange gain in the income statement, as illustrated by the following extract from Sipef:

Sipef (1993):
"The items of the assets and liabilities expressed in foreign currencies are converted into Belgian francs at the average monthly date of their booking.
On the closing date of the balance sheet:
- non-monetary items of the balance sheet, such as formation expenses, intangible and tangible fixed assets, financial fixed assets and stocks (on the assets side) and the items under own funds (on the liability side), are maintained at their acquisition value expressed in BEF, whatever the value at the balance sheet date of the currency in which the acquisition price was paid.
- monetary items of the balance sheet, such as amounts receivable after more than a year or within one year, cash investments, cash at bank and cash in hand and deferrals and accruals (on the asset side) and the provision items for liabilities and charges, amounts payable after more than a year or within one year and deferrals and accruals (on the liability side) are evaluated at the exchange rates retained for the foreign currencies at the date of closing the balance sheet.
The exchange variances resulting from these evaluations are accumulated per currency. The book keeping of these exchange variances is done using the method of integral accounting of the variances whereby the positive as well as the negative variances are booked into the result. The variances per currency are booked under the other financial charges or income. "

In France, several companies indicated different accounting policies in the parent company and consolidated accounts, by including only exchange losses in income in the parent company accounts while taking both losses and gains into the consolidated income statement. However, France made use of Art. 29.2 of the 7th Directive which provides Member States with the option to permit the use of valuation methods in consolidated financial statements other than those used in the annual accounts of the parent undertaking. As indicated by FEE (1993, p.116), this alternative treatment is applicable to French companies in the particular case of foreign exchange adjustments. The examples of Pernod Ricard and Matra Hachette illustrate this practice:

Pernod Ricard (1993):
Note to the parent company financial statements:
"Income and expenses arising from currency translation differences are recorded at their exchange value on the transaction date. Payables, receivables and cash equivalents in foreign currency are recorded on the balance sheet at their year-end exchange rates. The differences arising from the discounting of payables and receivables at these rates are recorded on the balance sheet as currency translation adjustments. Unrealized exchange losses are subject to a provision for risks, at full value."

Note to the consolidated financial statement:
"Foreign currency transactions are translated at the exchange rate prevailing at the transaction date. Gains and losses resulting from foreign currency translation up until December 31, 1993 are recorded in the statement of income."

Matra Hachette (1993):
Note to the consolidated financial statement:
"Receivables and payables in foreign currencies are translated into the local currency of each company on the basis of year-end exchange rates. Unrealised gains and losses are credited or charged to income. However when a transaction in foreign currency is hedged, the contracted rate will be used."

In Italy, a number of companies recorded all unrealised exchange differences in the profit and loss account, even though the CSPC recommends the deferral of unrealised exchange gains.

Sogefi (1993):
"Accounts receivable and payables denominated in a foreign currency are translated at the exchange rate ruling at the year end and the resulting exchange gains and losses are charged to the income statement."

The exceptional discretion which the Spanish Government accorded to utilities as a result of the peseta devaluations in 1992 and 1993 was described in Part Three of this chapter. The policy of defering and amortising not only unrealised exchange gains but also losses is illustrated by the Spanish company Endesa:

Endesa (1994):

"Foreign currency balances are recorded at the exchange rates prevailing at the transaction date. At December 31 of each year, the outstanding balances of these transactions are reflected in the balance sheet at the then current exchange rate. Exchange differences were recorded as follows: as stipulated by the Ministry of Economy and Finance Order dated March 12, 1993, adapting the Spanish National Chart of accounts for regulated entities, the exchange differences on each transaction arising in the year had to be allocated by the interest method over the transaction term. The exchange losses financially calculated as allocable to future years are recorded as "deferred charges" on the asset side of the balance sheet for allocation to income in future years on the basis of the financial calculation method used. Exchange losses allocable to the current year or to prior years are recorded as a financial expense in the year in which they arise, per the aforementioned Ministerial Order, recognition of the exchange gain revenue on each transaction is generally deferred until maturity thereof. However, the exchange gains arising in the current year which, based on the financial calculation, are allocable to prior years are recognized as revenues up to the limit of exchange losses arising on the same transaction which were allocated to income in prior year, the excess, if any, being recorded on the liability side of the balance sheet as deferred revenues. (...) A Ministry of Industry and Energy Order dated December 3, 1993, implemented by a subsequent resolution, specified the procedure for recovery of the exchange differences which arose in 1993 and 1994 through the electricity rate during the period from 1993 to 1997."

In the Netherlands, a similar exception exists for unrealised exchange gains on long term transactions. However, in contrast to Portugal, this policy is optional and the probable reversal of the unrealised gain is not a necessary condition for its adoption. Instead, the relevant gains are amortised until maturity and future unrealised losses can be offset against them. Such treatment for unrealised exchange gains and losses on long term transactions was reported in the annual report of Royal Nedlloyd, which also indicates the valuation of hedged transactions at the corresponding contracted rate:

Royal Nedlloyd (1993):

"Short-term receivables and payables in foreign currencies are translated into guilders at the rates prevailing on the balance sheet date, unless in specific cases the foreign currency position has been hedged by forward contracts. In that case the short-term receivables and payables are valued at the relevant forward rates. Exchange differences resulting from these short-term receivables and payables in foreign currencies are recognised in the operating result in the period in which they arise.

Profits on exchange arising in respect of long-term receivables and payables in foreign currencies other than from/to foreign subsidiaries are credited to the 'Equalization account currency exchange differences' forming part of 'Current liabilities'. Losses on exchange in respect of these assets and liabilities are charged to result unless they can be offset against prior-year gains on the same currency with the 'Equalization account currency exchange differences'. The profits credited to this equalization account are systematically allocated to the results during the remaining term of the receivables and payables concerned."

Foreign financial statements

European practice reflects the regulatory harmony that exists with regard to the content of translation methods for foreign financial statements. As shown in Table 6.6, the reporting practice in the sample confirms the dominant use of the closing rate method in each country, reported by 92 companies (76%) in 1987 and 149 companies (82%) in 1993. Few companies distinguished between integrated and non-integrated subsidiaries, where the temporal or monetary/non-monetary method must be applied to the former, while only the latter was translated using the closing rate method. Most groups that translated the balance sheet at the closing rate, translated revenues and expenses at average rates for the financial period (referred to as the 'modified closing rate method'). This increased from 71% of the companies using the closing rate method in 1987 to 83% in 1993, a trend which anticipated the regulatory move in the revised IAS 21. Since 1993, this standard has no longer recommended the use of the closing rate to translate the income statement of foreign subsidiaries. It may be noted that some of the companies which translated the income statement at the closing rate (referred to as the 'pure closing rate method'), did so even though its use is not permitted in national regulations. Finally, German practice deviated from the relatively uniform pattern throughout Europe, not only because German companies applied a variety of methods but also because they combined them in many ways, as will be illustrated next.

The diversity which exists in German consolidated statements in this area is illustrated by the following examples: (i) the functional currency approach, including a "modified" temporal method which was reported in one case by BASF; (ii) a version of the temporal method where the translation difference is not recognised in the profit and loss account, as reported by Bayer; and (iii) the use of the current/non-current method by Daimler Benz. In fact, translation methods are individualised by companies. For instance, Daimler Benz transfers translation differences to reserves and translates "borrowed capital" (presumably long-term loans) at the current rate, which is not consistent with the current/non-current method. BASF translates inventories at the closing rate under the "modified" temporal method. However the relevant note to the accounts remains silent on the treatment of the translation difference.

BASF (1993):

"Currency translation was based on the principle of functional currency. Because of the low direct or indirect effect of the German mark on the trading operations of our subsidiaries and affiliates in North America, Japan and Korea, the local currency is to be regarded as the functional currency. The financial statements of these companies are converted to German marks as follows:

-all income and expense and the profit/loss, at quarterly average rates

-all assets, liabilities and provisions at year-end current rates; (...)

-the equity is carried forward at the rates at the date of payment or accumulation; the adjustment to the values converted at year end current rates is shown separately in the balance sheet as translation adjustment in the equity.

The other companies, whose business operations are more markedly influenced, directly or indirectly, by changes in the parity of the German mark, are converted in accordance with the modified temporal method. This also applies in principle to companies in high inflation countries, or if the financial statements are influenced by national regulations regarding inflation accounting. In these cases, the financial statements are converted to German Mark as follows:

-fixed assets, except loans, at rates in effect at the date of acquisition or production (historical rates)

-all other assets, liabilities and provisions at year end current rates

-paid in capital at the rate at the date of payment or acquisition; the earned surplus is determined as a remaining balance in the balance sheets converted in accordance with these principles."

Bayer (1993):

"Foreign consolidated companies' financial statements are translated into DM according to a temporal method which does not affect net income. Foreign currency translation is made as follows:

-fixed assets, intangibles, investment in affiliated companies and other securities included in investments at the average DM exchange rate in the year of addition (historical average rate)

-all other balance sheet items and net income at the year-end rate

-all income and expenses at the weighted average rate for the year.

Bayer's portion of the adjustments resulting from the translation of foreign currency items in the balance sheet is included in capital reserves, while the minority stockholders' portions are included in minority interest."

Translation of foreign financial statements

Table 6.6

	Belgium 1987	1993	Denmark 1987	1993	France 1987	1993	Germany 1987	1993	Ireland 1987	1993	Italy 1987	1993	Netherland 1987	1993	Spain 1987	1993	UK 1987	1993	Total 1987	1993
Number of reporting companies	9	10	4	5	15	24	28	27	7	9	7	24	18	24	7	17	25	42	120	182
Closing rate method																				
1.Pure	2		2	4			4	3	1	3	1	3	5	3			12	10	27	26
2.Modified	5	8	2	1	14	21	5	14	4	6	5	16	11	16	6	9	13	32	65	123
Temporal method							2	2					1	3					3	5
Monetary/non-monetary method															1	3			1	3
Current/non-current method							5	4											5	4
Combination of methods					1		3	3					1	1					5	4
No disclosure	2	2				3	9	1	2		1	5		1		5			14	17

Daimler Benz (1992):

"The accounts of all foreign companies are translated to DM on the basis of historical exchange rates for non-current assets, and at the year end exchange rates for current assets, borrowed capital, and unappropriated profit. Stockholders' equity in DM is the remaining difference between translated assets less translated liabilities and unappropriated profit. The difference resulting from the translation of balance sheet items is recorded in consolidated retained earnings. Expense and income items are essentially translated at average annual exchange rates. To the extent that they relate to fixed assets (fixed asset depreciation, profit or loss from disposal of fixed assets), they are translated at historical cost. Net income, additions to retained earnings, and the unappropriated profit are translated at year end rates. The difference resulting from the translation of annual net income, between annual average rates and the exchange rate at the balance sheet date is reflected in other operating income. "

In the Netherlands several companies translated foreign financial statements in a manner that departs from the rules established by the Annual Reporting Council. Although the groups DAF and van Ommeren use the temporal method, van Ommeren transfers the exchange difference to reserves, which is not in agreement with the regulatory guidelines, while DAF recognises the translation difference correctly in the profit and loss account. However, DAF translates inventories at the closing rate with is not consistent with the temporal method. Neither company applies the temporal method only to integrated subsidiaries; both appear to apply it to independent subsidiaries as well, which is another difference between practice and regulation.

Van Ommeren (1993):

"For the purpose of consolidating annual accounts denominated in foreign currencies, fixed assets are generally translated at historical rates of exchange, that is at the rates applicable at the year of acquisition.
Other assets and liabilities of consolidated group companies are translated at the closing exchange rates. Income and expenses in the annual accounts denominated in foreign currencies are translated at the closing rate of exchange, except in the case of tangible fixed asset depreciation for which historical exchange rates apply.
Exchange differences relating to the opening balance of net investments in foreign consolidated participating interests are taken direct to reserves. "

DAF (1993):

"For foreign subsidiaries expenditure on fixed assets is translated at the exchange rates ruling at the moment of acquisition. Expenditure on financial assets, current assets and

liabilities denominated in foreign currency relating to both foreign subsidiaries and to the Company are translated at the exchange rate ruling on the balance sheet date.

Exchange differences arising from the use of the exchange rates ruling at the balance sheet date for translating capital components denominated in foreign currency (excluding fixed assets) and from the use of the average rate of exchange for translating profit and loss accounts denominated in foreign currency are incorporated directly in the profit and loss account."

In the UK, from 1987 to 1993, a significant proportion of the companies changed the translation of the income statement from the closing rate to the average rate for the financial period. While in 1987 the proportions of both rates were about 50/50 in the UK sample, by 1993 the proportion of the companies using the average rate was 76% and only 24% indicated the closing rate. A company which reported such a change in policy was Whitbread:

Whitbread (1987 and 1993):

in 1987

"Assets and liabilities located overseas or denominated in a foreign currency and profits and losses of foreign subsidiaries and branches are translated into sterling at the foreign exchange rates ruling at the balance sheet date. Exchange differences arising from the re-translation of the opening net investment in foreign subsidiaries and branches at the closing rates of exchange are recorded as a movement on reserves."

in 1993

"Assets and liabilities denominated in foreign currencies are translated into sterling at the rates of exchange quoted at the balance sheet date. Trading results are translated into sterling at average rates of exchange for the year.(...)Currency gains and losses arising from the retranslation of the opening net assets of overseas operations, less those arising from related currency borrowings to the extent that they are matched, are recorded as a movement on reserves."

Although regulations in Denmark refer to the use of the 'exchange rate at the dates of transactions' to translate the income statement of foreign subsidiaries, the use of the closing rate was observed in some Danish annual reports and is here illustrated by the company Danisco:

Danisco (1993):

"Assets and liabilities as well as accounts of foreign subsidiaries in foreign currencies are translated into DKK at the rates of exchange ruling at the balance sheet date or at forward rates. Exchange adjustments are included in the profit and loss account. (...) Exchange gains or losses arising from the translation of the subsidiaries' net asset values at the beginning of the accounting year are included directly in capital and reserves. On direct hedging of investments abroad, exchange adjustments of such hedging are also dealt with in capital and reserves."

The use of historic rates to translate equity capital was generally reported by Spanish groups. This reporting policy, which is in line with national regulations is illustrated by the Spanish company Metrovacesa.

Metrovacesa (1993):

"The financial statements of the group companies abroad were translated to pesetas at the exchange rate ruling at the year end, exept for:

1. Capital and reserves, which were translated at the historical exchange rates

2. Statements of income, which were translated at the average exchange rate for the year

The exchange difference arising as a result of application of this translation procedure is included under the "shareholder's investment translation gains" caption in the accompanying consolidated balance sheet."

6.5 Concluding remarks

A key factor in the regulation of foreign currency reporting has been the harmonising effect of IAS 21 which has progressively gained acceptance throughout Europe without the force of legislation. Instead, market forces appear to have led to the widespread adoption of this regulatory initiative of US origin, which was taken up by the IASC and has been applied by multinational companies in Europe. This was made possible by the lack of other international regulatory positions on this issue, particularly by the European Commission, although it may be noted that recently the Accounting Advisory Forum has recommended rules in line with IAS 21 for the translation of foreign financial statements. However, because of the linkage between accounting and taxation and because of the emphasis on prudence in many Member States, the harmonising influence of IAS 21 has been limited to consolidated accounts.

This chapter has attempted to compare the regulations governing foreign currency reporting in different European countries. It demonstrated the widespread consensus with respect to the use of the closing rate method to translate foreign financial statements in the consolidated accounts on the one hand and the diversity in accounting for foreign transactions in individual accounts on the other. With respect to the regulations concerning the recognition of unrealised exchange gains, countries could be divided into three groups - those which recognise unrealised exchange gains in income, those which defer it and those which do not recognise such gains. However, at a detailed level, differing regulatory positions were observed with regard to short term and long term monetary items, currency hedging, and setting-off positive and negative translation differences.

Examples from the published accounts of European companies confirmed the relative uniformity in consolidated accounts and the diversity in individual accounts in this area. It remains to be seen whether this difference in the reporting of foreign currency balances will continue in the future. In a number of instances, there was evidence of reporting practices which depart from local regulations. These included variation in the treatment of unrealised exchange gains and the use of a number of company specific translation methods.

CHAPTER 7

THE DEFINITION OF A SUBSIDIARY

7.1 Introduction

The distinction between formalism and anti-formalism was at the roots of controversy surrounding the drafting of the criteria defining group companies included in the Seventh Directive (van Hulle and van der Tas, 1995). The *de facto* 'economic' criteria rely on the recognition of broader notions of unified decision-making and a dominant influence by the parent undertaking over a subsidiary, while the more precise *de jure* 'legal' criteria require the existence of legally-defined rights to control another company.

Following the implementation of the Seventh Directive, differences in regulatory strategy across countries are clearly evident. Economic control was not adopted in France, Spain and Italy. It was adopted in addition to legal control in the UK, Belgium and Denmark, but without detailed definition. In Germany, on the other hand, the conditions under which economic control may be presumed were specified in some detail in the law. Finally, in the Netherlands, where both forms of control were also implemented, economic control takes precedence over legal control.

As for the effect of the Seventh Directive on member state law, it was either implemented in commercial legislation (Germany, the UK and the Netherlands) or in a separate consolidation decree (Belgium, Denmark and Ireland) or in both (France, Italy and Spain). In addition to the law, supplementary standards have been issued in the Netherlands, the UK and Ireland.

It is evident that some countries have been very imaginative in their interpretation of the Directive and the resulting differences in regulatory strategy have given rise to various ways in which the boundaries of a group may be demarcated. In fact, at the present time, no two countries apart from the UK and Ireland have an identical accounting group concept. To some extent, the differing industrial structures and organisational forms which have developed in European nations over time have resisted accounting harmonisation.

In an attempt to explore the different regulatory structures in European group accounting, this chapter first deals with the accounting traditions that influenced the development of Article 1 of the Seventh Directive. The analysis then considers the current legal framework in the EU by identifying and comparing the sources and design of consolidation rules concerning the definition of a subsidiary in each member state. The definition of a subsidiary adopted in practice is then examined, with particular reference to any changes in regulatory approach that might have taken place at the time of the implementation of the Directive. This is based on a review of annual financial statements for the years 1987 and 1993.

7.2 The definition of a subsidiary in European company law

The first country requiring consolidated accounts in Europe was the UK. The growth of large public corporations in the mid-1930s and the emerging separation of control from ownership (Bircher, 1988) led eventually to the first legal requirement for consolidated accounts in the Companies Act 1947. In this Act, the definition of a parent-subsidiary relationship was on an entirely legal basis (*de jure* control), specified (in section 154) as either a 'majority of the equity' or 'control of the composition of the board'. These two legalistic consolidation criteria were mirrored in SSAP 14 issued in 1978 and also remained unchanged in the Companies Act 1985 (section 736).

In Germany, consolidated accounts were also published by groups long before there was a legal requirement (Ordelheide, 1995). In 1950, the allied occupation authorities required newly created companies in the coal and steel industry to publish an audited consolidated balance sheet and income statement following American disclosure requirements, specified in Art. 16 (3) of the model articles of association (*Mustersatzung*). This influenced the voluntary publication of consolidated accounts by other companies which preceded the first legal consolidation requirement for corporations as set out in the 1965 *Aktiengesetz* (Busse von Colbe and Ordelheide, 1993). The *Aktiengesetz*, or AktG, adopted the concept of economic control of a group (*i.e. de facto* control), specifying that a company with the legal form of a *Aktiengesellschaft (AG)* or *Kommanditgesellschaft auf Aktien (KGaA)* had to prepare consolidated financial statements if a subsidiary existed under 'unified management' (*einheitliche Leitung*, Art.18). The *Aktiengesetz* did not define 'unified management' but specified that a majority-owned enterprise (*in Mehrheitsbesitz stehendes Unternehmen*, Art.16(1)) is presumed to be a dependent undertaking (*abhängiges Unternehmen*, Art.17(2)) and that any dependent undertaking is presumed to be a group undertaking (*Konzernunternehmen*) under 'unified management'. Furthermore 'unified management' is presumed to exist in the relationships of integration (*Eingliederung*, Art.319) or contractual control

(*Beherrschungsvertrag*, Art.291). However, whilst consolidation is required if either integration or contractual control exist, majority ownership is not a necessary condition for consolidation. That is, in the case where there is majority ownership but there is not 'unified management', consolidation is not required. In the German *Publizitätsgesetz (PublG)*, which extended the requirement to consolidate to large groups irrespective of their legal form in 1969, an identical definition of the parent-subsidiary relationship in terms of 'unified management' was codified. It should be noted that the consolidation requirements in the *Aktiengesetz* and *Publizitätsgesetz* were limited to the consolidation of the accounts of German subsidiaries only, a particular feature of German financial reporting until recently.

In Ireland, the Irish Companies Act of 1963 introduced the requirement to consolidate and defined a subsidiary undertaking in close accordance with the UK *de jure* control concept. However, the legal criteria given in this Act were not only the 'control of the composition of the board and a 'majority holding of the equity capital', but also 'majority holding of voting rights'.

In Denmark, a Parliamentary Commission in 1964 defined a subsidiary in terms of a 'majority of shares' as well as a '*bestemmende indflydelse*' (dominant influence), the latter being based on 'a majority of shares, voting rights or other rights in the articles of association or agreements'. These definitions eventually formed the basis of the 1973 Companies Act which contained the notion of a group for the first time in Danish accounting legislation, although it may be noted that proposals for group accounts actually date back to 1934, when the Nordic countries attempted to harmonise company law. This project was never completed because of the Second World War. According to Christiansen and Hansen (1995, p. 841), these initial proposals were based on *de facto* economic control and, they suggest, were influenced by the prevailing German definition of a group. The Financial Statements Act 1981, which implemented the 4th Directive, did not change the definition of a group, although it made obligatory the requirement to publish group accounts.

In the Netherlands, the definition of a subsidiary was referred to for the first time in the 1971 *Wet op de jaarrekening van ondernemingen* (Annual Accounts Act) which required (in Art.13 para.1) parent companies to include, in the explanatory notes on the financial statements, either consolidated statements or the financial statements of all subsidiaries, combined or individually. The definition of a subsidiary was based on a direct or indirect "majority share capital participation" (Klaassen and Hekers, 1995, p.2153). It only became obligatory to prepare consolidated accounts in the Netherlands in 1984 as a result of the legislation introducing the EC 4th Directive (through the Act of 7 December 1983).

In Belgium, regulations on consolidation evolved from the late 1960s until the mid-1980s as a result of initiatives by the Banking Commission and pressure from workers' councils, but they were related only to holding companies (*portefeuillemaatschappijen / sociétés à portefeuille*) at that time. Holding companies had been institutionalised under a separate legal statute (the 1967 Royal Decree), which defined holding companies as companies which hold shares in one or more companies and which "enable them (*de facto* or *de jure*) to direct the activities of the dependent companies" (Aerts and Theunisse, 1995, p.500). However, this Decree did not contain any requirement with respect to group accounts.

The first legal requirements in Belgium on the disclosure of group-related information were contained in the Royal Decree of 27 November 1973 concerning the economic and financial information to be disclosed to workers' councils. Although this legal text does not define group structures, it is interesting to note that trade union representatives and employer representatives disagreed on the issue of *de jure* and *de facto* control. Whilst the trade union representatives favoured economic control, legal control inherent in the 'majority participation' criterion was preferred by the employers' organisations. The notion of economic control was specified by the union representatives as "a lower limit of 10% of the equity capital, 10% of the voting rights, or the nomination of more than 25% of the number of delegates on the board of directors with negative proof of association to be provided by the company concerned" (Aerts and Theunisse, 1995, p.502). A Royal Decree in 1977 established the first legal requirement for consolidation. In the law of 20 January 1978, the definition of a subsidiary that was previously included in the Royal Decree of 1967 was modified to that of a company in which a holding company had "a majority in the capital or voting rights at the present or the last annual general meeting, or exercised control through a contract or other measures" (Lefebvre and Lin, 1991, p.140).

In France, no legal consolidation requirements existed in company law before the adoption of the Seventh Directive through Law 85-11 of 3 January 1985 and Decree No. 86-221 of 17 February 1986. However, groups had begun to publish consolidated accounts from the 1960s onwards and, in the absence of legislation, decided to apply U.S. standards (Richard, 1995). In fact, the *Commission des Opérations de Bourse* (COB, Stock Exchange Commission) since 1961 has required group accounts for any company that sought permission to issue shares or bonds for the first time (Pham, 1993). The National

Accounting Council had published the first official French text on consolidation on 20 March 1968: *Rapport sur la consolidation des bilans et des comptes* (Report on the Consolidation of Balance sheets and Accounts), which was optional however. The COB issued a reporting guideline for quoted companies in 1980.

In Spain, the 1973 Standard National Chart of Accounts called for information about group companies and defined a group as existing when "one company has a direct holding in the capital stock of another company of 25% or more" (Corona, 1992, p.229). A non-binding Ministerial Order of July 1982 concerning the preparation of consolidated accounts was based on the draft Seventh Directive and was issued by the Institute of Accounting Planning, the predecessor of the ICAC (López Díaz, Rivero Torre, 1995). In fact, consolidation regulation had existed for the purpose of computing tax on consolidated income since the Royal Decree Law No.15 was issued in 1977, and consolidation requirements were introduced by the regulatory bodies for the electricity industry in 1984 and for the banking industry in 1989. The legal obligation for all groups to consolidate was incorporated in commercial law with the implementation of the EU Directive following the publication of the *Real Decreto* No.1815 (Royal Decree) in 1991, which approved the *Normas para la formulación de las cuentas anuales consolidadas* (standards for the preparation of consolidated annual accounts).

In Italy, there was no legal obligation for companies to prepare consolidated accounts until the Seventh Directive was incorporated into legislation (Riccabboni and Ghirri, 1994, p.102).

The Seventh Directive

The coexistence of different approaches to group accounting within the EU and, at the same time, the lack in many Member States of specific regulations dealing with consolidated accounts led to action by the Community resulting in the adoption of the 7th Directive in 1983. The European Commission originally preferred an economic group approach, derived from German law, which was implicit in published drafts in the 1970s (Diggle and Nobes, 1994), but eventually, in the final text of the Directive, consolidation was made compulsory under legal power of control, and economic control was retained as a Member State option .

In fact, in the first draft of the Directive prepared by the European Commission (which resulted from the proposals of the *Groupe d'Etudes Droit des Sociétés des Experts Comptables de la CEE*) in 1971, consolidation was required

> "if more than 50% of the shares were held or if the shareholding was less than 50% but was combined with dominant influence" (van Hulle and van der Tas, 1995 p. 1054).

A second draft was published in 1974, following discussion with national experts from the member states, after the UK, Ireland and Denmark had joined the EC. Indeed, the criteria changed as a result of lobbying by the 'Anglo-Saxon' countries. Consolidation was now required

> "where an undertaking, directly or indirectly held the major part of the undertaking's subscribed capital, or where it controlled the majority of votes in the undertaking, or where it could appoint more than half of the board members" (idem, p.1054).

After further discussion, the first published proposal for the Seventh Directive was issued by the Commission on 4 May 1976. The proposal revealed the strong German influence, as it defined a group in terms of dominance and dependence as follows:

> "A dominant undertaking was stated to be any undertaking which exercised in practice its dominant influence to the effect that dependent undertakings were managed on a central and unified basis. The proposal laid down certain situations in which dominance and dependence would be presumed to exist (majority of the capital held, majority of the voting rights, appointment of more than half of the board members)" (idem, p.1055).

On 14 December 1978, the Commission issued an amended proposal after the European Parliament and Economic and Social Committee had given their opinions. In 1979, there were further amendments by the Council Working Party which led to the avoidance of the term 'group' in the text of the Directive in favour of 'the undertakings to be consolidated taken as a whole', to a change in its title from 'group accounts' to 'consolidated accounts' and to an agreement to introduce a list of circumstances in which consolidated accounts must be prepared. It was at this point that agreement was reached to make consolidation compulsory under legal power of control.

The Seventh Directive (83/349/EEC) was adopted by the Council of Ministers on 13 June 1983. In Article 1 of the final published text, the Directive specifies seven parent-subsidiary relationships. In accordance with this, Member States must require consolidation where a parent undertaking has the "legal power to control" another undertaking (van Hulle and van der Tas, 1995, p.1083), which is presumed in four cases:

- the holding of the majority of the voting rights (Art.1.1 (a));

- the right to appoint or to remove a majority of the board members (Art.1.1 (b));

- the right to exercise a dominant influence pursuant to a contract or a provision in articles of association (Art. 1.1 (c)); and

- the holding of a majority of the voting rights pursuant to an agreement with other shareholders (Art.1.1 (d)(bb)).

The final version of the Directive also specifies a further case in Article 1.1 where Member States may require consolidation on the grounds that a parent has the power to control which is not necessarily dependent on holding legal rights but, rather, as a matter of historical fact, evidenced by

- the appointment of a majority of the board members during two consecutive years, solely as a result of the exercise of voting rights (Art.1.1 (d)(aa)).

According to van Hulle and van der Tas (1995, p.1086), during the negotiations of the Directive, Art. 1.1 (d)(aa) was "strongly advocated by France, but opposed by many other countries."

Two other cases of *de facto* control are included in a separate article, as Member State options which may or may not be included in national law. Here, *de facto* control exists if a parent undertaking has a participating interest in the subsidiary and either

- the parent actually exercises a dominant influence on the subsidiary company (Art.1.2(a)); or

- the subsidiary and the parent undertaking are managed on a unified basis (Art.1.2(b)).

The inclusion of one *de facto* criterion in Art. 1.1 along with the *de jure* criteria seems to have resulted in ambiguity in what is now understood by *de facto* control. For instance, the term *de facto* is used by companies in their financial reports (and also in texts on financial reporting) to refer to all three criteria, or alternatively to the two criteria in Art. 1.2 or, indeed, to the specific criterion for which a Member State has opted. Furthermore, the *de jure* and *de facto* control concepts are not the same as the original legal and economic control criteria which used to distinguish the UK and Germany. In conclusion, as van Hulle and van der Tas (1995, p.1064) remark:

> "It is difficult to say whether the Directive finally adopts the legal or the economic approach. Although the Directive requires consolidation in the case of legal power of control, in its definition of the mandatory cases of consolidation, it goes beyond the traditional legal power of control approach. Consolidation is indeed also required in cases where the parent does not hold the majority of the voting rights. By allowing Member States to require the consolidation of certain minority shareholdings, the Directive has clearly borrowed from the economic approach."

Throughout the rest of this chapter, the term *de jure* control will be used to refer to the Directive's four criteria presuming legal control, and *de facto* control will refer to the three cases where effective control is presumed.

7.3 The current regulations

An overview of the implementation of the Seventh Directive into national company law is provided in Table 7.1. This shows the various ways in which the seven parent-subsidiary relationships have been treated in national laws and, hence, reveals the differences in the scope of a consolidated group between European states. The alternative combinations of the seven criteria result in the definition of the scope of an accounting group being unique in each country, except that the UK and Ireland have adopted the same definition.

De jure criteria

Majority of voting rights

Art. 1.1(a), requiring consolidation when there is a majority of voting rights in a subsidiary, is a compulsory criterion which has been implemented by all countries.

Right to appoint board members

Art. 1.1(b), which requires consolidation when the parent has the right to appoint or remove the majority of board members, was implemented in all countries except France and Italy. Even though it was compulsory under the Seventh Directive, the argument that has been put forward in France is that this right to appoint or remove board members is anyway consequent in French law to the holding of the majority of the voting rights (Pham, 1993). Elsewhere, there is evidence that such rights of appointment and removal may exist even in the absence of a majority of voting rights because they are attached to preferential shares in Belgium (see Aerts and Theunisse, 1995, p.516) and in the Netherlands (see Petite, 1984, p.90), or by articles and agreements in Germany, in particular for limited liability companies as indicated by Ordelheide (1995, p.1583).

Contractual right to exercise a dominant influence

In the final text of Art. 1.1(c), consolidation is required when a parent undertaking has the right to exercise a dominant influence over a subsidiary, pursuant to a contract or to a provision in its memorandum or articles of association. Art. 1.1(c) is compulsory except in cases where a Member State's law does not provide for such contracts and clauses, although a further option given in the Directive is that Member States may indicate that this criterion only applies if the parent is a shareholder in the subsidiary. It appears that this criterion was only included in the Directive after lengthy debate (Petite,1984, p.90).

All Member States, with the exception of Spain, implemented the requirement to consolidate when there is a dominant influence pursuant to a contract or clause, and Belgium, Denmark and France chose to limit it to those cases where the parent is a shareholder.

With regard to the nature of contracts giving the right to exercise a dominant influence, there seem to be significant differences in law across European countries. In Germany, a subordination contract (*Beherrschungsvertrag*), where one undertaking has the right to give direct instructions to the management of another undertaking, is subject to strict conditions in the case of *Aktiengesellschaften (AktG* Art.293, 294 - see Ordelheide, 1995, p.1584).

Although such contracts are illegal in certain other countries and German law appears to be unique in providing for such contracts (see FEE, 1993, p.80), other Member States were motivated nevertheless to adopt the criterion because a parent undertaking might conclude such a contract with a foreign subsidiary in a country where such contracts are lawful. In fact, in Belgium, the Report to the King accompanying the Consolidation Decree states explicitly that, although the type of contract "known in Germany as *Beherrschungsverträge* cannot be legally enforced in Belgian subsidiaries, it can however be relevant for foreign subsidiaries, especially for German group enterprises" (Aerts and Theunisse, 1995, p.516). In France, where dominant control by means of statutory clauses is also forbidden, the new law was written "to take account of conventions which are used abroad, especially in Germany" (Richard, 1995, p.1319). In Italy, where *contratti di dominazione* are again illegal, the same argument has been advanced (Riccaboni and Ghirri, 1994, p.158). Indeed, even though the Italian Civil Code (Art. 2359 para.3) refers to the subsidiary definition in terms of a dominant influence based on contractual ties (*influenza dominante di un'altra società in virtù di particolari vincoli contrattuali*), legislative decree No. 127 explicitly excludes this provision for consolidation purposes (Art. 26).

Thus, in countries such as Belgium, France and Italy, where subordination contracts are illegal, they are nevertheless recognised in law in the context of group accounting due to their legitimacy in other jurisdictions. The situation is not so clear cut in the UK and the Netherlands, where such contracts were not in conflict with established commercial law, yet appear not to be commonplace.

In the UK, for instance, there may be a risk that acceptance by directors of a contractual right of 'dominant influence' over them would be in breach of the common law duty to act in the best interest of their company (para 70, FRS 2). Gordon and Gray reason (1994, p.160) that "the general fiduciary duty of directors to conduct the affairs of the company in accordance with its own best interests makes it most unlikely that consolidation by virtue of a control contract will have much practical effect unless the power to enter into control contracts is explicitly conferred by a company's memorandum and articles."

The contractual right of group control is also referred to in the Netherlands (RJ 2.03.103), as noted by Klaassen and Hekers (1995), although the potential conflict in laws is not discussed by these authors.

Majority of voting rights through agreement with others

Art. 1.1(d)(bb) requires consolidation where a single shareholder controls the majority of voting rights in a subsidiary undertaking pursuant to an agreement with other shareholders or members. However, no detail concerning the form and content of such agreements is provided in Art.1.1(d)(bb) and, instead, the option to introduce more detailed provisions into the national law is granted to Member States.

It would appear that this article has been introduced in all Member States. However, according to the *Fédération des Experts Comptables Européens* (1993, p.81), no country took up the option of providing more information concerning the form and content of such agreements.

De facto criteria

Appointment of a majority of board members by exercise of voting rights

Art. 1.1(d)(aa) allows Member States to require consolidation where a parent company has appointed the majority on the supervisory board of a subsidiary undertaking during two consecutive years solely by exercising its voting rights. The article contains the option for Member States to make this criterion dependent on a holding of at least 20 % of the voting rights in the subsidiary. The provision has been implemented as a consolidation requirement in company law by France, Belgium and Spain.

Whilst the French Assembly adopted this *de facto* control criterion (see Scheid and Walton, 1992, p.328), French law was further refined such that a company's claim to have appointed the majority of the board is substantiated if two conditions are fulfilled: (i) the parent undertaking has held more than 40% of the voting rights during the two years and (ii) no other shareholder has held a higher proportion (Raffegeau et al., 1989). As noted by Richard (1995, p.1318): "as the nomination of directors frequently results from a secret vote of the shareholders, the proof of the origin of the votes can be difficult to show." Thus, as there may be no clear evidence, the presumption of *contrôle de fait* (*de facto* control) has led to a unique definition of control in France.

Similarly in Belgium, the presumption attached to Art. 1.1 (d)(aa) is articulated in law, where *de facto* control is based on the exercise of a majority of voting rights of the shares represented at the last and previous general assemblies. "This presumption, which may be refuted if there is evidence to the contrary, can lead to an enterprise being classified as a subsidiary in some years and in others not" (Lefebvre and Flower, 1994, p.136).

Spain also adopted Art. 1.1(d)(aa) but did not exercise the option to make the obligation to consolidate dependent on the ownership of 20 % of the voting rights (Gonzalo and Gallizo, 1992, p.227).

Actual exercise of a dominant influence and/or unified management

Art. 1.2 allows Member States the option to make consolidation compulsory where a parent undertaking holds a participating interest (as defined in Article 17 of the Fourth Directive) in a subsidiary undertaking and either (a) the parent actually exercises a dominant influence over the subsidiary or (b) the parent and the subsidiary are managed on a unified basis.

- Dominant influence only

Denmark chose to implement only the criterion in Art. 1.2(a) that a parent-subsidiary relationship exists when the parent actually exercises a dominant influence. Reference to dominant influence (*bestemmende indflydelse*), which already existed in law, occurs again in the Årsregnskapsbekendtgørelsen of 1990 (ÅRL, section 1(2) No.6). However, the notion of dominant influence is not defined in Danish law. Furthermore, as the option in Art. 1.2(b) was not taken up, the law does not refer to 'unified management'.

- Unified management only

Germany, on the other hand, was the only country to implement just the second criterion that *de facto* control exists if the parent and the subsidiary are managed on a unified basis (Art.1.2(b)). The notion of unified management existed already in German law (Art. 18 AktG) and its interpretation has not changed since (Odenwald, 1992). In Germany, *de facto* control continues to be based on the unified management of the parent and the subsidiary (Art. 290(1) HGB; Art. 11(1) PublG.). The additional requirement for there to be a participating interest, which is defined as a 20% shareholding (Art. 271(1) HGB), is only applicable if the parent is a corporation under the HGB. For enterprises of other legal forms, unified management creates a parent subsidiary-relationship even if there is no shareholding (as defined in Art. 271(1) HGB).

The law states (Art.18 AktG) that a *Konzern* exists if the controlling enterprise (*herrschendes Unternehmen*) and a dependent enterprise (*abhängiges Unternehmen*) are under unified management. The law (Art.17 AktG) also states that there is a presumption that a majority-owned enterprise will be dependent, although it is possible for unified management to be refuted (Art.18 (1) S.3 AktG). In fact, unified management is not defined in detail in the law, although the AktG 1965 specified conditions under which unified management may be presumed. These are where a dependent undertaking is controlled by a subordination agreement (*Beherrschungsvertrag*) or if it is integrated into the controlling enterprise (Art.291, 319 AktG), and in these cases the existence of unified management cannot be refuted (Art.18(1)S.2 AktG). The specific circumstance of integration (*Eingliederung*) of one AG into another AG in Germany, requires a 100% ownership of the share capital by the controlling AG (Art. 319 AktG).

A legal commentary (AktG Art.18) by Kropff (1965, p.33) states that "unified management must actually exist (factual unified management). However, it is not necessary that all important business segments are under unified management nor does the control depend on the right to give directions to the management of the dependent enterprise. Instead, it is sufficient if the group management coordinates the general business policy of the group undertakings. In fact, this may take the looser form of regular consultation or it can result from personal interaction between managers" (Odenwald, 1992, translated from original).

- Dominant influence and unified management

The countries which implemented both Art. 1.2 (a) and Art. 1.2 (b) were the UK, Ireland, the Netherlands and Belgium.

In the UK, the Companies Act 1989 (sec.258) introduced *de facto* control on the grounds of both dominant influence and unified management (see Gordon and Gray, 1994, p.245). The ASB (Accounting Standards Board) defined 'dominant influence' and 'unified management' in FRS 2 "Accounting for subsidiary undertakings" published in 1992. 'Dominant influence' is defined as

"influence that can be exercised to achieve the operating and financial policies desired by the holder of the influence, notwithstanding the rights or influence of any other party."

FRS 2 defines 'unified management' where

"two or more undertakings are managed on a unified basis, if the whole of the operations of the undertakings are integrated and they are managed as a single unit. Unified management does not arise solely because one undertaking manages another".

In Ireland, the application of FRS2 in 1992 anticipated the implementation of the Seventh Directive and hence the definition of a subsidiary. The Irish Regulation 4(1), Group Accounts Regulations 1992, followed the UK approach and adopted the two *de facto* control criteria of dominant influence and unified management.

In the Netherlands, there exists a difference between a group company and a subsidiary company which does not appear to mirror the distinctions between legal and economic control in the Seventh Directive. In fact, it seems confusing that under Dutch law, a subsidiary may not be included in the consolidated financial statements if it is not a group company, and a group company may be consolidated even though it is not a subsidiary (Art. 406 Civil Code). While a subsidiary is defined (Art. 2:24(a)) in accordance with *de jure* control in Articles 1.1(a) and 1.1(b) of the Seventh Directive, a group is defined (Art. 2:24(b)) as an economic whole (*economische eenheid*) in which legal entities are united, although the term 'economic whole' is not defined in the legislation. The Guidelines of the Council on Annual Reporting (RJ 2.03.103) specify that complementary economic activities and a collective financial policy indicate the existence of an 'economic whole' (Klaassen and Hekers, 1995, p. 2162).

In Belgium, group control adopted in legislation is *de jure* or *de facto* and Art. 1.2 of the Seventh Directive has been implemented in Art. 2(1) Royal Decree of 6 March 1990 (Lefebvre and Flower, 1994, p.241). In fact, *de facto* control is presumed in Belgium when a company has exercised a majority of the voting rights represented at the last two general shareholders' meetings. It is suggested by Aerts and Theunisse, however, that the group concept in Belgium is "mainly an economic one" (1995, p. 515). "If legal control is effectively exercised, group accounts should be prepared. If a legal control relationship exists, but some circumstances prevent effective economic control, this can be a reason for non-consolidation. If no legal control relationship exists but *de facto* control can be presumed, consolidation is compulsory."

In conclusion, the three criteria under which *de facto* control is referred to in Article 1 of the Seventh Directive (appointment of majority of board, dominant influence and unified management) have been implemented into national laws with considerable diversity. France and Spain do not refer to *de facto* control in terms either of dominant influence or of unified management and instead, as has been stated, consider *de facto* control only with respect to Art.1.1(d)(aa) of the Directive; that is, the case where a parent has appointed during a two year period a majority of the subsidiary's board. Denmark accorded the actual exercise of a dominant influence to *de facto* control, and thus enacted Art. 1.2(a) only. German law refers to *de facto* control where a parent and a subsidiary are under unified management and thus enacted only Art.1.2(b). Both, 'unified management' and 'dominant influence' comprise *de facto* control in Dutch, British and Irish accounting legislation. On the other hand, *de facto* control includes all three criteria in Belgium. It appears, that Italy is the only country, which adopted none of the three criteria specified as *de facto* control in the Seventh Directive (see Riccaboni and Ghirri, 1994, p.230).

De jure and de facto consolidation criteria in Member States' law

Table 7.1

EC Legislation	Belgium	Denmark	France	Germany	Ireland	Italy	Netherlands	Spain	UK
7 th Directive	Art. 2 1990 Royal Decree	Annual Accounts Act Sec.1(2),6; Sec.2b	Art.357.1-11 du Loi 85, Decrée 86-221	§290 HGB; §§16-18, §291§319 AktG	Group Accounts Law 1992	Art.2359 CivilCode Decree Law No. 127/91	Art.24a, 24b, Art.406 Book 2 Civil Code; RJ 2.03.103	Art. 42-49 Real Decreto	Companies Act 1989 Sec. 258
Date of compulsory compliance:	31/12/90	01/04/91	31/12/85	31/12/89	01/09/92	01/01/94	01/01/90	31/12/91	23/12/89
Definition of a subsidiary Obligation to prepare consolidated accounts (art.1.1.), if a company has the following rights over another company (subsidiary):									
Art.1.1(a) Majority of shareholders' voting rights	yes	yes	yes	yes	yes	yes	yes	yes	yes
Art.1.1(b) Right to appoint or remove a majority of board members, etc. and is a shareholder	yes	yes	not adopted	yes	yes	not adopted	yes	yes	yes
Art.1.1(c) Right to exercise a dominant influence pursuant to a contract, or a provision in its memorandum or articles of association (* Member States may require that the parent company also has a shareholding); no obligation where no provision in national law for such contracts and clauses	yes *	yes *	yes *	yes	yes	yes	yes	not adopted	yes

	Belgium	Denmark	France	Germany	Ireland	Italy	Netherlands	Spain	UK
Art.1.1(d) the parent company is a shareholder and									
(aa) A majority of the members of management, etc. who have held office during the financial year (and the preceding year) have been appointed solely by the exercise of its voting rights, or	yes	not adopted	yes[1]	not adopted	not adopted	not adopted	not adopted	yes	not adopted
(bb) Controls, pursuant to an agreement with other shareholders, a majority of voting rights	yes	yes	yes	yes	yes	yes	yes	yes	yes
Art.1.2 Consolidation may be required, if the parent company holds a participating interest (defined in art.17 4th Directive) and			not adopted			not adopted		not adopted	
(a) it actually exercises a dominant influence over the subsidiary, or	yes	yes		not adopted	yes		yes		yes
(b) it and the subsidiary undertaking are managed on a unified basis by the parent company	yes	not adopted		yes	yes		yes		yes

---

[1] control is presumed at > 40% of the voting rights, and no other shareholder has a larger holding

The diversity between Member States in the adoption of the *de facto* control criteria is clearly a result of the optional character accorded to them by the Directive. Moreover, the different interpretations of the *de facto* control concept are also attributable to the lack of definition of the terms 'unified management' and 'dominant influence' used in the Seventh Directive. The fundamental difference in Europe on the issue seems to be, however, that *de facto* control is referred to in some countries as the actual exercise of voting rights in the past, while in other countries de *facto* control signifies the effective existence of an economic group control relationship.

Implications

The different combinations of the *de jure* and *de facto* control criteria, discussed above, show the variability with which the Directive has been interpreted in the development of regional regulations for group accounting in Europe.

It appears that the development of different organisational group structures in Europe and their legal frameworks have created tensions between the national legislations. In fact, the differences in interpretation of Article 1 of the Seventh Directive have given rise to various ways in which the boundaries of a consolidated group may be demarcated. Below, this elusive concept of a group is further discussed with respect to

> (i) confusion between the 'legal' and the 'economic';

> (ii) resistance to harmonisation;

> (iii) subsequent developments in individual countries.

(i) Confusion between the 'legal' and the 'economic'

The distinction between 'legal' and 'economic' control is not always clear, particularly as economic control may be presumed in the light of certain legal relationships. For example, the German *Aktiengesetz* specifies the economic criterion of unified management by reference to legal parent-subsidiary relationships (namely the existence of integration or contractual control, or majority ownership of share capital, according to which the power to exercise economic control is presumed). Thus, in Germany, economic control may operate through legal criteria.

Alternative examples of this source of confusion exist where *de jure* control in one country operates as *de facto* in another. That is, while a certain parent-subsidiary relationship might be considered in one country as a legal criterion, it might be classified in another country as an economic criterion. For instance, in France the use of the term *contrôle exclusive* for consolidation purposes implies *maîtrise juridique* (legal power of control) only with respect to each of the different control concepts included in the amendment of 1985 (Art. 357.1), *i.e.* *contrôle de droit, contrôle contractuel* and *contrôle de fait* (Raffegeau et al. 1989, p.93). In each case, the definition relies upon voting power. *Contrôle de droit* simply involves a majority of voting rights. Furthermore, *contrôle contractuel* recognises only *conventions de vote*; that is, voting conventions in the collective interest of shareholders (Richard, 1995, p. 1319). Finally, *contrôle de fait* depends on the appointment of the majority of the board during two consecutive years, which in this case is presumed with the exercise of 40% of the votes, while at the same time, no other shareholder has hold a higher proportion. Hence, although the French legislator refers to *contrôle de fait* which is usually translated as *de facto* control, the concept is entirely legal since it is based on voting rights which either exist at present or were exercised in the past.

The ambiguity with which parent-subsidiary relationships might be classified as *de jure* or as *de facto* is in fact rooted within the Directive itself. In particular, confusion arises from Art. 1.1(d)(aa) which, although being a Member State option, was included as *de facto* control criterion in Art. 1.1 along with the mandatory *de jure* consolidation requirements. This ambiguity is acknowledged by van Hulle and van der Tas (1995, p.1086): "This gives this case the appearance of a requirement but also makes the text of the Seventh Directive Article 1 difficult to interpret." Indeed, this particular *de facto* control criterion (whereby an undertaking has during two consecutive financial years effectively appointed a majority of the board members in another undertaking solely as a result of the exercise of its voting rights) does not imply an economic parent-subsidiary relationship but, instead, a historical fact.

Finally, although the 'true and fair view' principle is excluded from the scope of consolidation and the Seventh Directive has made it clear in Art. 16(5) that the true and fair view does not relate to its Art. 1, in some specific instances the exclusion of subsidiaries from the consolidated accounts may be linked to the presentation of a true and fair view of a group's affairs. Thus, a *de facto* relationship may take precedence over a *de jure* relationship. This may depend not only on different definitions of 'true and fair' in Member States (Alexander, 1993), but also on the specific circumstances of the company concerned. Indeed, it may be noted that Art. 14, paras 1 and 2 which require exclusion of subsidiaries with dissimilar activities from the consolidated accounts where their inclusion would impair a true and fair view of the group accounts, has been identified as being in conflict with IAS 27 which does not allow such an exclusion (van Hulle and van der Tas, 1995, p.1089).

(ii) Resistance to harmonisation

Following the implementation of the Directive, some resistance to harmonisation has been observed arising from well-established institutional structures to which the new regulations could not easily be adapted. One example of this relates to the contractually-based group relationship known as *Vertragskonzerne,* developed in Germany in the inter-war period (Hadden, 1992), which could not transfer readily to other jurisdictions. As mentioned earlier, the legal provisions for contractual groups are still an important feature of German group law, whereas their acceptance within European company law has created major difficulties. Although the obligation to consolidate where control is exercised through a contract or a provision in the memorandum or articles of association (Article 1.1 (c)) has been implemented in most jurisdictions, some national legislation still prohibits subordination contracts. Nevertheless, contractual control based on clauses in the articles of association has become a legal criterion for control in most Member States.

A further example is found in the Netherlands, where economic group control takes precedence over legal power to control. In fact, even though the Seventh Directive has explicitly treated *de facto* control as a secondary criterion and has accorded primacy to legal control as the principal consolidation requirement (van Hulle and van der Tas, 1995, p. 1085), the Duch legislator has made it clear that the requirement for consolidation refers only to 'group companies' which form an economic whole. Indeed, it follows that if no economic control exists, "no obligation to consolidate a subsidiary would exist" (Klaassen and Hekers, 1995, p. 2158). Thus, legal control is subordinated to economic control in the Netherlands which seems clearly to be in conflict with Community law.

A final instance of resistance to harmonisation can be seen where the concept of *de facto* control already existed in law. Here, a single notion was usual, as in the case of dominant influence (*bestemmende indflydelse*) in Denmark and uniform management in Germany (*einheitlich Leitung*). Neither country widened the scope of *de facto* control, as Germany has not included reference to dominant influence as a *de facto* criterion for control and Denmark has not included reference to unified management.

(iii) Subsequent developments in individual countries

Although the approach adopted in the Directive does not allow for further parent-subsidiary relationships beyond those specified in Article 1, there is evidence that the *de facto* control criteria have been extended by national regulators. The UK (and Irish) standard setters widened the definition of a subsidiary, using what has been progressively termed 'non-subsidiary subsidiaries' (ED 42, 1988), 'controlled non-subsidiaries' (ED 49, 1990) and 'quasi-subsidiaries' (FRS 5, 1994). The intention was to respond to changing economic circumstances, allowing for 'substance over form' (Taylor, 1995). The ASB defined a 'quasi-subsidiary' (which should be accounted for as if it were a subsidiary) as a

> "... a company, trust, partnership, or other vehicle which, though not fulfilling the definition of a subsidiary, is directly or indirectly controlled by the reporting entity and gives rise to benefits for that entity that are in substance no different from those, that would arise were the vehicle a subsidiary" in (para.7) FRS 5 "Reporting the substance of transactions".

The UK definition of a quasi-subsidiary is clearly beyond the seven parent-subsidiary relationships specified in Article 1 of the Directive.

In summary, the different interpretations of *de jure* and *de facto* control in Europe imply that the boundaries of consolidated financial statements appear to vary internationally. While some jurisdictions such as France defined group control in a detailed (legal) manner, which depends solely on the existence or effective exercise of voting rights, other countries such as the Netherlands adopted a solely economic approach to group control, which indeed may exclude *de jure* relationships in certain circumstances. In contrast, a broader concept of group control has been adopted in countries such as the UK and Germany, where both effective economic control and the existence of certain rights of control are consolidation criteria.

7.4 The criteria used in practice to define a subsidiary

In order to investigate the definition of a subsidiary adopted in practice and to relate this to the differences which exist in regulations between member states, the accounting policies reported in the annual reports of European groups have been analysed with respect to the inclusion of subsidiaries in group accounts.

This analysis is based on an earlier investigation (Ebbers, 1997c) for the thesis sample of companies with multiple listings in Europe. The financial years 1987 (117 companies) and 1993 (223 companies) were chosen for the analysis as, during this period, most member states enacted the Seventh Directive in national laws.

Table 7.2 indicates the frequency with which consolidation criteria were reported in the sample. In 1993, 172 (87%) companies disclosed, with different degree of detail, criteria used to consolidate subsidiaries and 99 (85%) in 1987. As some groups stated that two or more criteria were applied to the definition of consolidated subsidiaries, the results for the different criteria do not add up to the total. In 1993, 159 (80%) companies specified one or more of the *de jure* control criteria, whilst 27 (14%) companies specified one of the *de facto* control criteria. In 17 (9%) cases, *de jure* and/or *de facto* consolidation was indicated but without specifying which criteria. These proportions did not change significantly between 1987 and 1993. Also, there were several discrepancies between reporting practices and requirements in law. These are indicated in Table 7.2 by the shaded boxes; that is, where a criterion is used in practice although it is not in the current national legislation.

De jure criteria

Majority of voting rights (1.1(a))

A majority of shareholders' voting rights was the dominant criterion used to define consolidated subsidiaries for both years. This was disclosed by 95 out of the 117 companies (81%) in the 1987 sample and 159 out of 198 companies (80%) in the 1993 sample.

Right to appoint majority of board members (1.1(b))

The right to appoint the majority of board members was reported by 6 companies in 1993, of which 5 were Dutch and 1 was a UK company. It may be noted here, that in the Netherlands a subsidiary is defined in accordance with the *de jure* control criteria in Articles 1.1(a) and 1.1(b) of the Directive, whilst a group is defined as an 'economic whole in which legal entities are united' (Art.2:24 (b) Civil Code). Only subsidiaries which are group companies are consolidated. This can be seen in practice as in the following extract from the annual report of Bols Wessanen:

Bols Wessanen (1993):
"(...) Group companies are defined as:
-companies of which more than half of the voting rights can be exercised in the annual general meeting, or
-companies of which the majority of the statutory directors or supervisory directors can be appointed or dismissed,
but only if these companies form an integral part of the economic entity."

Right based on a contract or clause 1.1(c)

The obligation to consolidate in cases where a dominant influence is exercised through a contract or clause was disclosed by 4 groups in 1993 (1 in 1987). Although the earlier discussion suggested that this is a special feature of German company law, it was not disclosed as a consolidation criterion by any of the German groups. This is in accordance with an earlier Treuarbeit study (Treuarbeit, 1990, p.44) in which 51 out of the 95 analysed groups disclosed their criteria for consolidation but none reported that consolidation was based on a contract.

However, the mention of contractual rights was found in 4 annual reports in other countries: in Italy (2 companies), where such contracts are illegal for consolidation purposes, and in the UK (2 companies), where the existence of the contract may give rise to the risk of being "in breach of the directors' duty to act in the best interest of their company' (FRS 2). This reference to contractual rights may be illustrated by the following extracts from the consolidation policies of the Italian group Montedison and the UK group Sema:

Montedison (1987):
"The consolidated financial statements include the accounts of Montedison S.p.A. and subsidiaries in which it has a direct or indirect interest of more than 50%. They also include the accounts of companies where the Group, although possessing 50% or less of the equity, has contractual power to control financial and operating policies."

Sema (1993):
"The Group's 50% holding in BAeSEMA limited and its 49% holding in Tibet SA have been fully consolidated as Group undertakings as defined by the Companies Act 1989. BAeSEMA is consolidated on the basis of a shareholders' agreement which gives the Group control of the board of directors. Tibet SA is consolidated on the basis of actual dominant influence exercised by the Group by virtue of a control contract."

Agreement with other shareholders (1.1(d)(bb))

The obligation to consolidate subsidiaries where control of a majority of voting rights is based on an agreement with other shareholders, was found in 8 annual reports in 1993 (3 in1987), comprising 3 (1) in Italy, 2 (1) in the Netherlands, 1(1) in the UK and 1(0) in Denmark.

De facto control

Actual appointment of the majority supervisory board (1.1(d)(aa))

No examples were found in the sample of the criterion to require consolidation where the parent-subsidiary relationship is based on the appointment of the majority of board members for two consecutive years. Nevertheless, this provision has been implemented in company law in Belgium, France and Spain.

Actual dominant influence (1.2(a))

The criterion to base consolidation on *de facto* dominant influence was reported in 14 annual reports in 1993 (3 in 1987), of which 5(1) were in Denmark, 6 (2) in the Netherlands and 3(0) in the UK. The Danish companies Novo and Great Nordic illustrate this policy, Novo referring to a 'dominating influence' *(dominerende indflydelse* in the Danish report) and Great Nordic to a 'controlling interest' *(bestemmende indflydelse* in the Danish report):

> **Novo (1987):**
> *"The consolidated financial statements include the accounts of the Company and all companies in which the group owns more than 50% of the voting rights or in some other way has a dominating influence."*

> **Great Nordic (1993):**
> *"The consolidated accounts comprise the Parent Company and all Danish and foreign subsidiaries, in which the Parent company, directly or indirectly, has a controlling interest."*

Unified management (1.2(b))

References to the parent-subsidiary relationship as unified management were found in the annual reports of 13 groups in 1993 (6 in 1987), including 9 out of

29 (31%) German groups, either together with a majority shareholding or as a single consolidation criterion. A study by Treuhand (1990) found the same proportion for the year 1989, where in 16 cases out of 51 (31%), disclosing groups based the consolidation of a subsidiary on *einheitliche Leitung*. In the following extracts, *einheitliche Leitung* is referred to as 'uniform control' by Bayer and as 'under the central direction of the parent company' by MAN in the English translation:

Bayer (1993):
"The Financial Statements of the Bayer Group include Bayer AG and 28 German and 135 foreign subsidiaries in which Bayer AG, directly or indirectly, has a majority of the voting rights or which are under its uniform control".

MAN (1993):
"Comprised in the group's consolidated financial statements are MAN AG, as well as 73 German companies and 63 non German companies under the central direction of MAN AG."

Although this criterion is not implemented in French legislation, 4 French annual reports referred to it in 1993 (1 in 1987). In fact, as described in part 3 of this chapter, the French notion of *contrôle exclusif* is based entirely on the existence or past exercise of voting rights. An example was reported by Rémy Cointreau which refers to 'effective management control' for which the French wording was *pouvoir effective de direction.*

Rémy Cointreau (1993):
"The companies over which Rémy Cointreau exercises exclusive control due to
-a direct or indirect holding of more than 50% of the share capital, or
-effective management control,
are fully consolidated."

De jure versus de facto control

In 1993, 17 companies (9%) and 11 in 1987 (9%) communicated '*de jure*' and '*de facto*' control as the basis for consolidation without further specification of the underlying criteria, of which 7 (3) were in Italy, 4 (3) in France, 4 (3) in Belgium and 2 (2) in Denmark. In some cases, the blanket terms '*de jure* control' and/or '*de facto* control' were used (see the Belgian group Sipef and the Italian group Fiat below); in others a term such as 'effective control' is used, still without specifying the underlying criterion (see the French group Total below). Given the conceptual conflict with respect to *de facto* control in Europe such reporting policies may be interpreted differently. Indeed, it may be noted that Italy adopted none of the three *de facto* control criteria of the Seventh Directive.

Sipef (1993):
"Global consolidation is applied for the subsidiaries where the Holding Company exerts control either de jure or de facto."

Fiat (1993):
"The consolidated financial statements include the financial statements of Fiat S.p.A., the parent company, and of all Italian and foreign subsidiaries which constitute the Fiat Group, in which Fiat S.p.A. holds, directly or indirectly, more than 50% of the voting capital or has de facto control."

Total (1993):
"All subsidiaries regarded as significant are fully consolidated in the consolidated financial statements. Companies in which the ownership is less than 50%, but over which the Company maintains effective control, are also fully consolidated."

7.5 Concluding remarks

In an attempt to evaluate the evolution of national regulations concerning the definition of a subsidiary prior to and following the implementation of the Seventh Directive, this chapter has explored the distinction between *de jure* and *de facto* control in Europe. Given the discretion concerning the four *de jure* consolidation criteria and the three *de facto* criteria, the legal definition of a subsidiary for consolidation has been implemented in a different manner in almost every country.

De jure and de facto consolidation criteria in Europe

Table 7.2

Criteria disclosed for consolidation	Belgium 1993	Denmark 1993	France 1993	Germany 1993	Ireland 1993	Italy 1993	Netherlands 1993	Spain 1993	UK 1993	Total 1993	% 1993	Total 1987	% 1987
1.1(a) Majority of votes	8	14	18	19	8	19	18	15	40	159	80%	95	81%
1.1(b) Appointment of board	0	0	0	0	0	0	5	0	1	6	3%	1	1%
1.1(c) Contract or Clause	0	0	0	0	0	2	0	0	2	4	2%	1	1%
1.1(d)(aa) Appointment of board by votes	0	0	0	0	0	0	0	0	0	0	0%	0	0%
1.1d(bb) Majority of votes by agreement	0	1	0	0	0	3	2	1	1	8	4%	3	3%
1.2 (a) De facto dominant influence	0	5	0	9	0	0	6	0	3	14	7%	3	3%
1.2 (b) De facto unified management	0	0	4	0	0	0	0	0	0	13	7%	6	5%
Groups reporting just 'de jure' and/or 'de facto'	4	2	4	0	0	7	0	0	0	17	9%	11	9%
More than 1 criterion	(4)	(5)	(6)	(7)	(0)	(7)	(9)	(2)	(5)	(45)	23%	(19)	16%
Groups reporting on control	**8**	**16**	**20**	**20**	**8**	**24**	**20**	**14**	**42**	**172**	**87%**	**99**	**85%**
Groups not disclosing	2	2	4	9	1	0	2	3	3	26	13%	18	15%
Sample size	**10**	**18**	**24**	**29**	**9**	**24**	**22**	**17**	**45**	**198**	**100%**	**117**	**100%**

□ not a legal requirement   □ corresponds to a legal requirement

Perhaps this was inevitable, given the controversy underlying the scope of consolidated accounts in Article 1 of the Directive (Petite, 1984). Moreover, it appears that structural differences in corporate group organisation which have developed over time have resulted in diverging approaches towards accounting for groups, and that these different structures act as a barrier to legal harmonisation, with the concept of 'control' remaining elusive at the national and international level.

With respect to *de jure* control, only the legal criterion of a majority of voting rights was implemented in each country's law. Resistance to uniformity was found at a number of levels with respect to each of the other *de jure* control rights. However, it is with particular respect to *de facto* control that legal barriers to harmonisation are evident. In fact, in certain countries the three *de facto* criteria were adopted in conjunction with additional *de jure* presumptions, thus resulting in some confusion in the interpretation of *de facto* control in the countries involved. It appears, that the lack of uniform definition of the 'unified management' and 'dominant influence' criteria in the Seventh Directive, and the discretion provided to countries with respect to the adoption of its provisions, has led to ambiguity of what is 'commonly' interpreted as *de jure* and *de facto* control in Europe.

Finally, financial reporting practices suggest that the considerable variety in accounting policies is attributable in part to the fact that harmonisation of laws is not complete.

PART III

STATISTICAL MODELLING OF COMPLIANCE WITH ACCOUNTING REGULATION

CHAPTER 8

A PROBABILITY MODEL OF COMPLIANCE IN

FINANCIAL REPORTING

8.1 Objective

The objective of the statistical analysis carried out for this study is to determine whether the avoidance of full compliance in accounting practice is influenced by regulatory factors, in particular the source of the regulation and the degree of formalism in the rules themselves. In this section the model used for the analysis is developed.

The nature of count data, such as multiple accounting choices, implies that conventional regression methods would be inappropriate for our purpose, as both the dependent response variable 'compliance' and the hypothesised explanatory factors are discrete rather than continous outcomes, with assigned qualitative values (Fienberg, 1977). For the purpose of our analysis a probability model is required to describe the odds that a company fully complies with the regulation, rather than avoids the regulation, as a function of regulatory regressors.

8.2 The binomial linear logistic model

The binomial distribution

The distributional properties of the response variable 'compliance' require a binomial modelling approach. As reported subsequently, in aggregate, the observed values were 38,5% full compliance with the regulations and 44.8% creative or partial compliance. Only 6.9% of the observations were non-compliant while 9.9% of the cases were unqualified data. By offsetting the decision to contravene the rule in question, a conditional probability model is required to describe the relative odds that a company chooses either to comply unambiguously with the regulations in force or to resort to some form of avoidance, either through creative compliance or partial disclosure. A suitable probability model for count data in the context of a binary response is provided by the binomial distribution[1] (Cox and Snell, 1989).

In the particular case of a binary response, the random variable Y can take only two values, which are conventionally assigned: the value 1 (for our purpose full compliance) and the value 0 (for our purpose creative or partial compliance). The probability p, that $Y = 1$ is denoted the compliance probability which can be written as $P(Y = 1) = p$ and the corresponding probability of creative or partial compliance is $P (Y = 0) = 1 - p$. Expressing the two probabilities in a single equation, where y, the observed value of the random variable Y, is either 1 or 0, leads to the following probability distribution which is known as the Bernoulli distribution: $P(Y = y) = p^{y}(1-p)^{1-y}, y = 0,1$.

---

[1] The Poisson distribution would be a suitable probability model for count data in the context of a multinomial response.

164

The mean, or expected value of the random variable Y is defined as $E(Y) = 0 \times P$ $(Y = 0) + 1 \times P(Y = 1) = p$. The variance of Y is given by $Var\ (Y) = p(1 - p)$. For n binomial observations of the form y_i / n_i, where $i = 1, 2,..., n$ and where $E(y_i) = n_i p_i$, p_i is the probability of full compliance corresponding to the ith observation.

The logistic transformation

The linear probability model relates Y to a set of factors X, which explain the response variable Y so that $P\ (Y = 1) = F\ (x, \beta)$ and $P\ (Y = 0) = 1 - F\ (x, \beta)$ and indeed, that $P(Y) = \alpha + \beta X$ with a set of parameters β reflecting the impact of changes in X on the probability P of full compliance. This model has the principal defect that the linear specification is not constrained to the limited range from 0 to 1, which is imposed on probabilities.

Instead, a model is required that will produce predictions for a given regressor so that

$$\lim_{\beta'x \to +\infty} P(Y = 1) = 1 \text{ and } \lim_{\beta'x \to -\infty} P(Y = 1) = 0.$$

In order to ensure that the fitted probabilities will lie between 0 and 1, the probability scale must be transformed so that it varies monotonically with X, yet remains within the boundaries 0 and 1. In principle, any continuous probability distribution is adequate. However, in econometric applications the probit and logit models have been used almost exclusively (Greene, 1990). The logistic function will be used for our application mainly due to its mathematical convenience.

Conventionally, the logistic transformation of a success probability p is log $[p/(1-p)]$, denoted as logit (p). The function presents a sigmoid curve that is symmetric about $p = 0.5$, and which is essentially linear between $p = 0.2$ and $p = 0.8^2$. The mathematical convenience of the logistic transformation is evident in its property that a value of logit (p) in the interval $(-\infty, +\infty)$ corresponds to a value of p in the range $(0,1)$. Indeed, as $p \rightarrow 0$, $logit (p) \rightarrow -\infty$; as $p \rightarrow 1$, $logit$ $(p) \rightarrow +\infty$; and for $p = 0.5$, $logit (p) = 0^3$. The relationship between p and x is sigmoidal, whereas logit (p) is linearly related to x.

For our purpose, $p/(1-p)$ is the odds of full compliance, relative to creative or partial compliance, and the logistic transformation of p is the log ratio of full compliance relative to regulatory avoidance. Consequently, we adopt the linear logistic regression model as the complement of the linear regression model in the case that the regressand is not a continous variable but, instead, a dichotomous variable in a given classification (Cramer, 1991). As explained later, the regressors of the equation have been assigned multinomial categories.

The linear logistic model

The associated linear logistic model for the dependence of p_i on the values of k explanatory variables, $x_{1i}, x_{2i}, ..., x_{ki.}$, is

---

[2] See Collett, p.54, (1991).
[3] Similarly, the probit transformation is also adequate, as the function is symmetric in p and represents a sigmoid curve. For any value of p in the range $(0,1)$, the corresponding value of the probit (p) will lie between $-\infty$ and ∞ and when $p = 0.5$, probit (p) = 0. The standard normal distribution function, usually denoted by Φ (ξ) serves as a

$$\text{logit}(p_i) = \log\frac{p_i}{(1-p_i)} = \beta_0 + \beta_1 x_{1i} + \beta_2 x_{2i} + \ldots + \beta_k x_{ki} \tag{1}$$

which can be rewritten as,

$$p_i = \frac{\exp(\beta_0 + \beta_1 x_{1i} + \ldots + \beta_k x_{ki})}{1 + \exp(\beta_0 + \beta_1 x_{1i} + \ldots + \beta_k x_{ki})} \tag{2}$$

or, writing $\eta_i = \sum_j \beta_j x_{ji}$,

$$p_i = \frac{e^{\eta_i}}{1 + e^{\eta_i}} \tag{3}$$

probit transformation, and so ξ is such that $\Phi(\xi) = p$, or $\xi = \Phi^{-1}(p)$, where the inverse function $\Phi^{-1}(p)$ is the probit transformation of p, written as probit (p).

8.3 Statistical modelling

The method of estimation: maximum likelihood

The preferred method of estimation of the $k + 1$ unknown parameters $\beta_0, \beta_1, ..., \beta_k$ for probability models is maximum likelihood (Colett, 1991). The likelihood function is given by

$$L(\beta) = \prod_{i=1}^{n} \binom{n_i}{y_i} p_i^{y_i} (1 - p_i)^{n_i - y_i} \qquad (4)$$

The estimation of the maximum likelihood estimates $\hat{\beta}$, is generated by equating the derivatives of log L to zero and by fitting parameters from a generalised linear model by using iterative proportional fitting (Aitken *et al.*, 1989). Accordingly, our analysis was carried out using the generalised linear modelling system GLIM 4 (Francis *et al.*, 1993). Once $\hat{\beta}$ has been obtained, the estimated value of the linear systematic component of the model, the linear predictor, is $\hat{\eta}_i = \hat{\beta}_0 + \hat{\beta}_1 x_{1i} + \hat{\beta}_2 x_{2i} + ... + \hat{\beta}_k x_{ki}$. From the linear predictor, the fitted probabilities $\hat{p}$ of full compliance can be found through equation (3).

Fit of a linear logistic model

Summary statistics that measure the discrepancy between observed binomial proportions y_i / n_i and fitted proportions $\hat{p}_i$, serve to test the adequacy of an estimated linear logistic model.

A measure of the fit of a current model is the value of the likelihood $\hat{L}_c$, when the values of the unknown parameters are set equal to their maximum likelihood estimates, which can be compared to the value of the maximum likelihood for a model for which the fitted values coincide with the actual observations, termed the full model. A full model, or saturated model, has the same number of unknown parameters as there are observations and is therefore not useful on its own, since it does not provide an abstract of the data. The maximised likelihood under the full model is denominated $\hat{L}_f$.

The deviance D is a summary statistic, which tests the goodness of fit of the current model by measuring the extent to which the current model deviates from the full model. The deviance is minus twice the logarithm of the ratio of these maximised likelihoods, so that

$$D = -2\log(\hat{L}_c / \hat{L}_f) = -2[\log \hat{L}_c - \log \hat{L}_f] \qquad (5)$$

A large D indicates that $\hat{L}_c$ is small in comparison to $\hat{L}_f$ and hence indicates the inadequacy of the current model. In contrast, a small D can be interpreted as evidence of the appropriateness of the current model.

In the relevant case of binary data, the deviance on fitting a model is not itself suitable as a measure of the goodness of fit as it depends only on the fitted probabilities and is uninformative with respect to the conformity between the actual observations and their corresponding fitted probabilities.

Instead of employing the deviance itself to evaluate the adequacy of an adopted model, the distribution of the deviance, under the assumption that the model is correct, is required. The deviance is asymptotically distributed as χ^2 with $(n-k)$ degrees of freedom, where n is the number of binomial observations and k is the number of unknown parameters included in the current linear logistic model. The D statistic can be compared to the χ^2 - distribution with $(n - k)$ degrees of freedom. If the observed value of the statistic exceeds the upper $100\alpha\%$ point of the χ^2 - distribution on the given number of degrees of freedom, where α is sufficiently small, the lack of fit is regarded as significant at the $100\alpha\%$ level. When the deviance on fitting a particular model is declared to be significantly large, the model is deemed to be an inappropriate summary of the data.

However, even though the D - statistic can be used to determine whether a current model can be regarded as adequate fit for the actual observations, the general approach to measure goodness of fit of linear logistic models is the comparison of a sequence of nested models, where one model encompasses additional variables in comparison to another[4].

---

[4] See Colett, pp. 67-74, (1991).

170

8.4 Comparing linear logistic models

The empirical analysis compares a hierarchy of nested linear logistic models to describe the odds of full compliance relative to creative or partial compliance as a function of different sets of regressors. In general, two models are defined as nested if one model includes additional variables with regard to another. The difference in the deviances of two nested models measures the relevance of the additional variables for the improvement of the fit of the model. The effect of each explanatory variable in a model cannot be estimated independently of the others, so the order in which the terms are included is important when interpreting the model.

In general, the comparison of model (1) which is nested within model (2), may be denoted as follows:

Model (1): $\log it(p) = \beta_0 + \beta_1 x_1 + ... + \beta_h x_h$

Model (2): $\log it(p) = \beta_0 + \beta_1 x_1 + ... + \beta_h x_h + \beta_{h+1} x_{h+1} + ... + \beta_k x_k$

The difference in deviance $D1 - D2$ which counts for the effect of the additional variables $x_{h+1}, x_{h+2}, ..., x_k$ after $x_1, x_2, ... x_h$ have already been taken into account, is denoted the deviance of fitting $x_{h+1}, x_{h+2}, ..., x_k$ adjusted for $x_1, x_2, ... x_h$.

Since the deviance for each model has an approximate χ^2 - distribution, the differences between two deviances will also approximately follow a χ^2 - distribution. Denoting the maximum likelihood under model (1), model (2) and the full model by $\hat{L}_{c1}, \hat{L}_{c2}$, and $\hat{L}_f$ respectively, the two deviances are $D_1 = -2[\log \hat{L}_{c1} - \log \hat{L}_f]$ and $D_2 = -2[\log \hat{L}_{c2} - \log \hat{L}_f]$.

When subtracting $D1$ - $D2$, the term $\hat{L}_f$ disappears, so that $D_1 - D_2 = -2[\log \hat{L}_{c1} - \log \hat{L}_{c2}]$ and the χ^2 approximation to the difference between two variances can be used to compare nested models.

F - Test

The relative goodness of fit of two nested models can be compared by examining the ratio of (i) the change in deviances from two models within a hierarchy divided by the change in degrees of freedom, to (ii) the deviance for the full model, for which the fitted values coincide with the actual observations, divided by its degrees of freedom.

Where the deviance of a higher order model is D_H on v_H degrees of freedom and the deviance of the lower order model, containing a subset of the terms in the higher order model, is D_L on v_L degrees of freedom, and D_F is the deviance of the full model on v_F degrees of freedom, the ratio

$$\frac{\left[(D_L - D_H)/(v_L - v_H)\right]}{(D_F / v_F)} \tag{6}$$

has an F-distribution[5] on $(v_L - v_H), (v_F)$.

8.5 Incorporating regulatory factors into the linear predictor of compliance

As noted earlier, the objective of our statistical analysis is to determine whether the avoidance of full compliance is influenced by regulatory factors, in particular the rule-issuing authority and the extent of formalism in the rules themselves. Compliance is also assumed to vary over different subject areas of accounting. Furthermore, we have substituted the country of incorporation as an alternative indicator, this time representing national regulatory systems, rather than the type of regulation.

The first model considers an outcome which is independent of regulatory factors but conditional on the decision not to violate the regulations. By offsetting the companies which decided to contravene the rule in question, the conditional probability model to describe the relative odds that a company chooses either to comply unambiguously with the regulations in force or to resort to some form of avoidance, either through creative compliance or partial disclosure is therefore as follows:

$$\text{logit}(p_i) = \log(\frac{p_i}{1-p_i}) = \beta_0 \qquad\qquad (7)$$

Given the binary response, a logistic transformation of the linear predictor is used to generate fitted probabilities p which lie between zero and one.[6]

The second model adds the effects of differences in regulatory design to the model of conditional independence. The associated linear model, where the probability that a company in the ith jurisdiction will fully comply with the regulations depends on regulatory design (RD_i) is therefore as follows:

$$\text{logit}(p_i) = \log(\frac{p_i}{1-p_i}) = \beta_0 + \beta_1 RD_i \qquad\qquad (8)$$

We define RD as a factor distinguishing between formal and anti-formal regulatory texts, and we also include an interaction term when a particular set of regulations combines both features.

---

[5] Since the deviance for each model has an approximate χ^2 - distribution, the differences between two deviances will also be approximately follow a χ^2 - distribution.
[6] See Collett (1991) and Cramer (1991) for further discussion of statistical modelling of binary data and logit analysis.

The third model adds to this the effects of differences in regulatory source. The associated linear model, where the probability that a company in the ith jurisdiction will fully comply with the regulations depends on regulatory design (RD_i) and regulatory source (RS_i) in that jurisdiction, is therefore as follows:

$$\text{logit}(p_i) = \log(\frac{p_i}{1-p_i}) = \beta_0 + \beta_1 RD_i + \beta_2 RS_i \qquad (9)$$

The second explanatory factor, RS, represents the source of regulations governing the relevant accounting issue in each jurisdiction, in the form of either legislation, accounting standard or recommendation, or the interactions of law with standards and law with recommendations.

In a fourth model we substitute the country of incorporation, C, as an alternative indicator, this time representing national regulatory systems. The associated linear model, where the probability that a company in the ith jurisdiction will fully comply with the regulations depends on regulatory design (RD_i) and the country of incorporation (C_i), is therefore as follows:

$$\text{logit}(p_i) = \log(\frac{p_i}{1-p_i}) = \beta_0 + \beta_1 RD_i + \beta_3 C_i \qquad (10)$$

175

The third explanatory factor, C, represents the European countries subject to our analysis and is therefore defined as a nine-level factor without interaction terms.

The empirical analysis will be carried out separately for each of the subject areas of accounting and also for the aggregated subsets for which we will add a factor representing the three areas of accounting regulation in a fifth model. The associated linear model, where the probability that a company in the ith jurisdiction will fully comply with the regulations depends on regulatory design (RD_i), and regulatory source (RS_i) in that jurisdiction, and on the particular area of accounting regulation(AR_i), is therefore as follows:

$$\text{logit}(p_i) = \log(\frac{p_i}{1 - p_i}) = \beta_0 + \beta_1 RD_i + \beta_2 RS_i + \beta_4 AR_i \qquad (11)$$

As explained earlier, the decrease in the goodness-of-fit statistic provides a suitable measure of the significance of the factors added when fitting these models in sequence. The estimated regression coefficients, being logits, indicate the relative effect of the different levels of each explanatory factor. These statistics form the basis of the tables presented and discussed in Chapter Ten. Before that, however, the data collected and the research design are described in Chapter Nine.

CHAPTER 9

RESEARCH DESIGN AND DATA

9.1 Introduction

This chapter sets out to define the research design for the empirical analysis of this thesis. It describes the criteria used in selecting the sample and presents the survey results obtained from the annual reports of European companies. Accounting policies were examined for compliance with the relevant regulations in the three accounting areas under investigation using annual report disclosures by companies in the years 1987, 1993 and 1995. This chapter goes on to define the criteria used in categorising compliance behaviour and for assigning different levels to the two explanatory variables: regulatory source and regulatory design. The chapter ends with a preliminary analysis of the distribution of compliance in the sample.

9.2 The sample

This section provides details on the sample and the criteria for its selection. The sample of companies was drawn from nine European countries. In addition to a domestic stock exchange listing, these companies also had to be quoted on another foreign stock exchange elsewhere in the European Union in at least two of the three years covered by the study. The countries in which the companies were incorporated were Belgium, Denmark, France, Germany, Ireland, Italy, The Netherlands, Spain and the United Kingdom. A total of 154 European companies were included in the sample, being all interlisted companies quoted on the relevant stock exchanges in 1993 fitting the selection criteria.

The appendix of the thesis contains a list of all companies selected for the analysis, which were chosen on the basis of the following criteria:

1 The published annual report and financial statements were available during at least two consecutive periods for the financial years 1987, 1993 and 1995.

2 The company is not a subsidiary of another company in the survey.

3 The company is registered in one of the following European countries: Belgium, Denmark, France, Germany, Ireland, Italy, The Netherlands, Spain or the United Kingdom
4 The company is an industrial company; that is, not a bank or insurance company.
5 The company has foreign transactions.
6 The company has an equity listing on the domestic stock exchange
7 The company has an equity listing on at least one foreign stock exchange in Europe

Company reports published by the selected companies were analysed for compliance behaviour. The starting year was taken as 1987. By 1993, financial statements could be expected to reflect the Fourth and Seventh Directives which had by then been implemented in all of the countries under study. In the same year, a number of International Accounting Standards were revised with the objective of narrowing their options, and these revised standards were to become effective two years later in 1995. In that year, the IASC agreed with IOSCO the potential recognition of IASs for companies listed on international stock exchanges and a change in EU regulatory strategy with respect to harmonisation was also announced. Consequently, the three years selected for the review of compliance were 1987, 1993 and 1995.

Table 9.1 provides a breakdown of the distribution of the sample cross-classified by countries and years. The table indicates that the sample sizes are unequal for each country which reflects the fact that in each country a different number of companies fulfilled the selection criteria. An equal number of companies for each year could not be obtained because during the period 1987 to 1995 a number of companies in the sample either became delisted or ceased to exist following acquisitions, mergers and bankruptcy, or else they were set up or became listed after 1987. However, for the majority of companies, all three accounting periods were analysed and at least two observations were collected from each company. While all sample companies are included for the year 1993, there were 36 missing observations in 1987 and 11 in 1995 due to the above-mentioned causes.

Table 9.1

Sample of companies, cross-classified by country and year

COUNTRIES	NUMBER OF COMPANIES		
	1987	1993	1995
BELGIUM	7	10	9
DENMARK	3	5	5
FRANCE	15	22	21
GERMANY	22	23	21
IRELAND	9	9	8
ITALY	8	10	9
SPAIN	8	11	11
THE NETHERLANDS	17	20	18
UNITED KINGDOM	29	44	41
TOTAL	118	154	143

Notes

The sampling frame comprised all European companies interlisted between two or more stock exchanges in the European Union in 1993, the eventual sample excluding companies for which it was not possible to obtain the necessary financial reports.

The difference in sample size from year to year is accounted for by new interlistings after 1987 but prior to 1993 (*i.e.* reports for 1993 and 1995 were included) and by delistings after 1993 (*i.e.* reports for 1987 and 1993 were included).

9.3 Observed accounting practices

This section describes the observed accounting practices for the three areas of accounting regulation under study: revaluation of fixed assets, foreign currency reporting and the definition of a subsidiary.

9.3.1 Revaluation of fixed assets

As can be seen in Table 9.2 historic cost accounting, rather than revaluation, was the dominant policy choice during each of the sample years. As the use of historic cost is accepted by all national regulators, companies using historic cost accounting fully complied with the national requirements. The French, Spanish and Italian companies did likewise, reporting a policy of historic cost which was periodically adjusted for inflation in accordance with laws which enabled price-level adjustment.

In Germany, a movement towards internationally accepted valuation rules, which remained within the boundaries of national requirements, was clearly observable. While assets were subject to maximum tax depreciation rates by the majority of German companies in 1987, by 1995 straight-line depreciation had been adopted by half of the companies. This creative avoidance of national valuation rules by a change in depreciation strategy in order to accommodate international rules is illustrated in the following examples.

Babcock 1995:
"In adaptation to international standards, depreciation of property, plant and equipment is now carried out uniformly throughout the Group according to the straight-line method. The lump-sum accruals for warranty obligations have been reduced. As a result, income before taxes has increased by DM 22 million due to the change in the method of depreciation and by 20 DM million caused by the reduction of lump-sum accruals for warranty obligations. Tax-allowable provisions shown in the subsidiaries' balance sheets have been reversed in the consolidated balance sheet likewise increasing income."

Wella 1995:
"In compliance with international accounting standards newly acquired fixed assets are written off uniformly following the straight-line method as from 1995 onwards."

Veba 1995:
"The following accounting principles applied to the VEBA consolidated financial statements have been modified to comply with U.S. GAAP effective January 1, 1995: To value fixed assets, depreciation periods for power plants and distribution units have been adjusted from the periods previously acceptable under tax law to those as defined by German Commercial Law for the depreciation of such assets. (...)"

In countries which refer in legislation to the general concepts of either current value accounting or revaluation of fixed assets, companies are required to revalue regularly and to disclose detail with respect to the relevant assets and revaluation basis. While some companies make use of the broadness of the law and avoid further substantiating it (see Pernod Ricard), other companies specify the detail and circumstances which the relevant rules require (see P&O):

Pernod Ricard 1995:
"Property, plant and equipment are valued at cost or when applicable, at a revalued cost in compliance with legal requirements."

P&O 1993:
"Investment properties and properties occupied by the Group companies are included in fixed assets at their latest valuations plus subsequent additions at cost, and surpluses and deficits on valuation are included in the revaluation reserve. A substantial proportion by value, including the largest properties, is valued annually by the Group chief surveyor and triennially by external valuers. (...) The valuation of properties at 31 December 1993 were all made on the basis of open market value by external valuers, principally Healey & Baker, totalling £1,465.2m, and by the Group chief surveyor R A Knight FRICS, totalling £54.3m."

9.3.2 Foreign transactions

Chapter Six of this thesis separated the issue of translating foreign transactions from the issue of translating foreign financial statements. For the empirical analysis the area of foreign currency reporting has been confined to the accounting for foreign transactions only. In fact, the analysis in Part Two demonstrates that, while IAS 21 has been widely adopted by regulators and used in practice with respect to the translation of foreign subsidiaries, this has not been repeated with respect to accounting for foreign transactions. In particular, the recognition of unrealised exchange gains has remained contentious among European countries. Moreover, even though considerably different authoritative sources implemented the content of the international standard for foreign subsidiaries this acceptance of IAS 21 has led to a relatively homogeneous rule design on this issue in Europe. In contrast, the rules for foreign transactions not only differ in their sources of authority but also in their rule design across Europe. Finally, in order to prevent an overrepresentation of observations for the issue of foreign currency reporting, the statistical analysis has been limited to one aspect only, that of accounting for foreign transactions.

As can be seen in Table 9.3, many different approaches exist in practice with regard to the reporting of foreign exchange differences and these do not always fully correspond to national requirements. For example, the majority of French companies included unrealised exchange gains in the consolidated profit and loss account and hence reported in line with the rules of IAS 21 instead of deferring such gain to the balance sheet as French regulations require. This practice was explained by a provision in French law which allows companies to employ different valuation methods in the consolidated financial statements than those used in the annual accounts. An example which illustrates this creative compliance with national law in practice is Thomson:

Thomson 1995:
"Monetary assets and liabilities denominated in foreign currencies are converted at the exchange rates prevailing at balance sheet dates. In accordance with an option of the French law on consolidation, the Company records the related unrealised exchange gains and losses under 'Other financial income (expense), net' in the accompanying consolidated statement of income."

In the German sample, not avoidance but violation of national rules for the treatment of foreign transactions occurred. Table 9.3 shows that for the years 1987 and 1993, all the German sample companies only valued foreign payables and receivables at the closing rate (unless hedged) if this resulted in a lower asset value and a higher liability value, in accordance with GoB. However, by 1995, some companies had relaxed this strict interpretation of GoB by applying it only to long term monetary items, while translating all short term payables and receivables at the closing rate. This non-compliance behaviour was observed in the annual report of Hoechst:

Hoechst 1995:

"For the first time, short term receivables and liabilities in foreign currency are uniformly stated in the 1995 Group financial statements at the buying or selling rate on the balance sheet date in accordance with IAS 21. In previous years, the closing rates were only used so long as no unrealised gains resulted. Due to this change in the currency translation method, the profit before taxes on income shown is DM 80 million higher in the year under review."

9.3.3 The definition of a subsidiary

National differences in regulatory design with respect to group control do not seem to constrain compliance behaviour in reporting practice. As can be seen in Table 9.4, in France, even though the regulator has issued narrow, detailed rules and emphasised their literal interpretation, companies avoid the criteria specified in the national law and, instead, report in an indeterminate manner. For instance, not a single French company referred to the formal consolidation criterion that a parent company exercised *'at least 40% of voting rights during two years whilst no other shareholder has held a higher proportion'*. Instead, the French sample companies disclosed in rather a broad and flexible way referring, for example, to 'controlling interest', as in the case of Carnaud Metalbox:

Carnaud Metalbox 1995:
"The group financial statements include the accounts of all significant subsidiaries in which Carnaud Metalbox holds, directly or indirectly a controlling interest."

Avoidance of regulation occurred most obviously by failure to disclose the accounting policy choice which had been made. In particular, the consolidation criteria were not specified in the UK, where the regulatory strategy was to adopt both legal and economic group control. Most companies did not describe the criteria upon which they decided to include a subsidiary into the consolidated accounts. This example of partial compliance is illustrated here by Guiness:

Guiness 1995:
"Basis of consolidation: The Group accounts include the accounts of the company and its subsidiary undertakings."

As described earlier, the French legislator adopted a legal concept of group control with emphasis on the literal interpretation of the defined control rights. However, a number of companies such as Rémy Cointreau referred to management control, thereby clearly contravening the national regulation:

Rémy Cointreau 1993:
"The companies over which Rémy Cointreau exercises exclusive control due to
- a direct or indirect holding of more than 50% of the share capital, or
- effective management control,
are fully consolidated."

Conversely, the Dutch legislator constrained group control to the cases of actual economic parent-subsidiary relationships. Yet by giving priority to the existence of legal control rights, some reporting companies violated the Dutch consolidation principles, as the following example of Wereldhave demonstrates:

Wereldhave 1995:
"Companies which form a group with Wereldhave are included in the consolidated annual accounts. Interests of less than 100% are consolidated on a proportional basis. Proportional consolidation provides a direct illustration of the magnitude of Wereldhave's investments, other related assets and liabilities, and results."

Table 9.2

Observed accounting practices: The revaluation of fixed assets

	1987	1993	1995
Historic cost (straight-line depreciation)	41	61	63
Belgium	5	7	6
Denmark	1	1	1
France	9	14	13
Germany	2	6	10
Ireland	1	1	1
Italy	0	0	0
Netherlands	11	16	16
Spain	0	0	0
UK	12	16	16
Historic cost (full use of tax depreciation)	20	17	11
Belgium	0	0	0
Denmark	0	0	0
France	0	0	0
Germany	20	17	11
Ireland	0	0	0
Italy	0	0	0
Netherlands	0	0	0
Spain	0	0	0
UK	0	0	0
Historic cost adjusted for inflation in accordance with enabling laws	17	23	22
Belgium	0	0	0
Denmark	0	0	0
France	4	4	4
Germany	0	0	0
Ireland	0	0	0
Italy	7	10	9
Netherlands	0	0	0
Spain	6	9	9
UK	0	0	0
Periodic revaluation (basis not defined)	7	10	10
Belgium	2	3	3
Denmark	2	3	3
France	3	4	4
Germany	0	0	0
Ireland	0	0	0
Italy	0	0	0
Netherlands	0	0	0
Spain	0	0	0
UK	0	0	0
Current cost accounting	9	4	3
Belgium	0	0	0
Denmark	0	0	0
France	0	0	0
Germany	0	0	0
Ireland	0	0	0
Italy	1	0	0
Netherlands	6	3	2
Spain	1	0	0
UK	1	1	1
Revaluation of land and buildings (by a surveyor)	25	39	34
Belgium	0	0	0
Denmark	0	1	1
France	0	0	0
Germany	0	0	0
Ireland	8	8	7
Italy	0	0	0
Netherlands	0	1	0
Spain	1	2	2
UK	16	27	24
Report not available	35	0	11
Belgium	3	0	1
Denmark	2	0	0
France	6	0	1
Germany	1	0	2
Ireland	0	0	1
Italy	2	0	1
Netherlands	3	0	2
Spain	3	0	0
UK	15	0	3
Total	154	154	154

185

Table 9.3

Observed accounting practices: The reporting of foreign exchange differences

		1987	1993	1995
Foreign exchange gain and loss in profit & loss account		70	101	96
	Belgium	4	4	4
	Denmark	3	5	5
	France	9	16	15
	Germany	0	0	2
	Ireland	9	9	8
	Italy	4	7	6
	Netherlands	12	15	14
	Spain	2	2	2
	UK	27	43	40
Foreign exchange short term gain and loss in profit & loss account, Long term gain and loss deferred in balance sheet		4	2	2
	Belgium	0	0	0
	Denmark	0	0	0
	France	1	0	0
	Germany	0	0	0
	Ireland	0	0	0
	Italy	0	0	0
	Netherlands	3	2	2
	Spain	0	0	0
	UK	0	0	0
Foreign exchange short term gain and loss in profit & loss account Long term gain deferred (or not recognised), long term loss in profit & loss account		1	3	4
	Belgium	0	0	0
	Denmark	0	0	0
	France	0	0	0
	Germany	0	0	2
	Ireland	0	0	0
	Italy	0	0	0
	Netherlands	1	3	2
	Spain	0	0	0
	UK	0	0	0
Foreign exchange loss in profit & loss account, gain deferred in Balance sheet (or not recognised)		26	31	26
	Belgium	3	4	4
	Denmark	0	0	0
	France	1	0	0
	Germany	17	21	16
	Ireland	0	0	0
	Italy	0	0	0
	Netherlands	0	0	0
	Spain	5	6	6
	UK	0	0	0
Foreign exchange gain and loss deferred in balance sheet		3	6	6
	Belgium	0	0	0
	Denmark	0	0	0
	France	0	0	0
	Germany	0	0	0
	Ireland	0	0	0
	Italy	2	3	3
	Netherlands	0	0	0
	Spain	1	3	3
	UK	0	0	0
Method not disclosed		15	11	9
	Belgium	0	2	1
	Denmark	0	0	0
	France	5	6	6
	Germany	5	2	1
	Ireland	0	0	0
	Italy	2	0	0
	Netherlands	1	0	0
	Spain	0	0	0
	UK	2	1	1
Report not available		35	0	11
	Belgium	3	0	1
	Denmark	2	0	0
	France	6	0	1
	Germany	1	0	2
	Ireland	0	0	1
	Italy	2	0	1
	Netherlands	3	0	2
	Spain	3	0	0
	UK	15	0	3
Total		154	154	154

186

Table 9.4

Observed accounting practices: The definition of a subsidiary

		1987	1993	1995
Solely legal criteria		37	33	36
	Belgium	3	3	3
	Denmark	1	2	1
	France	4	1	2
	Germany	12	8	12
	Ireland	0	0	0
	Italy	2	4	4
	Netherlands	8	3	2
	Spain	7	9	9
	UK	0	3	3
Solely economic criteria		2	5	5
	Belgium	0	0	0
	Denmark	0	0	0
	France	0	0	0
	Germany	1	1	1
	Ireland	0	0	0
	Italy	1	0	0
	Netherlands	0	3	3
	Spain	0	0	0
	UK	0	1	1
Legal and economic criteria combined		13	25	27
	Belgium	1	1	1
	Denmark	1	2	3
	France	2	5	5
	Germany	1	5	5
	Ireland	0	0	0
	Italy	4	5	4
	Netherlands	3	5	6
	Spain	0	0	0
	UK	0	2	3
Indeterminate consolidation criteria		11	25	21
	Belgium	3	6	4
	Denmark	0	1	1
	France	8	14	11
	Germany	0	0	0
	Ireland	0	0	0
	Italy	0	1	1
	Netherlands	0	3	4
	Spain	0	0	0
	UK	0	0	0
Consolidation criteria not specified / indication of principal subsidiaries		56	67	53
	Belgium	0	0	1
	Denmark	1	0	0
	France	2	3	2
	Germany	8	9	3
	Ireland	8	9	8
	Italy	1	0	0
	Netherlands	6	6	3
	Spain	1	2	2
	UK	29	38	34
Report not available		35	0	11
	Belgium	3	0	1
	Denmark	2	0	0
	France	6	0	1
	Germany	1	0	2
	Ireland	0	0	1
	Italy	2	0	1
	Netherlands	3	0	2
	Spain	3	0	0
	UK	15	0	3
Total		154	154	154

9.4 Classification of compliance behaviour

This section describes the characteristics of accounting practices which are classified according to different levels of compliance and on which the following statistical analysis is based. Following the comparison of the reported policies with the relevant national accounting regulations to which the reporting company was subject, compliance behaviour was assigned to one of three categories: either (i) full compliance, (ii) the avoidance of regulations or (iii) non-compliance with the regulations. Avoidance of regulations comprises either creative or partial compliance.

Full compliance with the accounting regulation is assigned when a company's reported policy corresponds unambiguously with the national regulatory requirement. Creative compliance applies when the reported policy is not strictly in conformity with the rule but, at the same time, does not violate the rule. Partial compliance refers to the case in which a company provides insufficient information. Finally, non-compliance is defined as those instances when there is a clear indication by the company in its annual report that the rule in question is contravened.

A detailed analysis of the criteria assigning reported accounting policies into one of the three compliance levels, together with the regulatory requirements in each area of accounting policy for each country is provided in Tables 9.5 to 9.7.

Table 9.5

Revaluation of fixed assets

Country	Source	Form	Content	Full compliance	Creative / partial compliance	Non-compliance
Belgium	Arrêté royal 8 October 1976, amended by Arrêté royal 12 September 1983, Chapter II, Section III, Art. 34	Anti-formal	Tangible fixed assets, participating interest and shares under financial fixed assets or specific categories of such assets may be revalued when the value of the asset by reference to the enterprise clearly and permanently exceeds its carrying value. The revaluation must be justified by reference to profitability.	Revaluation is determined and disclosed by reference to the usefulness and profitability to the enterprise, the relevant assets are specified; historic cost accounting.	Disclosure of "revaluation", but no justification with respect to its usefulness and profitability to the enterprise is provided, the relevant assets and the revaluation amounts are not specified.	The revaluation of intangible fixed assets.
Denmark	Regnskabslov 1981, chapter 5 section 30 (U 11 Regnskabsvejledning 11, 1995)	Anti-formal	Tangible and financial fixed assets may be revalued if their value is materially and permanently higher than the book value.	Detail with respect to the assets concerned and the revaluation amount is disclosed. Historic cost accounting.	"Revaluation" has been carried out, without informing the reader about the relevant assets, year, basis and amount of the revaluation.	The revaluation of intangible fixed assets.
France	Code de Commerce 1984, Art. 12 Ordonnance du 15 août 1945, Loi du 28 décembre 1959 Loi des Finances pour 1977 OEC Avis, CNCC Norme	Anti-formal	The Commercial Code allows the revaluation of tangible and financial fixed assets. If a company decides to revalue, it must comprise all tangible and financial fixed assets. Fiscal revaluation laws authorized the revaluation of certain specified fixed assets in accordance with inflation indices.	Revaluation in accordance with specific price-level adjustment law in 1977/78; detailed disclosure if commercial law revaluation has been carried out. Historic cost accounting.	"Revaluation" has been carried out, without providing information on the assets concerned, the amount, the basis and the year of revaluation.	The revaluation of individual fixed assets; the revaluation of intangible assets.
Germany	Handelsgesetzbuch 1985, Art.253 sec.1 and 2	Formal	The upper value of fixed assets is limited to acquisition or production cost.	Historic cost accounting.	Change of depreciation methods from tax depreciation to the straight-line depreciation.	The revaluation of fixed assets.

Country	Legal references	Classification	Description			
Ireland	Companies Act (1986); SSAP 19 Accounting for Investment Properties (1981); ED 51 Accounting for Fixed Assets and Revaluations (1990)	Anti-formal	The Companies Act permits the valuation of intangible fixed assets (other than goodwill) at current cost, tangible fixed assets at market value or current cost and financial fixed assets at market value or at a basis which appears to the directors to be appropriate. SSAP 19 requires the valuation of investment property at open market value. ED 51 requires the valuation of an asset at either current value or historic cost on a regular basis. The valuation basis should be the open market value, or the net replacement cost, determined by professional experts at regular intervals (at least every five years).	Pure current cost accounting, historic cost accounting or regular revaluation of all fixed assets or individual assets carried out by professional valuers, detail with respect to the relevant assets and the revaluation amount is disclosed	Revaluation of individual assets is carried out on an irregular basis; insufficient information is provided with respect to the relevant assets, the basis, amount and year of revaluation.	The use of foreign GAAP to revalue.
Italy	Legge: -91 of 01/04/1949 -74 of 11/02/1952 -576 of 02/12/1975 -72 of 19/03/1983 -408 of 29/12/1990 -413, 30/12/1991	Formal	The revaluation of fixed assets is limited to explicit permission by tax laws, authorizing the adjustment of specific assets in line with inflation indices.	Revaluation in accordance with specific price-level adjustment laws. Historic cost accounting.	Revaluation of assets on the occasion of internal group restructurings, acquisitions and mergers.	Revaluation of fixed assets without explicit permission by a tax law.
Netherlands	Title 9 Book 2 Burgerlijk Wetboek Art.384.1., Art.390; General Administrative Order (22 December 1983)	Anti-formal	The Civil Code allows the application of current values for tangible and financial fixed assets. The General Administrative order defines three different types of current value: (i) replacement value, if it is assumed that the asset will be replaced in due course, (ii) economic value, if replacement of the asset is unlikely and (iii) net realizable value if the business will not continue in the future.	A company describes the criteria for the establishment of the replacement value, economic value or net realizable value and discloses the assets subject to revaluation; consistent valuation of an asset at either current value or historic cost.	Insufficient information is provided with respect to the revaluation (the asset concerned, the revaluation basis); inconsistent valuation of assets.	The use of foreign GAAP to revalue. The revaluation of intangible fixed assets.
Spain	Fiscal revaluation laws: 76 in 1961; 41 in 1964; 12 in 1973; 50 in 1977; 1 in 1979; 74 in 1980; 9 in 1983; 6 in 1996	Formal	The revaluation laws authorise the adjustment of specific fixed assets in accordance with published inflation indices.	Revaluation in accordance with specific revaluation laws. Historic cost accounting.	Revaluation of assets on the occasion of internal group restructurings, acquisitions and mergers.	Revaluation of fixed assets without explicit permission by a tax law.

| UK | Companies Act (1981) Para. 29-34, Schedule 4; SSAP 19 Accounting for Investment Properties (1981); ED 51 Accounting for Fixed Assets and Revaluations (1990) | Anti-formal | The Companes Act permits the valuation of intangible fixed assets (other than goodwill) at current cost, tangible fixed assets at market value or current cost and financial fixed assets at market value or at a basis which appears to the directors to be appropriate. SSAP 19 requires the valuation of investment property at open market value. ED 51 requires the valuation of an asset at either current value or historic cost on a regular basis. The valuation basis should be the open market value, or the net replacement cost, determined by professional experts at regular intervals (at least every five years). | Pure current cost accounting, historic cost accounting or regular revaluation of all fixed assets or individual assets carried out by professional valuers, detail with respect to the relevant assets and the revaluation amount is disclosed. | Revaluation of individual assets is carried out on an irregular basis; insufficient information is provided with respect to the relevant assets, the basis, amount and year of revaluation. | The use of foreign GAAP to revalue. |

191

Table 9.6

Translation of foreign transactions

Country	Source of regulations	Form	Content	Full compliance	Creative / partial compliance	Non-compliance
Belgium	*Avis* (Bulletin No. 20) of the Commission des Normes Comptables (1987)	Formal	At the balance sheet date unsettled foreign payables and receivables are translated at the closing rate. Unrealised gains are deferred, unrealised losses are charged to the P&L account.	Use of closing rate, charge of unrealised loss to the P&L account, deferral of unrealised gain to the balance sheet.	Partial or no disclosure of method used.	Unrealised gain is credited to the profit and loss account.
Denmark	Foreningen af Statsautoriserende Revisorer Regnskabsvejledning no. 9 (1994)	Formal	At the balance sheet date unsettled foreign payables and receivables are translated at the closing rate. Unrealised gains or unrealised losses are credited or charged to the P&L account.	Use of closing rate, charge of unrealised loss and credit of unrealised gain to the P&L account.	Partial or no disclosure of method used.	Deferral of exchange differences to the balance sheet.
France	Plan Comptable Général p. II. 12-13 (1982)	Formal	At the balance sheet date unsettled foreign payables and receivables are translated at the closing rate. Unrealised gains are deferred, unrealised losses are charged to the P&L account.	Use of closing rate, charge of unrealised loss to the P&L account, deferral of unrealised gain to the balance sheet.	All unrealised translation difference, including gain, are reported in the P&L account.	Distinction between short term and long term monetary items.
Germany	Grundsätze ordnungsmäßiger Buchführung Institut der Wirtschaftsprüfer HfA Stellungnahme (1986)	Anti-formal	GoB: Prudence principle and historic cost principle, interpreted as follows: At the balance sheet date unsettled foreign payables are translated at the lower of the closing rate and unsettled foreign payables are translated at the higher of the closing or historic rate. Unrealised losses are charged to the income statement, unrealised gains are not recognised.	Foreign payables (receivables) are translated at the higher (lower) of the closing or historic rate. Exchange loss is charged to the P&L account, gain is not recognised	Partial or no disclosure of method used.	Distinction between short term and long term monetary items. Unrealised translation gain reported in the P&L account for all or short term monetary items.
Ireland	Statement of Standard Accounting Practice No. 20 (1983)	Formal	At the balance sheet date unsettled foreign payables and receivables are translated at the closing rate. Unrealised gains or unrealised losses are credited or charged to the P&L account.	Use of closing rate, charge of unrealised loss and credit of unrealised gain to the P&L account.	Partial or no disclosure of method used.	Deferral of unrealised translation gain to the balance sheet.

Country	Source	Type	Description		Disclosure	Effect
Italy	Commissione per la Statuizione dei Principi Contabili Documento N. 9 (1988) Art. 72 Income Tax Law	Anti-formal	At the balance sheet date unsettled foreign payables and receivables are translated at the closing rate. Unrealised gains are deferred, unrealised losses are charged to the P&L account. Option not to recognise gain or loss on long term transactions.	Use of closing rate, charge of unrealised loss to the P&L account, deferral of unrealised gain to the balance sheet. Exception for long term monetary transactions.	Partial or no disclosure of method used.	Unrealised gain is credited to the profit and loss account. Unrealised loss is deferred to the balance sheet. Gain or loss on short term transactions not recognised
Netherlands	Raad voor de Jaarverslaggeving Richtlijnen 1.03.906.-12 (1986)	Formal	At the balance sheet date unsettled foreign payables and receivables are translated at the closing rate. Unrealised gains or unrealised losses are credited or charged to the P&L account. Option to defer unrealised translation gains on long term transactions whilst offsetting future losses on long term transactions.	Use of closing rate, charge of unrealised loss and credit of unrealised gain to the P&L account. Gain or loss on long term items deferred to the balance sheet.	Deferral of exchange gain in the balance sheet for long term transactions without offsetting losses.	Deferral of exchange gain and loss in the balance sheet for short term transactions.
Spain	Plan General de Contabilidad part V, 14a (1983) Ministerial Orders 1991,1992	Formal	At the balance sheet date unsettled foreign payables and receivables are translated at the closing rate. Unrealised gains are deferred, unrealised losses are charged to the P&L account. Companies operating in the utility industries may defer unrealised loss since 1991.	Use of closing rate, charge of unrealised loss to the P&L account, deferral of unrealised gain to the balance sheet. Exception for utility industries.	Partial or no disclosure of method used.	Credit of unrealised translation gain to the P&L account. Deferral of exchange loss to the balance sheet for companies not operating in the utility industry.
UK	Statement of Standard Accounting Practice No. 20 (1983)	Formal	At the balance sheet date unsettled foreign payables and receivables are translated at the closing rate. Unrealised gains or unrealised losses are credited or charged to the P&L account.	Use of closing rate, charge of unrealised loss and credit of unrealised gain to the P&L account	Partial or no disclosure of method used.	Deferral of unrealised translation gain or loss to the balance sheet.

Table 9.7

The definition of a subsidiary

Country	Source of regulations	Form	Content	Full compliance	Creative / partial compliance	Non-compliance
Belgium	Arrêté royal 6 March 1990, Art. 2	Formal and anti-formal	Legal control is defined as: (1) a majority of voting rights, (2) the right to appoint a majority of the board members, (3) a dominant influence pursuant to a contract (4) the appointment of a majority of the board for two consecutive years by exercise of voting rights, (5) majority of voting rights is based on an agreement; Economic control is defined as participating interest and (6) actual dominant influence, or (7) unified management.	The reporting of one or several legal or economic criteria referred to in the regulation.	The reported criterion does not correspond to the provis on in the regulation. The reader is unable to judge whether the company has complied with the legislator or violated it.	The non-consolidation of either de jure or de facto controlled subsidiaries.
Denmark	Årsregnskabsbekendtgørelsen, section 1(2), 6, section 2b	Formal and anti-formal	Legal control is defined as: (1) a majority of voting rights, (2) the right to appoint a majority of the board members, (3) a dominant influence pursuant to a contract (4) majority of voting rights is based on an agreement; Economic control is defined as participating interest and (5) actual dominant influence.	The reporting of one or several legal or economic criteria referred to in the regulation.	Indeterminate reporting, which does not correspond to the legal provisions.	The non-consolidation of either de jure or de facto controlled subsidiaries.
France	Loi 85, Art. 357.1 Decrée 86-221	Formal	Legal control is defined as: (1) a majority of voting rights, (2) a dominant influence pursuant to a contract (3) the appointment of a majority of the board for two consecutive years by exercise of voting rights, which is presumed where the parent company holds more than 40% of the voting rights, (4) majority of voting rights is based on an agreement.	The reporting of one or several legal criteria referred to in the regulation.	The reported criterion is indeterminate and does not correspond to the provision in the regulatior. The reader is unable to judge whether the company has complied with the legislation or violated it.	The consolidation of subsidiaries based on the economic control criteria of dominant influence or unified management.

Country	Regulation	Classification	Definition	Reporting criterion	Consolidation criterion status	Consequence
Germany	Handelsgesetzbuch §§ 290, 291, §§ 16-18, Aktiengesetz § 319	Formal and anti-formal	Legal control is defined as: (1) a majority of voting rights, (2) the right to appoint a majority of the board members, (3) a dominant influence pursuant to a contract, (4) majority of voting rights is based on an agreement; Economic control is defined as participating interest and (5) unified management.	The reporting of one or several legal or economic criteria referred to in the regulation.	No consolidation criterion is specified.	The non-consolidation of either de jure or de facto controlled subsidiaries.
Ireland	Group Accounts Law 1992 FRS 2 Accounting for subsidiary undertakings	Formal and anti-formal	Legal control is defined as: (1) a majority of voting rights, (2) the right to appoint a majority of the board members, (3) a dominant influence pursuant to a contract, (4) majority of voting rights is based on an agreement; Economic control is defined as participating interest and (5) actual dominant influence, or (6) unified management. FRS 2 defines dominant influence as the achievement of desired operating and financial policies; and unified management as the integration of the whole of the operations of two undertakings	The reporting of one or several legal or economic criteria referred to in the regulation.	No consolidation criterion is specified, instead, a list with principal subsidiaries is provided which may hide the exclusion of effectively controlled subsidiaries from consolidation.	The non-consolidation of either de jure or de facto controlled subsidiaries.
Italy	Codice Civile Art. 2359 Decreto legislativo 127/1991	Formal	Legal control is defined as: (1) a majority of voting rights, (2) a dominant influence pursuant to a contract, (3) majority of voting rights is based on an agreement;	The reporting of one or several legal criteria referred to in the regulation.	Indeterminate reporting which does not correspond to the legal provisions.	The consolidation of subsidiaries based on the economic control criteria of dominant influence or unified management.
Netherlands	Burgerlijk Wetboek Art. 24a, 24b, 406 Raad voor de Jaarverslaggeving Richtlijnen 2.03.103	Anti-formal	A subsidiary is defined as: (1) a majority of voting rights, (2) the right to appoint a majority of the board members, A subsidiary is a group company, if it belongs to an economic whole. The RJ specifies that complementary economic activities and collective financial policies indicate an economic whole.	The reporting of economic control as the decisive criterion for consolidation.	The reported criterion is indeterminate and does not correspond to the provision in the regulation. The reader is unable to judge whether the company has complied with the legislation or violated it.	The reporting of legal control as the decisive criterion for consolidation.
Spain	Real Decreto 1815/1991 Art. 42-49	Formal	Legal control is defined as: (1) a majority of voting rights, (2) the right to appoint a majority of the board members, (3) the appointment of a majority of the board for two consecutive years by exercise of voting rights, (4) majority of voting rights is based on an agreement;	The reporting of one or several legal criteria referred to in the regulation.	Indeterminate reporting, which does not correspond to the legal provisions.	The consolidation of subsidiaries based on a control contract or on the economic control criteria of dominant influence or unified management.

					The non-consolidation of either de jure or de facto controlled subsidiaries.
UK	Companies Act 1989 Sec. 258 FRS 2 Accounting for subsidiary undertakings	Formal and anti-formal	Legal control is defined as: (1) a majority of voting rights, (2) the right to appoint a majority of the board members, (3) a dominant influence pursuant to a contract, (4) majority of voting rights is based on an agreement; Economic control is defined as participating interest with (5) actual dominant influence, or (6) unified management. FRS 2 defines dominant influence as the achievement of desired operating and financial policies; and unified management as the integration of the whole of the operations of two undertakings.	The reporting of one or several legal or economic criteria referred to in the regulation.	No consolidation criterion is specified, instead, a list with principal subsidiaries is provided which may hide the exclusion of effectively controlled subsidiaries from consolidation.

9.5 Classification of the regulatory variables

The aim of the empirical analysis is to analyse the relationship between compliance in financial reporting practice and the regulatory factors of accounting and, in particular, to examine whether (i) the authority issuing the regulation and (ii) the degree of formalism are statistically associated with companies' compliance behaviour regarding accounting rules.

Sources of accounting regulation

Tables 9.8-9.10 summarise the sources of authority of accounting regulation in the nine European countries under study for the three accounting areas fixed asset revaluation, foreign currency reporting and the definition of a subsidiary. For the purpose of our statistical analysis, the variable 'regulatory source' has been classified into the three main types of regulatory instruments which have been described in Part One of this thesis. These are: (i) laws, (ii) standards and (iii) recommendations. As has been seen, the different regulatory authorities act either individually or in interaction with each other. Accordingly, the factor 'regulatory source' has been assigned five levels comprising three main effects and two interactions; that is (1) law, (2) standard, (3) recommendation, (4) law and standard, (5) law and recommendation.

Table 9.8

THE REVALUATION OF ASSETS

		Source of Accounting Regulation			
	Parliamentary Law	Government Decree	Ministerial Legislation	Professional Standard	Professional Opinion
Belgium		*Arrêté Royal*			
Denmark	*Regnskabslov*				
France	*Code de Commerce*				*OEC Avis* *CNCC* *Norme*
Germany	*Handelsgesetz-buch*				
Ireland	*Companies Act*			*SSAP 19* *ED 51*	
Italy			*Legge fiscale*		
Netherlands	*Burgerlijk Wetboek*		*General Administrative Order*		
Spain			*Ley*		
UK	*Companies Act*			*SSAP 19* *ED 51*	

Table 9.9

FOREIGN TRANSACTIONS

	Source of Accounting Regulation				
	Ministerial Order	Accounting Plan	Governmental Guideline	Professional Standard	Professional Opinion
Belgium			*Bulletin No. 20 CNC*		
Denmark				*Regnskabsvej -ledning No.9*	
France		*PCG p. II. 12-13*			
Germany					*IdW Stellungnahme*
Ireland				*SSAP No. 20*	
Italy				*Documento No.9 CSPC*	
Netherlands				*RJ Richtlijnen 1.03.906-12*	
Spain	*Ordenes ministeriales*	*PGC p. V. 14a*		*Documento No. 10 AECA*	
UK				*SSAP No.20*	

Table 9.10

THE DEFINITION OF A SUBSIDIARY

	Source of Accounting Regulation		
	Parliamentary Law	Government Decree	Professional Standard
Belgium		*Arrêté Royal*	
Denmark		*Årsregnskabsbekendt-gørelsen*	
France	*Loi*	*Decrée*	
Germany	*Handelsgesetzbuch*		
Ireland		*Group Accounts Law*	*Financial Reporting Standard No.2*
Italy	*Codice Civile*	*Decreto Legislativo*	
Netherlands	*Burgerlijk Wetboek*		*RJ Richtlijnen 2.03.103*
Spain		*Real Decreto*	
UK	*Companies Act*		*Financial Reporting Standard No.2*

In order to ensure that the empirical analysis is not unduly influenced by the classification into law, standard and recommendation, the regression estimates were obtained using three different approaches to classification. First, law is defined as parliamentary legislation, government decree and ministerial legislation, while standards comprise rules issued by a standard setting agency which is either government-controlled or a self-regulated professional body, and recommendations are publications by all other 'non-authoritative' associations. In contrast, the second classification confines standards to those issued by a self-regulated accountancy body, while defining governmental standardisation as part of law. The third alternative classification differentiates between public regulation, on the one hand, and private regulation on the other. Public rules consist of parliamentary legislation, government decrees, ministerial orders, national accounting plan and governmental guidelines, while private rules comprise professional standard setting and recommendations.

Degree of formalism of accounting rules

Figures 9.1 to 9.3 summarise the grouping of countries relative to the factor regulatory design for the three accounting areas. As can be seen, policy design is either (i) formal, (ii) anti-formal or both (iii) formal and anti-formal. Accordingly, the factor regulatory design has been categorised into two main effects and one interaction effect.

Table 9.11 summarises the classifications of the variables 'regulatory source' and 'regulatory design' for the three accounting policies under study. The table shows clearly that regulatory strategies not only vary between countries, but also between different accounting policies within the same country.

Figure 9.1

THE REVALUATION OF ASSETS

<u>Countries</u>   <u>Design of rules</u>

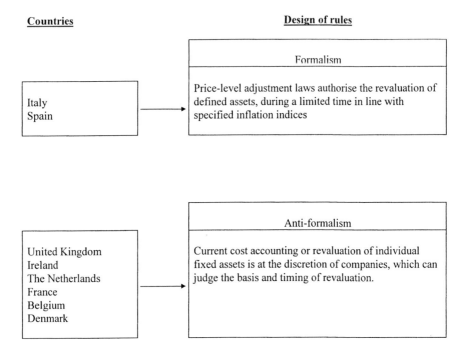

Formalism
Price-level adjustment laws authorise the revaluation of defined assets, during a limited time in line with specified inflation indices

Italy
Spain

Anti-formalism
Current cost accounting or revaluation of individual fixed assets is at the discretion of companies, which can judge the basis and timing of revaluation.

United Kingdom
Ireland
The Netherlands
France
Belgium
Denmark

Figure 9.2

FOREIGN TRANSACTIONS

<u>Countries</u>   <u>Design of rules</u>

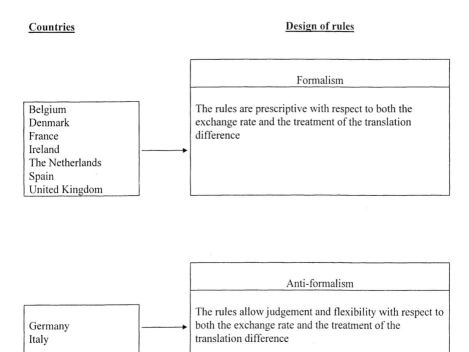

	Formalism
Belgium Denmark France Ireland The Netherlands Spain United Kingdom	The rules are prescriptive with respect to both the exchange rate and the treatment of the translation difference

	Anti-formalism
Germany Italy	The rules allow judgement and flexibility with respect to both the exchange rate and the treatment of the translation difference

Figure 9.3

THE DEFINITION OF A SUBSIDIARY

Countries

Design of rules

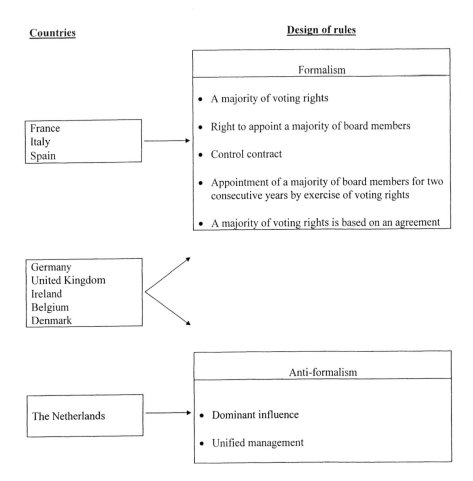

Formalism

- A majority of voting rights

France
Italy
Spain

- Right to appoint a majority of board members

- Control contract

- Appointment of a majority of board members for two consecutive years by exercise of voting rights

- A majority of voting rights is based on an agreement

Germany
United Kingdom
Ireland
Belgium
Denmark

Anti-formalism

The Netherlands

- Dominant influence

- Unified management

Table 9.11

A comparison of regulatory strategies

Country	Revaluation of Fixed Assets — Source of Regulations	Degree of Formalism	Accounting for Foreign Transactions — Source of Regulations	Degree of Formalism	Definition of a Subsidiary — Source of Regulations	Degree of Formalism
Belgium	Arrêté royal 8 October 1976, amended by Arrêté royal 12 September 1983, Chapter II, Section III, Art.34 — L	A	Avis (Bulletin No. 20) of the Commission des Normes Comptables (1987) — S	F	Arrêté royal 6 March 1990, Art. 2 — L	F / A
Denmark	Regnskabslov 1981, chapter 5 section 30 (U 11 Regnskabsvejledning 11, 1995) — L	A	Foreningen af Statsautoriserede Revisorer Regnskabsvejledning no. 9 (1994) — S	F	Årsregnskabsbekendtgørelsen, section 1(2), 6, section 2b — L	F / A
France	Code de Commerce 1984, Art. 12 Ordonnance du 15 août 1945, Loi du 28 décembre 1959 Loi des finances pour 1977 OEC Avis , CNCC Norme — L / R	A	Plan Comptable Général p. II. 12-13 (1982) — L / S	F	Loi 85, Art. 357.1 Décret 86-221 — L	F
Germany	Handelsgesetzbuch 1985, Art.253 sec.1 and 2 — L	F	Grundsätze ordnungsmäßiger Buchführung Institut der Wirtschaftsprüfer HFA Stellungnahme (1986) — R	A	Handelsgesetzbuch §§290, 291 §§ 16-18. § 319 Aktiengesetz — L	F / A
Ireland	Companies Act (1986) SSAP 19 Investment Properties(1981); ED 51 Fixed Assets & Revaluation (1990) — L / S	A	Statement of Standard Accounting Practice No. 20 (1983) — S	F	Group Accounts Law 1992 FRS 2 Accounting for subsidiary undertakings — L / S	F / A
Italy	Legge: -91 of 01/04/1949; -74 of 11/02/1952 -576 of 02/12/1975; -72 of 19/03/1983 -408 of 29/12/1990; -413, 30/12/1991 — L	F	Commissione per la Statuzione dei Principi Contabili Documento N. 9 (1988) Art. 72 Income Tax Law — L / S	A	Codice Civile Article 2359 Decreto legislativo 127 of 09.04.1991 — L	F
Netherlands	Title 9 Book 2 Burgerlijk Wetboek Art.384 1. Art.390; General Administrative Order (1983) — L	A	Raad voor de Jaarverslaggeving Richtlijnen 1.03.906.-12 (1986) — S	F	Burgerlijk Wetboek Art. 24a, 24b, 406 Raad voor de Jaarverslaggeving Richtlijnen 2.03.103 — L	A
Spain	Fiscal revaluation laws: 76 in 1961; 41 in 1964; 12 in 1973; 50 in 1977; 1 in 1979; 74 in 1980; 9 in 1983; 6 in 1996 — L	F	Plan General de Contabilidad part V., 14a (1983) Ministerial Orders 1991,1992 — L / S	F	Real Decreto 1815/1991 Art. 42-49 — L	F
UK	Companies Act (1981) Paragraphs 29-34 of Schedule 4; SSAP 19 Investment Properties (1981); ED 51 Fixed Assets & Revaluation (1990) — L / S	A	Statement of Standard Accounting Practice No. 20 (1983) — S	F	Companies Act 1989 Sec. 258 FRS 2 Accounting for subsidiary undertakings — L / S	F/A

Key: A=Anti-formalism, F= Formalism, L=Legislation, S=Standard, R=Recommendation.

9.6 Preliminary analysis of compliance

This section provides some preliminary comparisons of the distribution of compliance in the sample. The analysis is concerned with the frequency of full compliance (FC), creative compliance (CC) / partial compliance (PC) and non-compliance (NC) for the different areas of accounting policy, the nine countries, the three years, the different classes of regulatory sources and regulatory design.

Areas of accounting regulation

Table 9.12 presents the distribution of full-compliance, creative compliance / partial compliance and non-compliance cross-classified for the different areas of accounting. As can be seen, there are different distributions of compliance for the accounting subjects under study.

Table 9.12 Compliance across areas of accounting policy

Compliance across subjects	FC %	CC % & PC %	NC %	NR %	Total %
Revaluation of fixed assets	59.09	29.00	1.95	9.96	100
Definition of a subsidiary	23.81	58.44	7.79	9.96	100
Foreign transactions	60.17	18.18	11.69	9.96	100

Note. FC = full compliance, CC = creative compliance, PC = partial compliance,

NC = non-compliance

The initial investigation suggests that the area of consolidation; *i.e.,* the definition of a subsidiary, has a higher rate of creative/partial compliance than the areas of revaluation and translation. The rate of non-compliance is smallest for revaluation (1.95%), higher for consolidation (7.79) and highest for translation (11.69%).

Countries

Table 9.13 presents the distribution of full-compliance, creative/partial compliance and non-compliance for the different countries in the data set. The table is restricted to the combined data set rather than the individual areas of accounting under study.

Table 9.13 Compliance across countries

Compliance across countries	FC %	CC % & PC %	NC %	NR %	Total %
Belgium	33.33	40.00	13.33	13.33	100
France	26.26	58.59	4.55	10.61	100
Denmark	55.56	31.11	0.00	13.33	100
Germany	73.91	19.81	1.93	4.35	100
Ireland	39.51	56.79	0.00	3.70	100
Italy	27.78	17.78	44.44	10.00	100
The Netherlands	60.00	18.89	12.78	8.33	100
Spain	59.60	20.20	11.11	9.09	100
United Kingdom	44.70	41.67	0.00	13.64	100

The table indicates considerable variation in the extent of compliance in the countries under study. While German accounting practice follows the national requirements to a large extent, French companies are the foremost in avoiding control. In fact, the proportion of full compliance ranges from 73.91% for Germany to 26.26% for France, while the rate of creative compliance ranges from 58.59% for France to 19.81% for Germany. The rate of non-compliance is generally small, except in Italy where it reaches 44.44%. Similarly to Germany, full compliance dominates creative compliance in the Netherlands, Denmark, Italy, the United Kingdom and Spain. However, creative compliance dominates full compliance in Belgium, France and Ireland.

Years

Table 9.14 indicates the distribution of full-compliance, creative/partial compliance and non-compliance, cross-classified for the different accounting periods under investigation.

Table 9.14 Compliance across years

Compliance across years	FC %	CC %	NC %	NR %	Total %
1987	39.83	30.52	6.93	22.73	100
1993	52.70	40.17	7.13	0.00	100
1995	50.54	34.92	7.38	7.16	100

It appears that there are no major changes in compliance behaviour between the accounting periods investigated. In all the years under consideration full compliance dominates creative compliance while the rate of non-compliance is around 7%. The relatively high rate of non-availability of the annual report in 1987 (22.73%) explains the increase of both full compliance and creative compliance in 1993 and 1995.

Regulatory Source

Table 9.15 presents the distribution of full compliance, creative/partial compliance and non-compliance for the different institutional authorities issuing the relevant regulation.

Table 9.15 Compliance and the sources of regulations

Compliance across regulatory source	FC %	CC % & PC %	NC %	NR %	Total %
Legislation	45.05	40.11	5.86	8.97	100
Standard	73.86	3.41	11.74	10.98	100
Recommendation	65.66	11.11	16.16	7.07	100
Legislation & Standard	26.03	57.91	4.87	11.19	100
Legislation & Recommendation	72.73	16.67	0.00	10.61	100

The table shows considerable variation between the different regulators. The analysis distinguishes regulation which has been issued by a single regulator taking the form of either legislation, standard or recommendation from regulations which exist as a combination of these different regulators. It appears that regulation in the form of individual standards is most successful in achieving full compliance with the proportion at 73.86. Also regulations in the form of recommendation and in the form of combined legislation and recommendation appears to have a relatively high rate of full compliance and a relatively low rate of creative compliance. In contrast, creative compliance is higher if rules have the authority of legislation (40.11%). The least successful combination for achieving compliance appears to be the one where an accounting area is governed by legislation and a standard together, as indicated by the proportions of 26.03% for full compliance and 57.91% for creative compliance.

Regulatory design

Table 9.16 presents the distribution of full compliance, creative/partial compliance and non-compliance for the different forms of regulatory design identified in the data set.

Table 9.16 Compliance and the design of regulations

Compliance across regulatory design	FC %	CC %	NC %	NR %	Total %
Formal	56.41	25.16	8.49	9.94	100
Anti-formal	50.31	30.47	9.41	9.82	100
Formal & Anti-formal	23.08	66.67	0.00	10.26	100

As can be seen in Table 9.16, full compliance dominates creative compliance if an accounting rule is formulated in either a formal or an anti-formal manner, while in cases where an accounting rule includes both formal and anti-formal approaches, creative compliance (66.67%) clearly dominates full compliance (23.08%). A formal rule appears to be the most successful in achieving full compliance with a proportion of 56.41%, while only 50.31% of the companies fully complied with an anti-formal rule.

As can be seen in the preceding tables, the probabilities of non-compliance are relatively small when compared to the distributions of either creative or full compliance. Therefore the following analysis will be concerned with modelling the impact of different regulatory factors on the ratio of full compliance relative to regulatory avoidance; *i.e.*, either creative or partial compliance. Hence, as indicated in Chapter Eight the statistical modelling is based on a binomial probability model treating non-compliance as non-stochastic.

CHAPTER 10

A STATISTICAL ANALYSIS OF COMPLIANCE

IN EUROPEAN FINANCIAL REPORTING PRACTICE

10.1 Introduction

Following the theoretical modelling approach for binary data which was described in Chapter Eight, the empirical analysis sets out to analyse whether compliance behaviour in European reporting practice is associated with regulatory variables, particularly the source and the design of the regulations. A separate statistical analysis is carried out for each of the accounting policies under study and also after aggregating these subsets. In order to verify that the empirical results are not influenced by the selected categories of the variable 'regulatory source', the impact of different classifications of regulatory sources on compliance behaviour is analysed as outlined in the previous Chapter. Finally, the question of whether the source of the regulation exercises a stronger explanatory power on compliance than do the differences between national accounting regimes is analysed.

Non-compliance is treated as non-stochastic in the analysis[1], which assumes that accounting policy choice is restricted to either full compliance or creative / partial compliance. Similarly, the non-availability of the annual report for a particular year due to censoring in 1987 and 1995 is introduced as a non-stochastic component.

The analysis is carried out by comparing linear logistic models. Starting with the factor 'regulatory design', the models add successively the factors 'regulatory source' and 'country of incorporation' in order to compare their relative explanatory power over the dependent variable 'compliance'. The reduction in deviance of each model indicates the contribution of regulatory factors to compliance behaviour.

---

[1] The distribution of compliance in the sample is dominated by full and creative compliance which comprise 83.3% of the counts whilst featuring a generally low count for non-compliance. For the aggregate of all accounting subjects under study, 38.5% of the companies fully complied with the regulation, 44.8% of the companies creatively complied, whilst 6.9% of the companies did not comply with the regulation and in 9.9% of cases there was missing data due to censoring. A binary, rather than a multinomial modelling approach was therefore adopted.

Following the comparison of models for each accounting policy, the models for the aggregated set of accounting policies are described with regard to both their reduction in deviance and their parameter estimates for the different levels of each explanatory factor.

10.2 Comparison of models

Tables 10.1a-c present the results of comparing nested linear logistic models. The models vary with respect to three regulatory factors: (i) regulatory design; *e.g.,* the rule's degree of formalism, (ii) regulatory source; *e.g.,* the authority issuing a particular rule and (iii) the country where the reporting company is incorporated, as an alternative to regulatory source.

The tables themselves differ with respect to the categories of the explanatory factor 'regulatory source'. In fact, Table 10.1a shows the results when the type of regulation has been categorised into (i) legislation, including both parliamentary legislation and delegated legislation, (ii) standards issued by a standard setting agency which is either government-controlled or a self-regulated professional body and (iii) recommendations circulated by all the other 'non-authoritative' associations. Table 10.1b, on the other hand, presents the results when the type of regulation has been classified into (i) legislation, in this instance including parliamentary legislation, delegated legislation and provisions enacted in an accounting plan, (ii) standards issued by a professional accountancy body and (iii) recommendations published either by non-authoritative private associations or public bodies in an advisory function. Finally, Table 10.1c presents the result when the type of regulation is either (i) private or (ii) public. In this case the distinction between law, standard and recommendation is less relevant. Public regulations may be enacted by parliament, ministers, or a governmental accounting agency, while private regulations may be issued by authoritative or non-authoritative professional associations. It should be noted that combinations of the different levels occur within each of the above categorisations.

Model 0: Complete independence

In linear logistic modelling the lowest-order model is generally denoted the model of complete independence. Under this model, which is not reported in Tables 10.1a-c, the probabilities of full compliance are entirely independent of the regulatory source, the degree of formalism and the country of incorporation. Furthermore, the model is unconstrained by the statistical design which is confined to binary data analysis; that is, in the model of complete independence, the alternative outcomes of the response variable compliance, which can be full compliance, creative / partial compliance, non-compliance or no response due to censored data are treated as stochastic. Thus, the model of complete independence has no descriptive validity, and will be modified according to our research design in Model 1.

Model 1: Conditional independence

Model 1 reflects the constraints imposed by the statistical design of binary data modelling. These constraints are twofold. Firstly, the statistical analysis will be restricted to the counts of full compliance and creative / partial compliance only. As has been noted earlier, the reporting of full compliance and creative or partial compliance comprises 83.3% of the total counts in the sample and therefore the binary data design permits us to model more precisely the relative odds of compliance with regulation. Secondly, the model is restricted to the counts where the annual report was actually available for analysis.

Model 1 may be described as the model of conditional independence. While the fitted values of full compliance and creative / partial compliance are conditional on both the actual compliance (full or creative / partial) and the availability of the annual report for analysis, the probability of compliance is entirely independent of regulatory factors. Thus the model of conditional independence predicts the odds of full compliance with the regulations rather than avoidance of full compliance, given the decision not to contravene the regulation. The model of conditional independence is the model against which the influence of regulatory factors on the relative odds of full compliance and creative / partial compliance is assessed.

Model 2: Regulatory design

The extent to which the regulatory design affects compliance behaviour is evaluated in Model 2. The design of a regulation has been categorised as either formal, anti-formal or a combination of the two. By adding the factor to the model of conditional independence, the reduction in deviance indicates the contribution of regulatory design to compliance behaviour. As indicated in Table 10.1a, the regulatory design has a significant effect on the probability of full compliance in the case of revaluation ($F=6.826$) but not in the case of foreign currency accounting ($F=1.037$) and consolidation ($F=0.755$). Combining the three areas together, it can be seen that the design of regulation is not itself a significant factor in explaining compliance behaviour ($F=1.278$).

However, before concluding that the regulatory design is irrelevant for explaining compliance with accounting regulations, it is necessary to consider whether the factor may be significant if combined with other regulatory effects; namely, the source of regulation and the country of incorporation.

Model 3a: Regulatory design and regulatory source

In the third model, compliance behaviour is described as a function not only of the regulatory design but also of the source of regulation. As has been noted earlier, three different modes of classification of the factor regulatory source were analysed to verify the results. The analysis presented in Table 10.1a distinguishes between (i) legislation, (ii) a standard issued by a governmental or professional standardisation agency and (iii) a recommendation released by a 'non-authoritative' association. The analysis incorporated combinations of regulatory sources, acting either dependently or independently; that is, (iv) legislation and standard and (v) legislation and recommendation.

As can be seen in Table 10.1a the source of regulation is highly significant in explaining compliance behaviour for all areas of accounting regulation under study, both individually and combined. When making a comparison, we find that the change in deviance when adding the effect of regulatory source to Model 2 is greatest in the case of foreign currency accounting (F=60.081), less strong in the case of consolidation (F=19.183) and smallest in the case of revaluation (F=5.477). In comparison with regulatory design, the authority issuing a regulation dominates regulatory design in explaining compliance in reporting practice, except for the individual policy of revaluation. Combining the three policy areas together, the reduction in deviance is significantly higher when the source of regulation (F=25.495) is added to the model containing only the factor regulatory design (F=1.278).

Following the analysis presented in Table 10.1a, the explanatory factor regulatory source has been modified into two other justifiable classifications. As can be seen in Tables 10.1b and 10.1c, the interpretation of the impact of the modified factor on compliance behaviour does not differ. Hence, the empirical results are robust with respect to the different valid approaches to classifying the source of regulation.

In Table 10.1b, which treats standardisation plans as legislation rather than as standards, the reduction in deviance which occurs if the effect of regulatory source is added to Model 2 remains highest in the case of foreign currency accounting (F=60.033) and is still significant after pooling the subsets (F=20.815). Similarly, in Table 10.1c, which presents the results of the analysis distinguishing between public and private regulation, the effect of the regulatory source is highest in the case of foreign currency accounting (F=63.158) and is again highly significant after pooling the subsets (F=33.924).

Model 3b: Regulatory design and country of incorporation

In the final model presented in Tables 10.1a-c, the impact of different national regulatory regimes across European countries on compliance is assessed as an alternative to regulatory source, in addition to the factor regulatory design. When compared with Model 3a it can be seen that differences between the regimes of various countries contribute less to an explanation of compliance behaviour than do the sources of regulation. This result holds for all three subject areas, both individually and combined. Moreover, this finding is confirmed across different classifications of the factor regulatory source.

As can be seen in Table 10.1a, if we combine the three policy areas together, the reduction in deviance is significantly higher when the source of regulation (F=25.495) is added to Model 2 than it is when differences between countries (F=8.343) are added to Model 2. For the individual policy of revaluation, the dominance of the source of regulation in comparison to the differences between countries is shown by a value of F=5.477 compared to F=3.194. Regarding foreign currency accounting, the dominance of the source of regulation in comparison to the differences between countries is shown by F=60.081 compared to F=29.763. Finally, in the case of consolidation the dominance of the source of regulation in comparison to the differences between countries is indicated by F=19.183 compared to F=9.108.

Table 10.1a(Law, agency, recommendation)

Statistical analysis of the impact of regulatory design, regulatory structure and country of incorporation on compliance in Europe

Models	Revaluation of fixed assets			Translation of foreign transactions			Definition of a subsidiary			Combined		
	Deviance	DF	F-ratio	Deviance	DF	F-ratio	Deviance	DF	F-ratio	Deviance	DF	F-ratio
1. Model of conditional independence	171.93	151		130.74	151		152.43	151		455.10	457	
2. Degree of formalism	164.45	150	6.826 (p = 0.009)	129.84	150	1.037 (p = 0.310)	150.90	149	0.755 (p = 0.471)	452.56	455	1.278 (p = 0.279)
Reduction in deviance	- 7.48	-1		- 0.90	-1		- 1.53	-2		- 2.54	-2	
3a. Degree of formalism + type of regulation	153.12	148	5.477 (p = 0.005)	71.66	148	60.081 (p < 0.001)	133.58	148	19.183 (p < 0.001)	369.10	451	25.495 (p < 0.001)
Reduction in deviance	- 11.33	-2		-58.18	-2		- 17.32	-1		-83.46	-4	
3b. Degree of formalism + country of incorporation	142.21	143	3.194 (p = 0.004)	52.84	143	29.763 (p < 0.001)	109.17	143	9.108 (p < 0.001)	393.76	447	8.343 (p < 0.001)
Reduction in deviance	- 22.24	-7		-77.00	-7		- 41.73	-6		-58.80	-8	

Notes

The model of conditional independence predicts the odds of full compliance with the regulations rather than avoidance of full compliance, given the decision not to contravene the regulation. The extent to which regulatory design affects compliance behaviour is evaluated in the second model by classifying regulations as either formal, anti-formal or a mixture of the two (i.e. 2 main effects and 1 interaction). In the third model, compliance behaviour is described as a function not only of the degree of formalism but also the type of regulation which is either legislation, accounting standard or recommendation, or legislation combined with standard or recommendation (i.e. 3 main effects and 2 interactions). This is then compared in the final model with the alternative where variation across countries is assessed rather than regulatory structure.

The deviance (i.e. total binomial error) is averaged over three years. The contribution of the explanatory factors added to a model is given by the reduction in deviance. The F-ratio expresses the average change in deviance obtained from each additional explanatory factor (i.e. the reduction in deviance divided by the reduction in degrees of freedom) proportional to the scaled deviance after fitting the model (i.e. residual error divided by residual degrees of freedom). Low p-values indicate significant explanatory power.

Table 10.1b(Law, professional standard, recommendation)

Statistical analysis of the impact of regulatory design, regulatory structure and country of incorporation on compliance in Europe

Models	Revaluation of fixed assets			Translation of foreign transactions			Definition of a subsidiary			Combined		
	Deviance	DF	F-ratio	Deviance	DF	F-ratio	Deviance	DF	F-ratio	Deviance	DF	F-ratio
1. Model of conditional independence	171.93	151		130.74	151		152.43	151		455.10	457	
2. Degree of formalism	164.45	150	6.826 (p = 0.009)	129.84	150	1.037 (p = 0.310)	150.90	149	0.755 (p = 0.471)	452.56	455	1.278 (p = 0.279)
Reduction in deviance	- 7.48	-1		- 0.90	-1		- 1.53	-2		- 2.54	-2	
3a. Degree of formalism + type of regulation	153.12	148	5.477 (p = 0.005)	58.35	147	60.033 (p < 0.001)	133.58	148	19.183 (p < 0.001)	382.03	451	20.815 (p < 0.001)
Reduction in deviance	- 11.33	-2		- 71.49	-3		- 17.32	-1		- 70.53	-4	
3b. Degree of formalism + country of incorporation	142.21	143	3.194 (p = 0.004)	52.84	143	29.763 (p < 0.001)	109.17	143	9.108 (p < 0.001)	393.76	447	8.343 (p < 0.001)
Reduction in deviance	- 22.24	-7		-77.00	-7		- 41.73	-6		-58.80	-8	

Notes

The model of conditional independence predicts the odds of full compliance with the regulations rather than avoidance of full compliance, given the decision not to contravene the regulation. The extent to which regulatory design affects compliance behaviour is evaluated in the second model by classifying regulations as either formal, anti-formal or a mixture of the two (i.e. 2 main effects and 1 interaction). In the third model, compliance behaviour is described as a function not only of the degree of formalism but also the type of regulation which is either legislation, accounting standard or recommendation, or legislation combined with standard or recommendation (i.e. 3 main effects and 2 interactions). This is then compared in the final model with the alternative where variation across countries is assessed rather than regulatory structure.

The deviance (i.e. total binomial error) is averaged over three years. The contribution of the explanatory factors added to a model is given by the reduction in deviance. The F-ratio expresses the average change in deviance obtained from each additional explanatory factor (i.e. the reduction in deviance divided by the reduction in degrees of freedom) proportional to the scaled deviance after fitting the model (i.e. residual error divided by residual degrees of freedom). Low p-values indicate significant explanatory power.

217

Table 10.1c (Public versus private regulation)

Statistical analysis of the impact of regulatory design, regulatory structure and country of incorporation on compliance in Europe

Models	Revaluation of fixed assets			Translation of foreign transactions			Definition of a subsidiary			Combined		
	Deviance	DF	F-ratio	Deviance	DF	F-ratio	Deviance	DF	F-ratio	Deviance	DF	F-ratio
1. Model of conditional independence	171.93	151		130.74	151		152.43	151		455.10	457	
2. Degree of formalism	164.45	150	6.826 ($p = 0.009$)	129.84	150	1.037 ($p = 0.310$)	150.90	149	0.755 ($p = 0.471$)	452.56	455	1.278 ($p = 0.279$)
Reduction in deviance	- 7.48	-1		- 0.90	-1		- 1.53	-2		- 2.54	-2	
3a. Degree of formalism + type of regulation	153.12	148	5.477 ($p = 0.005$)	70.06	148	63.158 ($p < 0.001$)	133.58	148	19.183 ($p < 0.001$)	393.61	453	33.924 ($p < 0.001$)
Reduction in deviance	- 11.33	-2		- 59.79	-2		- 17.32	-1		- 58.95	-2	
3b. Degree of formalism + country of incorporation	142.21	143	3.194 ($p = 0.004$)	52.84	143	29.763 ($p < 0.001$)	109.17	143	9.108 ($p < 0.001$)	393.76	447	8.343 ($p < 0.001$)
Reduction in deviance	- 22.24	-7		- 77.00	-7		- 41.73	-6		- 58.80	-8	

Notes

The model of conditional independence predicts the odds of full compliance with the regulations rather than avoidance of full compliance, given the decision not to contravene the regulation. The extent to which regulatory design affects compliance behaviour is evaluated in the second model by classifying regulations as either formal, anti-formal or a mixture of the two (i.e. 2 main effects and 1 interaction). In the third model, compliance behaviour is described as a function not only of the degree of formalism but also the type of regulation which is either legislation, accounting standard or recommendation, or legislation combined with standard or recommendation (i.e. 3 main effects and 2 interactions). This is then compared in the final model with the alternative where variation across countries is assessed rather than regulatory structure.

The deviance (i.e. total binomial error) is averaged over three years. The contribution of the explanatory factors added to a model is given by the reduction in deviance. The F-ratio expresses the average change in deviance obtained from each additional explanatory factor (i.e. the reduction in deviance divided by the reduction in degrees of freedom) proportional to the scaled deviance after fitting the model (i.e. residual error divided by residual degrees of freedom). Low p-values indicate significant explanatory power.

10.3 Comparison of parameter estimates

Tables 10.2a-c set out the regression estimates obtained from each model described above when the data are aggregated across the three areas of accounting policy. As in the previous section, the three tables differ with respect to the classification of the factor regulatory source.

While the reduction in deviance is a measure of the significance of the explanatory factors on compliance, the estimated regression coefficients indicate the <u>relative</u> impact on compliance of the different categories within each explanatory factor.

It is important to note that, in contrast to conventional regression analysis, the calculated parameter estimates are logits; that is, they are log-relatives with respect to the first category of the relevant explanatory variable. The standard errors of the logistic regression coefficients are given in brackets, and significant parameter values at the 1% level are marked with an asterix in the tables.

A fourth explanatory factor, accounting policy, has been added to the comparison of parameter estimates. The inclusion of this factor permits investigation of whether compliance behaviour differs not only among the regulatory factors design, source and national reporting regime, but also from one individual accounting policy to another.

Different areas of accounting policy

The reported estimates are logits relative to asset revaluation. As indicated by the asterix in Table 10.4, in all four models the tendency towards avoidance is significantly greater in the case of the definition of a subsidiary, than in the other policy areas. For example, in the model incorporating the factors regulatory design and regulatory source the area of consolidation induces significantly more avoidance (logit = -1.426*) than asset revaluation. Moreover, the models, which do not contain the factor 'regulatory source', suggest that the area of consolidation is comparatively more subject to creative compliance.

Table 10.2a (Law, agency, recommendation)
Estimates of regulatory effects on compliance

Models	Conditional Independence	Regulatory design	Regulatory design + regulatory structure	Regulatory design + country of incorporation
Deviance	455.10	452.56	369.10	393.76
Degrees of freedom	457	455	451	447
Accounting policies				
(logit relative to asset revaluation):				
Translation of foreign transactions	+0.485*	+0 298	-0.905	+0 038
	(0.163)	(0 187)	(0 396)	(0 187)
Definition of a subsidiary	-1.609*	-1.490*	-1.426*	-1.736*
	(0.154)	(0.224)	(0.248)	(0 224)
Add: regulatory design				
(logit relative to formalism):				
Anti-formalism		-0.350	+0.231	-0.716*
		(0.171)	(0 278)	(0.171)
Formalism + anti-formalism		-0 535	-0 028	-1 097*
		(0 237)	(0.257)	(0 237)
Add: regulatory structure				
(logit relative to legislation):				
Standard			+2 800*	
			(0.470)	
Recommendation			+1.453	
			(0.637)	
Legislation + standard			-1.529*	
			(0.218)	
Legislation + recommendation			+0 111	
			(0 393)	
Add: country of incorporation				
(logit relative to UK):				
Germany				+1.724*
				(0 252)
Netherlands				+1.166*
				(0 292)
France				-1 382*
				(0 230)
Denmark				+0.710
				(0.416)
Belgium				-0.089
				(0.314)
Ireland				-0 576
				(0.291)
Italy				-0 117
				(0 432)
Spain				+0.711
				(0.378)

Notes
The model of conditional independence predicts the odds of full compliance with the regulations rather than avoidance of full compliance, given the decision not to contravene the regulation. The extent to which regulatory design affects compliance behaviour is evaluated in the second model. In the third model, compliance behaviour is described as a function not only of the degree of formalism but also the type of regulation. The final model includes variation across the countries in which the sample companies are incorporated.

The logits reported above are obtained from a binomial logistic regression, and are reported as log-relatives with respect to one of the categories of each explanatory variable. The (1,0) dependent variable is an indicator of full or partial compliance, non-compliance being offset in the regression. The vector of observed values comprises outcomes for 154 European multilisted companies in 3 areas of accounting policy. The standard errors of the logistic regression coefficients are given in brackets, and significant parameter values at the 1% level are marked with an asterix.

Table 10.2b (Law, professional standard, recommendation)
Estimates of regulatory effects on compliance

Models	Conditional Independence	Regulatory design	Regulatory design + regulatory structure	Regulatory design + country of incorporation
Deviance	455 10	452.56	382.03	393.76
Degrees of freedom	457	455	451	447
Accounting policies				
(logit relative to asset revaluation):				
Translation of foreign transactions	+0 485*	+0 298	-2.219*	+0 038
	(0 163)	(0.187)	(0 334)	(0 187)
Definition of a subsidiary	-1 609*	-1 490*	-1.495*	-1.736*
	(0.154)	(0.224)	(0 245)	(0 224)
Add: regulatory design				
(logit relative to formalism):				
Anti-formalism		-0 350	-0.247	-0.716*
		(0 171)	(0 254)	(0 171)
Formalism + anti-formalism		-0 535	-0 267	-1 097*
		(0.237)	(0.254)	(0 237)
Add: regulatory structure				
(logit relative to legislation):				
Standard			+4.130*	
			(0 436)	
Recommendation			+3 033*	
			(0.484)	
Legislation + standard			-0.899*	
			(0.194)	
Legislation + recommendation			+0 554	
			(0 381)	
Add: country of incorporation				
(logit relative to UK):				
Germany				+1.724*
				(0 252)
Netherlands				+1.166*
				(0 292)
France				-1 382*
				(0.230)
Denmark				+0 710
				(0.416)
Belgium				-0.089
				(0 314)
Ireland				-0.576
				(0.291)
Italy				-0.117
				(0 432)
Spain				+0 711
				(0.378)

Notes
The model of conditional independence predicts the odds of full compliance with the regulations rather than avoidance of full compliance, given the decision not to contravene the regulation. The extent to which regulatory design affects compliance behaviour is evaluated in the second model. In the third model, compliance behaviour is described as a function not only of the degree of formalism but also the type of regulation. The final model includes variation across the countries in which the sample companies are incorporated.

The logits reported above are obtained from a binomial logistic regression, and are reported as log-relatives with respect to one of the categories of each explanatory variable. The (1,0) dependent variable is an indicator of full or partial compliance, non-compliance being offset in the regression. The vector of observed values comprises outcomes for 154 European multilisted companies in 3 areas of accounting policy. The standard errors of the logistic regression coefficients are given in brackets, and significant parameter values at the 1% level are marked with an asterix.

Table 10.2c (Public versus private regulation)
Estimates of regulatory effects on compliance

Models	Conditional Independence	Regulatory design	Regulatory design + regulatory structure	Regulatory design + country of incorporation
Deviance	455.10	452.56	393.61	393.76
Degrees of freedom	457	455	453	447
Accounting policies *(logit relative to asset revaluation):*				
Translation of foreign transactions	+0.485*	+0 298	-2.068*	+0.038
	(0.163)	(0 187)	(0.298)	(0.187)
Definition of a subsidiary	-1.609*	-1.490*	-1.720*	-1.736*
	(0.154)	(0 224)	(0.244)	(0.224)
Add: regulatory design *(logit relative to formalism):*				
Anti-formalism		-0.350	-0 426	-0.716*
		(0.171)	(0.242)	(0.171)
Formalism + anti-formalism		-0.535	-0.367	-1.097*
		(0 237)	(0.253)	(0.237)
Add: regulatory structure *(logit relative to public standard setter):*				
Private standard setter			+3 491*	
			(0.351)	
Private & public standard setter)			-0.664*	
			(0 183)	
Add: country of incorporation *(logit relative to UK):*				
Germany				+1.724*
				(0 252)
Netherlands				+1.166*
				(0 292)
France				-1.382*
				(0.230)
Denmark				+0.710
				(0 416)
Belgium				-0 089
				(0.314)
Ireland				-0.576
				(0.291)
Italy				-0.117
				(0 432)
Spain				+0.711
				(0.378)

Notes
The model of conditional independence predicts the odds of full compliance with the regulations rather than avoidance of full compliance, given the decision not to contravene the regulation. The extent to which regulatory design affects compliance behaviour is evaluated in the second model. In the third model, compliance behaviour is described as a function not only of the degree of formalism but also the type of regulation. The final model includes variation across the countries in which the sample companies are incorporated.

The logits reported above are obtained from a binomial logistic regression, and are reported as log-relatives with respect to one of the categories of each explanatory variable. The (1,0) dependent variable is an indicator of full or partial compliance, non-compliance being offset in the regression. The vector of observed values comprises outcomes for 154 European multilisted companies in 3 areas of accounting policy. The standard errors of the logistic regression coefficients are given in brackets, and significant parameter values at the 1% level are marked with an asterix.

Regulatory design

The reported estimates are logits relative to formalism. When incorporating variations between countries, rather than differences between regulatory sources, anti-formal rules induce significantly greater avoidance (logit = -0.716*) in reporting practice, than do formal rules.

However, regulations which combine both formal and anti-formal elements, contribute to an even greater probability of avoidance in reporting practice (logit = -1.097*) than do rules which are either formal or anti-formal.

As suggested earlier, the factor 'regulatory design' is insignificant when added to the factor 'regulatory source'. This result is confirmed by the non-significant parameter estimates in Model 3 in Tables 10.2a-c. It is important to note that the interpretation of the parameter estimates remains identical across all the different classifications of regulatory source.

Regulatory source

The reported estimates are logits relative to legislation. As can be seen in Table 10.2a, when compared to law, a standard issued by a accounting standard setter induces a significantly higher rate of full compliance (logit = +2.800*). However, when an issue is addressed in both law and standard, this induces a significant tendency towards avoidance of regulations (logit = -1.529*).

When regulation exists only in the form of a voluntary recommendation, this results in a greater tendency towards full compliance, than does legislation. However in comparison to standards, recommendations contribute less to full compliance (logit = +1.453), although this result is only significant at the 5% significance level.

Tables 10.2b and 10.2c present the corresponding results after the variable regulatory source has been re-classified. Similarly, the results in Table 10.2b suggest that regulation issued by a professional standard setting body leads to a significantly higher rate of full compliance (logit = +4.130*) than does legislation. Recommendations induce a significantly greater proportion of full compliance (logit = +3.033*) than legislation but not as much as a professional standard. As before, when a policy is regulated by both law and professional standard, the tendency towards avoidance of regulations is significantly higher (logit = -0.899*) than under any of the other regulatory sources.

In accordance with the results indicated in Tables 10.2a and 10.2b, the results presented in Table 10.2c suggest that regulation issued by a private standard setter leads to a significantly higher rate of full compliance (logit = +3.491*) than does public accounting regulation. When an area of accounting regulation has been addressed by both public and private regulators, regulatory avoidance in the form of creative / partial compliance is significantly higher (logit = -0.664*) when compared to either public or private rules.

Hence, the interpretation of the results has been confirmed after controlling for different valid classifications of the factor regulatory source.

Country of incorporation

The reported estimates are logits relative to the UK. Tables 10.2a-c show that full compliance with regulations tends to be significantly higher in Germany (logit = +1.724*), followed by the Netherlands (logit = +1.166*). On the other hand, the avoidance of regulations tends to be significantly higher in France (logit = -1.382*).

The last chapter of the thesis will be concerned with the interpretation of the statistical analysis and will endeavour to explain the empirical results and to draw conclusions which are relevant to the regulation of accounting.

CHAPTER 11

INTERPRETATION OF RESULTS AND CONCLUSIONS

This thesis has examined the different forms of accounting regulation and their association with compliance behaviour in financial reporting. The aim of this chapter is to interpret and explain the empirical results obtained from the logistic regression analysis and, furthermore, to draw conclusions for the regulation of accounting. Each of the following sections evaluates the impact of the different explanatory factors; that is, the source of regulations, rule design, the different accounting policies and, finally, the ways in which compliance varies from one country to another.

11.1 The source of regulations

The empirical analysis suggests that compliance by European companies with accounting regulations is systematically associated with the type of institution issuing the relevant accounting regulation. Thus, the nature of the regulatory authority could constitute an important influence over compliance behaviour. This result proved to be significant in all three areas under investigation, both individually and combined. Moreover, the regulatory source was found to be the most powerful explanatory factor associated with compliance behaviour after controlling for rule design and differences in national regulatory regimes. This remained so when alternative classifications were used.

Thus, irrespective of whether a rule is highly detailed or open-textured, the source of regulation is systematically associated with compliance behaviour. In all three areas of accounting policy, the source of regulation has a stronger influence on compliance than the country of incorporation. This finding suggests that the institutional structure of the rule-issuing authority would be more decisive in influencing compliance behaviour than intercountry differences in their approaches to rule-making.

As depicted in Figure 11.1, the results suggest that full compliance with accounting regulation is significantly higher when such regulation has been issued by a standard setting agency. Conversely, full compliance is relatively lower when the governing rules have been promulgated in the form of legislation, either by the legislature itself or in the form of delegated legislation.

Hence, full compliance is lower and, therefore, creative compliance is higher when the governing rules are written as law. However, when the rules of accounting are contained jointly in both legislation and a standard, creative compliance in financial reporting is at its highest. These results could support the arguments in favour of delegating accounting regulation to a separate standard setting agency, which acts independently. The arguments for delegating the function of regulating accounting to a specialised agency have been noted in Chapter Two.

11.2 Regulatory design

The empirical results suggest that the degree of formalism in accounting regulation is only a systematic explanatory factor in certain policy areas. While the design of rules significantly affects compliance behaviour in the area of valuation, there is no systematic relationship in the areas of foreign currency reporting and consolidation.

When compared to the source of regulation, the design of rules was seen to be less important in explaining compliance behaviour. Nevertheless, accounting regulation drafted in a formalistic, highly detailed manner was found to generate a higher rate of compliance than did accounting rules drafted in a general, open-textured manner. Hence, discretion and judgement in accounting regulation is associated with a greater probability of creative compliance than is prescription and formalism. However, when the regulator has adopted a compromise in drafting, in that the rule contains elements of both precise and open formulations, this is associated with even greater regulatory avoidance. A regulatory text which is drafted in both precise and general language indicates that the accounting issue in question was itself controversial requiring a compromise by the regulators themselves. As was evident for the definition of a subsidiary, accounting practice is able to take advantage when such compromises are in the form of mixed regulatory strategies.

Figure 11.1

Regulatory avoidance and regulatory structure

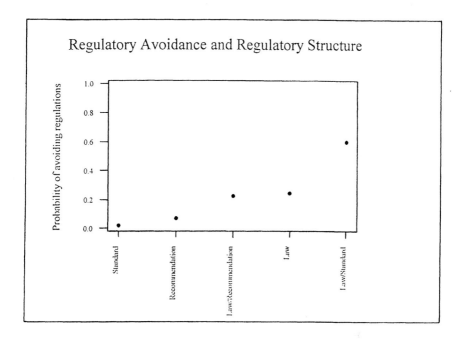

It has been suggested earlier that formalism in accounting regulation leads to a higher degree of compliance because a precise rule eliminates discretion and uncertainty. This advantage (at least for the issue of revaluation) could overcome the obvious disadvantages of precise rules: that is, inflexibility and the fact that they cannot be accommodated to the variety of circumstances to which they might need to be applied. Therefore, despite the criticism that very precise rules in accounting are likely to be either over-inclusive or under-inclusive, judgemental rules which are adaptable to the individual circumstances of a commercial transaction seem less optimal for the disclosure of financial information.

11.3 Accounting policies

Of the three areas of accounting included in the analysis, it was found that the issue of consolidation, or to be precise, the definition of a subsidiary for consolidation gave rise to the lowest rate of compliance. This finding was highly significant, and remained so after controlling for other explanatory factors: namely, the differences between countries, the design of regulations and the source of regulations.

This result suggests that, in accounting, irrespective of whether a regulation is detailed or general and, furthermore, irrespective of whether a regulation takes the form of legislation, professional standard or recommendation, there are certain accounting policies that are more susceptible to creative compliance than others.

The reason why the issue of defining a subsidiary for consolidation is more likely to be avoided in practice than other accounting policies might be its potential for off-balance sheet financing (Tweedie and Whittington, 1990) and its aptness for avoiding regulatory control without violating the letter of the regulation (McBarnet and Whelan, 1991). Moreover, as the consolidation decision is only an issue of recognition, not one of measurement, it only impacts the notes to the financial statements, and not the balance sheet or the profit and loss account. In contrast, both the revaluation of assets and accounting for foreign transactions are measurement issues. In general, however, the main result reported here with respect to the influence of regulatory strategies show the same tendencies across the three areas of accounting policy investigated.

11.4 Country differences

Notwithstanding earlier conclusions, the empirical results suggest that there are significant differences in compliance behaviour between nation-states, even after controlling for different areas of accounting policy and for different approaches to rule design. Even though the source of regulation is a more important explanatory factor than the country of incorporation, the results indicate that compliance with accounting regulations was at its highest in Germany during the period of the research study. Conversely, compliance was lowest in France. This result supports the suggestions of *vagabondage comptable* mentioned in our earlier discussion of creative compliance by French companies, which prompted a new regulatory structure for accounting in France in 1998.

Figure 11.2 summarises the probabilities of regulatory avoidance for the different European countries under study. A possible explanation for the compliant behaviour of German multinational companies might be the strong influence of tax law on financial accounting, despite the finding that the general tendency in other countries is to avoid regulations which take the form of law rather than of standards. It is worth commenting that this high degree of compliance with the national requirements appears to have dissuaded German multinational companies in the past, in contrast to their French competitors, from seeking equity listings on international capital markets. (Ebke, 1997).

Finally, it is important to note that the period under investigation in this research study was the years 1987 to 1995. During that time a large number of French multinational companies were already applying IAS or US GAAP. This was long before the recent regulatory reforms in the French accounting regime, which have allowed such companies to use IAS for consolidated accounts, which have been endorsed and translated into French by the new CRC only since 1998. In contrast, the move towards IAS or US GAAP by German multinational companies did not occur until the end of the investigation period and then accelerated during the years 1996 and 1997. In March 1998 a law was passed which enabled German companies listed on international stock exchanges to use IAS or US GAAP for consolidated financial statements, rather than the national accounting rules.

Figure 11.2

Avoidance of regulation in European financial reporting

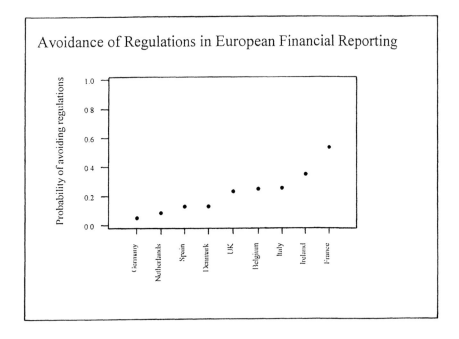

In conclusion, while this thesis has identified variations in the probability of compliance from one country to another, the main finding is that a more decisive factor associated with compliance is the source of regulation involved; that is, whether it is legislation, a standard, a recommendation or some combination of these. To a lesser extent, the degree of formalism present in the drafting of accounting regulations is also associated with compliance behaviour.

In the context of international accounting research, the thesis has addressed the issue of compliance (full compliance, creative compliance, partial compliance and non-compliance) using a specifically comparative approach. The research issues raised should be of some interest, as it is shown that simple classifications at the country level are inappropriate; that is, over the areas of accounting policy investigated, the type of regulation and the manner in which it is drafted is shown to vary not only across countries but within countries. Moreover, a mixture of regulatory instruments is also observed in some cases (*i.e.* a standard or a recommendation is sometimes issued in addition to legislation) and certain legal texts contain some provisions which are precise and others which are more flexible. The methodological contribution of the thesis therefore, is to use a probability model with a factor structure permitting interactions between these main effects. This approach leads to conclusions about compliance in accounting which may be generalised across countries, thus placing less emphasis on international differences at a superficial level and greater emphasis on the effect of regulatory strategies on corporate reporting when the details of regulatory texts are taken into consideration.

REFERENCES

Accountancy, UK Edition 1985, October, p. 4.

Accountancy, International Edition, 1997, July, p. 6.

Accountancy, International Edition, 1997, November, p. 7.

Accountancy, International Edition, 1998, January, p. 17.

Adelberg, A. H. (1979) 'A Methodology for Measuring the Understandability of Financial Report Measures', *Journal of Accounting Research*, pp. 565-592.

Aerts, W. and Theunisse, H. (1995) 'Belgium - Group Accounts' in Ordelheide, D. and KPMG (eds) *Transnational Accounting*. London: MacMillan, pp. 493-570.

Alexander, D. (1993) 'A European true and fair view?', *The European Accounting Review*, Vol. 2, No. 1, pp. 59-80.

Alexander, D. and Archer, S. (1992) *The European Accounting Guide*. London: Academic Press.

Archer, S., Delvaille, P. and McLeay, S. (1995) 'The Measurement of Harmonization and the Comparability of Financial Statement Items: Whithin-Country and Between-Country Effects', *Accounting and Business Research*, Spring.

Archer, S., Delvaille, P. and McLeay, S. (1996) 'A Statistical Model of International Accounting Harmonisation', *ABACUS*, Vol. 32, No.1, pp. 1-29.

Baggott, R. (1989) 'Regulatory Reform in Britain: The Changing Face of Self-Regulation', *Public Administration*, Vol. 67, pp. 435-453.

Baldwin, R. and McCrudden, C. (1987) *Regulation of Public Law*.

Ball, R. and Brown, P. (1969) 'Portfolio Theory and Accounting', *Journal of Accounting Research*, Autumn, pp. 300-323.

Ballwieser, W. (1995) 'Germany - Individual Accounts', in Ordelheide, D. and KPMG (eds.), *Transnational Accounting*, London: MacMillan, pp. 1395-1546.

Beaver, W., Kenelly, J. W. and Voss, W. M. (1968) 'Predictive Ability as a Criterion for the Evaluation of Accounting Data', *Accounting Review*, Vol. 44, No.3, pp. 675-683.

Beaver, W. and Demski, J. (1974) 'The Nature of Financial Accounting Objectives: A Summary and Synthesis, Studies on Financial Accounting Objectives', Supplement to *Journal of Accounting Research*, pp. 170-187.

Bircher, P. (1988) 'The Adoption of Consolidated Accounting in Great Britain', *Accounting and Business Research*, Vol. 19, No. 72, pp. 3-13.

Bollen, L. H. H. and Lin-Van Nuffel, L. (1997) 'Financial Reporting Regulation in Belgium and the Netherlands: a Comparative Study', in Flower, J. and Lefebvre, C. (eds.), *Comparative Studies in Accounting Regulation in Europe*, Leuven, Acco, pp. 49-80.

Brennan, N., O'Brien, F. J. and Pierce, A. (1992) *A Survey of Irish Published Accounts*. 2nd edition, Dublin & Cork: Oak Tree Press.

Brennan, N., O'Brien F. J. and Pierce, A. (1992) *European Financial Reporting: Ireland*. London Routledge/ICAEW.

Brink, H. L. (1992) 'A history of Philips' accounting policies on the basis of its annual reports', *The European Accounting Review*, Vol. 1, No. 2, pp. 255-275.

Bromwich, M. (1986) *The Economics of Standard Setting*, London: Prentice Hall.

Bromwich, M. and Hopwood, A. (1983) *Accounting Standards: an International Perspective*, London: Pitman.

Bromwich, M. and Hopwood, A. (1992) *Accounting and the Law*, Prentice Hall.

Buijink, W. and Eken, R. (1998) 'Accounting Regulation in the Netherlands', in McLeay, S. (ed.), *Accounting Regulation in Europe*, London: MacMillan (forthcoming).

Burchell, S., Clubb, C., Hopwood, A., Hughes, J. and Nahapiet, J. (1980) 'The Role of Accounting in Organizations and Societies', *Accounting Organizations and Societies*, pp. 5-27.

Busse von Colbe, W. (1972) 'Zur Umrechnung der Jahresabschlüsse ausländischer Konzernunternehmen für die Aufstellung von Konzernabschlüssen bei Wechselkursänderungen', *Finnish Journal of Business Economics*, Vol. 21, pp. 306-333.

Busse von Colbe, W. (1992) 'Relationships between Financial Accounting Research, Standards setting and Practice in Germany', *The European Accounting Review*, Vol. 1, No. 1, pp. 27-38.

Busse von Colbe, W. and Ordelheide, D. (1993) *Konzernabschlüsse*. 6th edition, Wiesbaden: Gabler.

Cahill, E. (1998) 'Accounting Regulation in Ireland: the Interdependence with the United Kingdom', in McLeay, S. (ed.), *Accounting Regulation in Europe*, London: MacMillan (forthcoming).

Cairns, D. (1995) 'IASC - International Accounts & Group Accounts', in Ordelheide, D. and KPMG (eds.) *Transnational Accounting*, London: MacMillan, pp. 1661-1804.

Cairns, D. (1997) 'The Future Shape of Harmonization: a Reply', *The European Accounting Review*, Vol. 6, No. 2, pp. 305-348.

Camfferman, K. (1995) 'The history of financial reporting in the Netherlands', in Walton P. (ed) *European Financial Reporting: A History*. London: Academic Press.

Camfferman, K. and Zeff, S. A. (1994) 'The contributions of Theodore Limperg Jr (1879-1961) to Dutch accounting and auditing', in Edwards, J. R (ed) *Twentieth-Century Accounting Thinkers*. London: Routledge/ICAEW.

Cane, P. (1987) 'Self-regulation and Judicial Review', *Civil Justice Quarterly*, Vol. 6, pp. 324-333.

Canibano, L. and Cea J.-L. (1998) 'Accounting Regulation in Spain', in McLeay, S. (ed.), *Accounting Regulation in Europe*, London: MacMillan (forthcoming).

CCAS - Deloitte Touche Tohmatsu, Ernst & Young Audit - GCC - Viala, G. (1994) *100 groupes industriels et commerciaux*. Paris: CPC, Meylan.

Chambers, R. (1966) *Accounting, Evaluation & Economic Behaviour.* Englewood Cliffs, NJ: Prentice-Hall.

Christensen, C. (1983) 'The Methodology of Positive Accounting', *The Accounting Review*, pp. 1-22.

Christiansen, M. and Elling, J. O. (1993) *European Financial Reporting: Denmark.* London: Routledge/ICAEW.

Christiansen, M. and Hansen, C. K. (1995) 'Denmark - Individual Accounts' in Ordelheide D. and KPMG (eds) *Transnational Accounting.* London: MacMillan, pp. 729-836.

Christiansen, M. and Hansen, C. K. (1995) 'Denmark - Group Accounts', in Ordelheide, D. and KPMG (eds) *Transnational Accounting.* London: MacMillan, pp. 837-920.

Christiansen, M. (1995) 'The history of financial reporting in Denmark', in Walton P. (ed) *European Financial Reporting: A History.* London: Academic Press.

Christiansen, M. (1998) 'Accounting Regulation in Denmark', in McLeay, S. (ed.), *Accounting Regulation in Europe*, London: MacMillan (forthcoming).

Clarke, F. and Dean, G. (1994) 'Fritz Julius August Schmidt', in Edwards, J. R. (ed) *Twentieth-Century Accounting Thinkers.* London: Routledge/ICAEW.

Coase, R. (1937) 'The Nature of the Firm', *Economica*, pp. 386-405.

Coenenberg, A. G. and Machariza, K. (1976) 'Accounting for price changes: An analysis of current developments in Germany', *Journal of Business, Finance and Accounting*, Vol. 3, No. 1, pp. 53-68.

Coenenberg, A. G. (1991) *Jahresabschluß und Jahresabschlußanalyse.* 12th edition, Landsberg am Lech: Verlag moderne Industrie.

Collett, D. (1991) *Modelling Binary Data*, London: Chapman and Hall.

Collins, L. (1994) 'Revaluation of assets in France: The interaction between professional practice, theory and political necessity', *The European Accounting Review*, Vol. 3, No. 1, pp. 122-131.

Cooke, T. E. and Wallace, R. S. O. (1995) 'United Kingdom - Individual Accounts', in Ordelheide, D. and KPMG (eds) *Transnational Accounting*. London: MacMillan, pp. 2627-2800.

Cooper, D. J. and Sherer, M. (1984) 'The Value of Corporate Accounting Reports: Arguments for a Political Economy of Accounting', *Accounting, Organization and Society*, Vol. 9, No. 3/4, pp. 207-232.

Cooper, D. J. and Hopper, T. M. (1990) *Critical Accounts*, London: MacMillan.

Corona, E. (1992) 'Consolidation in Spain', in Gonzalo, J. A. (ed) *Accounting in Spain 1992*. Book prepared for the 15th Annual Congress of the EAA.

Cramer, J. S. (1991) *The Logit Model for Economists*, London: Edward Arnold.

Dearing, Sir Ron (Chairman) (1988) (The Dearing Report) *The Making of Accounting Standards*, Report of the Review Committee, presented to the Consultative Committee of Accountancy Bodies, ICAEW.

De Kerviler, I. and Standish, P. (1992) 'French Accounting Law: Origins, Developments and Scope', in Bromwich, M. and Hopwood, A. (eds.), *Accounting and the Law*, Hertfordshire: Prentice Hall, pp. 130-158.

Delavelle, E. (1924) *La Comptabilité en Francs-Or*. Paris: Nouvelle Libraire Nationale.

Demski, J. (1973) 'The General Impossibility of Normative Accounting Standards', *Accounting Review*, Vol. 49, pp. 718-723.

Demski, J. (1974) 'Choice Among Financial Reporting Alternatives', *The Accounting Review*, April, pp. 221-232.

De Rongé, Y., Henrion, E. and Vael, C. (1995) 'The history of financial reporting in Belgium', in Walton, P. (ed) *European Financial Reporting: A History*. London: Academic Press.

Diver, C. S. (1983) 'The Optimal Precision of Administrative Rules', *The Yale Law Journal*, Vol. 93, No.1, pp. 65-109.

Diggle, G. and Nobes, C. (1994) 'European Rule making in Accounting: The Seventh Directive as a Case Study', *Accounting and Business Research*, Vol. 24, No. 96, pp. 319-333.

Dijksma, J. and Hoogendoorn, M. (1994) *European Financial Reporting: The Netherlands*. London: Routledge/ICAEW.

Ebbers, G. (1997a) 'Fixed Asset Revaluation in Europe: Interaction between Theory, Practice and Fiscal Policies', in Flower, J. and Lefebvre C. (eds.) *Comparative Studies in Accounting Regulation in Europe*, Leuven: Acco.

Ebbers, G. (1997b) 'Foreign Currency Reporting in Europe: Consensus and Conflict', in Flower, J. and Lefebvre C. (eds.) *Comparative Studies in Accounting Regulation in Europe*, Leuven: Acco.

Ebbers, G. (1997c) 'The Elusive Concept of a Group: *de jure* and *de facto* Criteria that Define a Subsidiary for Consolidation in Europe', in Flower, J. and Lefebvre C. (eds.) *Comparative Studies in Accounting Regulation in Europe*, Leuven: Acco.

Ebbers, G. and McLeay, S. (1997), "Accounting and *Volksgeist* - Territorial Claims on Accounting Regulation", *Journal of Management and Governance*, Vol. 1, No. 1 pp. 67-84.

Ebke, W. (1997) 'Rechnungslegung und Abschlußprüfung im Umbruch', *Wirtschaftsprüferkammer Mitteilungen*, Special issue on 'Financial Accounting and Auditing in Global Capital Markets', June, pp.12-24.

Edwards, E. and Bell, P. (1961) *The Theory and Measurement of Business Income*, University of California Press.

Ehrlich, I. and Posner, R. (1974) 'An Economic Analysis of Legal Rulemaking', *The Journal of Legal Studies*, pp. 257-286.

Elling, J. O. and Hansen, C. K. (1984) 'The Fourth Directive and Denmark', in Gray, S. and Coenenberg, A. G. (eds) *EEC Accounting Harmonisation: Implementation of the Fourth Directive*. Amsterdam: North-Holland.

Ernst and Young (1994) *UK GAAP*. London: MacMillan, 4th edition.

Fama, E. F. (1976) *Foundations of Finance*. Basic Books.

Faure, G. (1926) *Bilans et Comptes en Francs-Or*. Paris: La Nouvelle Libraire Nationale.

FAZ, Fankfurter Allgemeine Zeitung (14 February 1998), p. 13.

FAZ, Frankfurter Allgemeine Zeitung (28 March 1998), p. 13.

Fédération des Experts Comptables Européens (1991) *European Survey of Published Accounts 1991*. London: Routledge/FEE.

Fédération des Experts Comptables Européens (1993) *Seventh Directive Options and their Implementation*. London: Routledge/FEE.

Fernandes Ferreira, L. (1994) *European Financial Reporting: Portugal*. London: Routledge/ICAEW.

Fernandes Ferreira, R. (1992) 'Free Revaluations of Tangible Fixed Assets', Paper presented at the *15th Annual Congress of the EAA in Madrid*.

Fernandez Peña, E. (1992) 'Accounting in Spain in the 20th Century', in Gonzalo, J. A. (ed) *Accounting in Spain*. Book prepared for the *15th Annual Congress of the EAA*, pp. 39-56.

Flower, J. (1976) *Accounting Treatment of Overseas Currencies - A Backround Study*. London: ICAEW in conjunction with Arthur Andersen & Co.

Flower, J. (1994) *The Regulation of Financial Reporting in the Nordic Countries*, CE Fritzes AB.

Flower, J. (1995) 'Foreign currency translation', in Nobes, C. and Parker, R. (eds) *Comparative International Accounting*. 4th edition, London: Prentice Hall, pp. 348-389.

Flower, J. (1997) 'The Future Shape of Harmonization: the EU versus the IASC versus the SEC, *The European Accounting Review*, Vol. 6, No. 2, pp. 281-303.

Flower, J. and Lefebvre, C. (1997) *Comparative Studies in Accounting Regulation in Europe*, Leuven: Acco.

Foster, G. (1978) *Financial Statement Analysis*. Englewood Cliffs, NJ: Prentice-Hall.

Foster, G. (1980) 'Accounting Policy Decisions and Capital Market Research', *Journal of Accounting and Economics*, March, pp. 29-62.

Frank, W. G. (1979) 'An Empirical Analysis of International Accounting Principles', *Journal of Accounting Research*, Autumn.

Freedman, J. and Power, M. (1991) 'Law and Accounting: Transition and Transformation', *The Modern Law Review*, Vol. 54, No. 6, pp. 769-791.

Garrod, N. and McLeay, S. (1996) *Accounting in Transition: The Implications of Political and Economic Reform in Central Europe*, London: Routledge.

Gebhardt, G. (1987) Vereinheitlichung der Recheneinheit durch Währungs-umrechnung, in Castan, E. et al. (eds) *Beck'sches Handbuch der Rechnungs-legung*. Band II, C310, München: C. H. Becksche Verlagsbuchhaltung.

Gebhardt, G. (1988) 'Zur Aussagefähigkeit von Währungserfolgen in Einzel- und Konzernabschlüssen', in Domsch, M. et al. (eds) *Unternehmenserfolg, FS für W. Busse von Colbe.* pp. 169-185.

Gonedes, N. and Dopuch, N. (1974) 'Capital Market Equilibrium, Information Production and Selecting Accounting Techniques: Theoretical Framework and Review of Empirical Work, Studies on Financial Accounting Objectives', Supplement to *Journal of Accounting Research*, pp. 48-129.

Gonzalo, J. A. and Gallizio, J. L. (1992) *European Financial Reporting: Spain.* London: Routledge/ICAEW.

Gray, S. and Gordon, P. (1994) *European Financial Reporting: the United Kingdom.* London: Routledge/ICAEW.

Griffin, P. A. (1979) 'What Harm has FASB Actually Done?', *Harvard Business Review*, July-August, pp. 8-18.

Griffith, I. (1986) *Creative Accounting: How to Make your Profits What You Want Them To Be*, London: Sidgwick & Jackson.

Griziaux, J.-P. (1995) 'France - Individual Accounts', in Ordelheide, D. and KPMG (eds) *Transnational Accounting*. London: MacMillan, pp. 1135-1286.

Hadden, T. (1992) 'Regulating Corporate Groups: An International Perspective', in McCahery, J., Picciotto, S. and Scott, C. (eds), *Corporate Control and Accountability*. Oxford: Clarendon Press, pp. 343-370.

Hagerman, R. and Zmijewski, M. (1979) 'Some Economic Determinants of Accounting Policy Choice', *Journal of Accounting and Economics*, pp. 141-161.

Henisse, P.(1997) 'Loi comptable: les députés font entendre leur différence', *Les Echos*, 24.01.1997.

Hirschleifer, J. (1971) 'The Private and Social Value of Information & The Reward to Incentive Activity', *American Economic Review*, September, pp. 561-574.

Holthausen, R. (1981) 'Evidence on the effect of bond covenants and management compensation contracts on the choice of accounting techniques: The case of the depreciation switch-back', *Journal of Accounting and Economics*, pp. 73-109.

Hopwood, A. (1992) 'Discussion on: International Corporate Finance and the Challenge of Creative Compliance', McBarnet, D. and Whelan, C., in Fingleton, J. (ed.) *The Internationalisation of Capital Markets and the Regulatory Response*, Graham and Trotman. pp. 129-146.

Hopwood, A. and Vieten, H. (1998) 'Accounting Regulation in the United Kingdom', in McLeay, S. (ed.), *Accounting Regulation in Europe*, London: MacMillan (forthcoming).

Hoskin, K. (1994) 'Boxing Clever: For, Against and Beyond Foucault in the Battle For Accounting Theory', *Critical Perspectives on Accounting*, pp. 57-85.

Inchuasti, B.G. (1995) 'The History of Financial Reporting in Spain' in P.Walton (ed) *European Financial Reporting: A History*, Academic Press, pp.203-220.

Institute of Chartered Accountants of England and Wales (1949) *Rising Price Levels in Relation to Accounts*, ICAEW.

Institute of Chartered Accountants of England and Wales (1952) *Accounting in Relation to the Purchasing Power of Money*, ICAEW.

Institut der Wirtschaftsprüfer (1975) *Zur Berücksichtigung der Substanzerhaltung bei der Ermittlung des Jahresergebnisses*, IdW: Düsseldorf.

Johnston, E. (1991) 'Uncertainty, Chaos and the Torts Process: An Economic Analysis of Legal Form', *Cornell Law Review*, pp. 297-342.

Jorissen, A. and Block, H. (1995) 'Belgium - Individual Accounts', in Ordelheide, D. and KPMG (eds) *Transnational Accounting*. London: MacMillan, pp. 379-492.

Kay, J. (1988) 'The Forms of Regulation' in Seldon, A. (ed.) *Financial Regulation - or Over - Regulation.*

Kirkman, P. (1995) 'Inflation Accounting', in Nobes, C. and Parker, R. (eds) *Comparative International Accounting*. London: Prentice Hall.

Klaassen, J. and Hekers, T. (1995) 'Netherlands - Individual Accounts', in Ordelheide, D. and KPMG (eds) *Transnational Accounting*. London: MacMillan, pp. 2049-2148.

Klaassen, J. and Hekers, T. (1995) 'The Netherlands - Group Accounts' in Ordelheide, D. and KPMG (eds) *Transnational Accounting*. London: MacMillan, pp. 2149-2184.

Knorr, L. (1998) 'Europe Opens to IAS', *IASC Insight*, March 1998, p. 1.

Kress, K. (1989) 'Legal Indeterminacy', *California Law Review*, Vol. 77, pp.283-337.

Lamb, M. (1995) 'When is a group a group? Convergence of concepts of 'group' in European Union corporate tax', *The European Accounting Review*, Vol. 4, No. 1, pp. 33-78.

Laughlin, R. and Broadbent, J. (1993) 'Accounting and Law: Partners in the Juridification of the Public Sector in the UK?, *Critical Perspectives on Accounting*, pp. 337-368.

Lee, T. A. and Tweedie, D. P. (1977) *The Private Shareholder and the Corporate Report*, ICAEW.

Lefebvre, C. and Flower, J. (1994) *European Financial Reporting - Belgium*, London: Routledge.

Lefebvre, C. J. L. (1984) 'The Fourth Directive and Belgium', in Gray, S. and Coenenberg, A. G. (eds) *EEC Accounting Harmonisation: Implementation of the Fourth Directive*. Amsterdam: North-Holland.

Lefebvre, C. and Lin, Q.-L. (1991) 'On the Scope of Consolidation: A Comparative Study of the EEC 7th Directive, IAS 27 and the Belgian Royal Decree on Consolidation', *The British Accounting Review*, Vol. 23, pp. 133-147.

Lefebvre, C. and van Nuffel, L. (1998) 'Accounting Regulation in Belgium', in McLeay, S. (ed.), *Accounting Regulation in Europe*, London: MacMillan ' (forthcoming).

Leftwich, R., Watts, R. L., Zimmerman, J. L. (1981) 'Voluntary Corporate Disclosure: The Case of Interim Reporting', Supplement to *Journal of Accounting Research*, pp. 50-77.

Leftwich, R. (1983) 'Accounting Information in Private Markets: Evidence from Private Lending Agreements', *Accounting Review*, pp. 23-42.

Lev, B. (1979) 'The impact of Accounting Regulations on the Stock Market: The Case of Oil and Gas Companies', *The Accounting Review,* July, pp.79-122.

Lewis, N. (1990) 'Corporatism and Accountability: The Democratic Dilemma', in Crouch, C. and Dore, R. (eds), *Corporatism and Accountability: Organized Interests in British Public Life.*

Limperg Jr, T. (1937) 'De gevolgen van de depreciatie van de gulden voor de berekening van waarde en winst in het bedrijf', *Maandblad voor accountancy en bedrijfshuishoudkunde.* Vol. 14, pp. 1-8.

López Díaz, A. and Rivero Torre, P. (1995) 'Spain - Individual Accounts', in Ordelheide, D. and KPMG (eds) *Transnational Accounting*. London: MacMillan, pp. 2185-2304.

López Díaz, A. and Rivero Torre, P. (1995) 'Spain - Group Accounts', in Ordelheide, D. and KPMG (eds) *Transnational Accounting*. London: MacMillan, pp. 2305-2370.

MacDonald, G. (1991) 'Substance, Form and Equity in Taxation and Accounting, *The Modern Law Review,* Vol. 54, pp.830-847.

Macve, R. (1981) *A Conceptual Framework for Financial Accounting and Reporting*, ICAEW.

Mahlberg, W. (1923), *Bilanztechnik und Bewertung bei schwankender Währung*. 3rd edition, Leipzig: Glöckner.

McBarnet, D. and Whelan, C. (1991) 'The Elusive Spirit of the Law: Formalism and the Struggle for Legal Control', *The Modern Law Review*, Vol. 54, No. 6, pp. 848-873.

Mikol, A. (1995) 'The history of financial reporting in France', in Walton, P. *European Financial Reporting: A History*. London: Academic Press.

Miller, P. B. (1985) 'The Conceptual Framework: Myths and Realities', *Journal of Accountancy*, March, pp.62-71.

Miller, P. B. (1986) 'Accounting for Progress - National Accounting and Planning in France: A Review Essay', *Accounting, Organizations and Society,* pp. 83-104.

Mitchell, A. and Sikka, P. (1993) 'Accounting for Change: The Institutions of Accountancy', *Critical Perspectives on Accounting*, pp. 29-52.

Mitchell, A., Puxty, T., Sikka, P. and Willmott, H. (1994) 'Ethical Statements as Smokescreens for Sectional Interests: The Case of the UK Accountancy Profession', *Journal of Business Ethics,* Vol. 13, pp. 39-51.

Mora, A. (1997) 'A Comparative Analysis of the Accounting Systems of Italy and Spain: the Explanatory Variables of their Similarities and Differences', in Flower, J. and Lefebvre C. (eds.), *Comparative Studies in Accounting Regulation in Europe*, Leuven: Acco.

Most, K.S. (1977) *Accounting Theory.* Ohio: Grid Inc., Columbus.

Muis, J. S. (1975) 'Current Value Accounting in the Netherlands: Fact or Fiction', *The Accountant's Magazine*, November, pp. 377-379.

Mumford, M. (1979) 'The end of a familiar inflation accounting cycle', *Accounting and Business Research*, Spring, pp. 98-104.

Nair, R. D. and Frank, W. G. (1980) 'The Impact of Disclosure and Measurement Practices on International Accounting Classifications', *The Accounting Review*, July.

Napier, C. (1995) 'The History of Financial Reporting in the UK' in P.Walton (ed.) *European Financial Reporting: A History*, Academic Press, pp.259-284.

Naser, K. H. M. (1994) *Creative Financial Accounting: Its Nature and Use*, New York: Prentice Hall.

Neal, D. (1997) 'Locating Accounting Regulation in Greece', in Flower, J. and Lefebvre C. (eds.) *Comparative Studies in Accounting Regulation in Europe*, Leuven: Acco, pp. 127-158.

Nobes, C. (1980) 'A Review of the Translation Debate', *Accounting and Business Research*, Autumn, pp. 421-431.

Nobes, C. (1983) 'A Judgemental International Classification of Financial Reporting Practices', *Journal of Business, Finance and Accounting*, Spring.

Nobes, C. (1993) 'The True and Fair View Requirement: Impact on and of the Fourth Directive', *Accounting and Business Research*, Vol.24, No.93, pp.35-48.

Nobes, C. and Parker, R. (1984) 'The Fourth Directive and the UK', in Gray, S. and Coenenberg, A. G. (eds) *EEC Accounting Harmonisation: Implementation of the Fourth Directive.* Amsterdam: North-Holland.

Nobes, C. and Parker, R. (1995) *Comparative International Accounting.* 4th edition, London: Prentice Hall.

Odenwald, O. (1992) 'Aufstellungspflichten eines Konzernabschlusses', in Castan, E., Heymann, G., Müller, E., Ordelheide, D. and Scheffer, E. (eds) *Beck'sches Handbuch der Rechnungslegung*. München: Beck'sche Verlagsbuchhaltung, Band II, Stand: April 1995.

Ogus, A. I. (1994) *Regulation: Legal Form and Economic Theory*, Clarendon Law Series, Oxford: Clarendon Press.

Ohlson, J. and Buckman, G. (1981) 'Toward a Theory of Financial Accounting: Welfare and Public Information', *Journal of Accounting Research*, Autumn, pp. 399-433.

Olivero, B. (1997) 'The Accounting Standardisation Process in Italy: a French View', in Flower, J. and Levebvre, C. (eds.), *Comparative Studies in Accounting Regulation in Europe*, Leuven, Acco, pp. 219-246.

Ordelheide, D. and Pfaff, D. (1994) *European Financial Reporting: Germany*. London: Routledge/ICAEW.

Ordelheide, D. (1994) 'Gefährdung der Nominalkapitalerhaltung durch die Währungsumrechnung von Auslandsinvestitionen', in *Zeitschrift für Betriebswirtschaft*, Vol.46, pp. 795-818.

Ordelheide, D. and KPMG (1995) *Transnational Accounting*. London: MacMillan.

Ordelheide, D. (1995) 'Germany - Group Accounts' in Ordelheide, D. and KPMG (eds) *Transnational Accounting*. London: MacMillan, pp. 1547-1658.

Ordelheide, D. (1998) 'Accounting Regulation in Germany', in McLeay, S. (ed.), *Accounting Regulation in Europe*, London: MacMillan (forthcoming).

Page, A. C. (1986) 'Self-Regulation: The Constitutional Dimension', *Modern Law Review*, Vol. 49, pp. 141-163.

Page, A. and Ferguson, R. (1992) *Investor Protection*.

Papas, A. A. (1993) *European Financial Reporting: Greece*. London: Routledge/ICAEW.

Parker, R. H. (1989) 'Importing and Exporting Accounting: The British Experience', in Hopwood, A. (ed.) *International Pressures for Accounting Change*, Prentice Hall.

Peasnell, K. V. and Yaasnah, R. A. (1988) 'Off-balance sheet financing', *Certified Research Report 10*, The Chartered Association of Certified Accountants.

Petite, M. (1984) 'The Conditions for Consolidation under the 7th Company Law Directive', *Common Market Law Review*, Vol. 21, pp. 81-121.

Pham, D. (1993) 'France and the Seventh Directive', in Gray, S. and Coenenberg, A. G. (eds*) International Group Accounting*. London: Crom Helm.

Potthoff, E. and Sieben, G. (1994) 'Eugen Schmalenbach', in Edwards J. R. (ed) *Twentieth-Century Accounting Thinkers*. London: Routledge/ICAEW.

Power, M. (1992) 'The Politics of Brand Accounting in the United Kingdom', *The European Accounting Review*, Vol. 1, pp. 39-68.

Power, M. (1993) 'Auditing and the Politics of Control in the UK Financial Service Sector', in McCahery, J., Picciotto, S. and Scott, C. (eds), *Corporate Control and Accountability*, Oxford: Clarendon Press, pp.188-202.

Power, M. (1996) 'Making Things Auditable', *Accounting, Organizations and Society*, Vol. 21, pp. 289-315.

Puxty, A. G., Willmott, H. C., Cooper, D. J. and Lowe, T. (1987) 'Modes of Regulation in Advanced Capitalism: Locating Accountancy in Four Countries', *Accounting, Organization and Society*, Vol. 12, No. 3, pp. 273-291.

Puxty, A. G., Willmott, H. C., Robson, K., Cooper, D. J. and Lowe, T. (1992) 'Regulation of Accountancy and Accountants: A Comparative Analysis of Accounting for Reserach and Development in Four Advanced Capitalist Countries', *Accounting, Auditing & Accountability Journal,*Vol. 5, pp. 32-56.

Raffegeau, J., Dufils, P., Corre, J. and Lopater, C. (1989) *Memento Pratique Francis Lefebvre: Comptable 1990*. Paris: Francis Lefebvre.

Raffegeau, J., Dufils, P., Corre, J. and de Ménonville, D. (1989) *Comptes Consolidés*. Paris: Francis Lefebvre.

Rezaee Z. (1990) 'Capital Market Reactions to Accounting Policy Deliberations: an Empirical Study of Accounting for Foreign Currency Translation 1974-1982', *Journal of Business, Finance and Accounting*, pp. 635-648.

Riccaboni, A. and Ghirri, R. (1994) *European Financial Reporting: Italy*. London: Routledge/ICAEW.

Riccaboni (1998) 'Accounting Regulation in Italy', in McLeay, S. (ed.), *Accounting Regulation in Europe*, London: MacMillan (forthcoming).

Richard, J., Simons, P. and Bailly, J-M. (1987) *Comptabilité et Analyse Financière des Groupes*. Paris: Economica.

Richard, J. (1995) 'France - Group Accounts' in Ordelheide, D. and KPMG (eds) *Transnational Accounting*. London: MacMillan, pp. 1287-1394.

Robson, K. (1993) 'Accounting Policy Making and "Interest": Accounting for Research and Development', *Critical Perspectives on Accounting*, pp. 1-27.

Robson, K., Willmott, H., Cooper, D. J. and Puxty, T. (1994) 'The Ideology of Professional Regulation and the Markets for Accounting Labour: Three Episodes in the Recent History of the U.K. Accountancy Profession', *Accounting, Organizations and Society*, pp. 527-553.

Schauer, F. (1988) 'Formalism', *The Yale Law Journal*, Vol. 97, No. 4, pp.509-548.

Scheid, J. C. and Walton, P. (1992) *European Financial Reporting: France*. London: Routledge/ICAEW.

Scheid, J. C. and Lande, E. (1998) 'Accounting Regulation in France', in McLeay, S. (ed.), *Accounting Regulation in Europe*, London: MacMillan (forthcoming).

Schlesinger, R.B.(1988) *Comparative Law*, 5th edition, The Foundation Press.

Schmalenbach, E. (1921) 'Geldwertausgleich in der Bilanzmässigen Erfolgsrechnung', *Zeitschrift für handelswissenschaftliche Forschung*, October, pp. 401-417.

Schmidt, F. (1921) *Die Organische Bilanz im Rahmen der Wirtschaft*, Leipzig.

Schmidt, F. (1931) 'Is Appreciation Profit?', *The Accounting Review*, Vol. 6, pp. 289-293.

Schneider, D. (1995) 'The history of financial reporting in Germany', in Walton, P. (ed) *European Financial Reporting: A History*. London: Academic Press.

Selto, F. H. and Neuman, B. R. (1981) 'A Further Guide to Research on the Economic Consequences of Accounting Information', *Accounting and Business Research*, Autumn, pp. 317-322.

Shah, A. K. (1996) 'Creative Compliance in Financial Reporting, *Accounting, Organizations and Society*, Vol. 21, No. 1, pp. 23-39.

Sikka, P. and Willmott, H. (1995a) 'Illuminating the State-Profession Relationship: Accountants Acting as Department of Trade and Industry Investigators', *Critical Perspectives on Accounting*, pp. 341-369.

Sikka, P. and Willmott, H. (1995b) 'The Power of "Independence": Defending and Extending the Jurisdiction of Accounting in the United Kingdom', *Accounting, Organization and Society*, Vol. 20, pp. 547-581.

Skerrat, L. C. L. and Tonkin, D. J. (1995) 'Financial Reporting 1994-95: A Survey of UK Reporting Practice', ICAEW.

Smith, T. (1992) *Accounting for Growth: Stripping the Camouflage from Company Accounts*, London: Century Business.

Solomons, D. (1978) 'The Politicisation of Accounting', *Journal of Accounting*, November, pp. 65-72.

Soo, B. and Soo, L. (1994) 'Accounting for the Multinational Firm: Is the Translation Process Valued by the Stock Market?', *The Accounting Review*, Vol. 69, No. 4, pp. 617-637.

Stamp, E. (Study Group on the Objectives of Corporate Reporting, 1980) *Corporate Reporting: Its Future Evolution*, Canada Institute of Chartered Accountants.

Standish, P. (1997) *The French Plan Comptable: Explanation and Translation*, Paris: Expert Comptable Média.

Sterling, R. R. (1970) *Theory of the measurement of Enterprise Income*. University Press of Kansas.

Sterling, R. R. (1972) 'Decision Orientated Financial Accounting', *Accounting and Business Research*, Summer, pp. 198-208.

Sterling, R. R. (1990) 'Positive Accounting Theory: An Assessment', *ABACUS*, pp.97-135.

Sunstein, C. (1987) 'Constitutionalism After the New Deal', *Harvard Law Review*, Vol. 101, pp. 421-453.

Sweeney H. W. (1927) 'Effects of Inflation on German Accounting', *Journal of Accountancy*, July. Reprinted in Zeff, S. A. (ed) (1976) *Asset Appreciation, Business Income and Price-Level Accounting: 1918-1935*. Arno Press Collection.

Tay, J. S. W. and Parker, R. H. (1990) 'Measuring International Harmonization and Standardization', *ABACUS*, Vol. 26, No. 1, pp. 71-88.

Taylor, P. A. (1995) 'United Kingdom - Group Accounts', in Ordelheide D. and KPMG (eds) *Transnational Accounting*. London: MacMillan, pp. 2801-2956.

Theunisse, H. and Aerts, W. (1995) 'Belgium - Group Accounts', in Ordelheide, D. and KPMG (eds) *Transnational Accounting*. MacMillan, pp. 493-570.

Tinker, A. M. (1980) 'A Political Economy of Accounting', *Accounting, Organizations and Society*, Vol. 5, No. 2, pp. 147-160.

Tinker, A. M. (1985) *Paper Prophets: a Social Critique of Accounting*, Holt, Rinehart, Winston. London.

Tinker, A. M., Merino, B. D. and Niemark, M. D. (1982) 'The Normative Origins of Positive Accounting Theories', *Accounting, Organizations and Society*, Vol. 7, No.2, pp. 167-200.

Took, L. (1995) 'The History of Financial Reporting in Italy' in P.Walton (ed) *European Financial Reporting: A History*, Academic Press, pp.157-168.

Treuarbeit (1990) *Konzernabschlüsse '89*. Düsseldorf: IdW-Verlag GmbH.

Turley, S. (1992) 'Developments in the Structure of Financial Reporting in the United Kingdom', *The European Accounting Review*, Vol. 1, pp. 105-124.

Tushnet, M. (1984) 'Perspectives on Critical Legal Studies', *George Washington Law Review*, Vol. 52, pp.239-257.

Tweedie, D. P. and Whittington, G. (1984) *The Debate on Inflation Accounting*. Cambridge University Press.

Tweedie, D. and Whittington, G. (1990), "Financial Reporting: Current Problems and their Implications for Systematic Reform", *Accounting and Business Research*, Vol.21, pp. 87-97.

Van der Tas, L. G. (1988) 'Measuring Harmonisation of Financial Reporting Practice', *Accounting and Business Research*, Spring, pp.157-169.

Van der Tas, L. G. (1992) 'Evidence of EC Financial Reporting Practice Harmonisation: The Case of Deferred Taxation', *The European Accounting Review*, May, pp. 69-104.

Van Hoepen, M. A. (1984) 'The Fourth Directive and the Netherlands', in Gray, S. and Coenenberg, A. G. (eds) *EEC Accounting Harmonisation: Implementation of the Fourth Directive*. Amsterdam: North-Holland.

Van Hulle, K. (1992) 'Harmonisation of Accounting Standards: A View from the European Community', *The European Accounting Review*, Vol.1, No.1, pp.161-172.

Van Hulle, K. and van der Tas, L. G. (1995) 'European Union - Individual Accounts', in Ordelheide, D. and KPMG (eds) *Transnational Accounting*. London: MacMillan, pp. 921-1046.

Van Hulle K. and van der Tas (1995), 'European Union - Group Accounts', in Ordelheide, D. and KPMG (eds.), *Transnational Accounting*, London: MacMillan, pp. 1047-1134.

Van Hulle, K. (1997a) 'The True and Fair View Override in the European Accounting Directives', *The European Accounting Review*, Vol.6. pp. 711-720.

Van Hulle, K. (1997b) 'International Harmonisation of Accounting Principles: A European Perspective', *Wirtschaftsprüferkammer Mitteilungen*, Special issue on 'Financial Accounting and Auditing in Global Capital Markets', June, pp. 44-50.

Von Wysocki, K. (1987) 'Zur Berichterstattung über die Grundlagen der Umrechnung von Fremdwährungspositionen nach § 284 Abs. 2 Nr.2 HGB', *ZfB-Ergänzungsheft* 1/87, pp. 221-233.

Von Wysocki, K. (1988) 'Zur Berichterstattung über die Grundlagen der Umrechnung von Fremdwährungspositionen nach § 313 Abs. 1 Satz 2 Nr. 2 HGB', in Domsch, M. et al. (eds) *Unternehmenserfolg FS für W. Busse von Colbe*. pp. 401-412.

Walker, R. G. and Robinson, S. P. (1993) 'A Critical Assessment of the Literature on Political Activity and Accounting Regulation', *Research in Accounting Regulation* 7, pp. 3-40.

Wallace, R. S. O. and Gernon, H. (1991) 'Frameworks for International Comparative Financial Accounting', *Journal of Accounting Literature*, pp. 209-264.

Walton, P. (1995) *European Financial Reporting - A History*, London: Academic Press

Wassermann, M. J. (1931) 'Accounting practice in France during the period of monetary inflation, *Accounting Review*, March.

Watson, A. (1974) *Legal Transplants - An Approach to Comparative Law*, The University of Georgia Press, London.

Watts, R. L. (1977) 'Corporate Financial Statements: A Product of the Market and Political Processes', *Australian Journal of Management*, April, pp.53-75.

Watts, R. L. and Zimmerman, J. (1978) 'Towards a Positive Theory of the Determination of Accounting Standards', *The Accounting Review*, January, pp. 112-134.

Watts, R. L. and Zimmerman, J. (1986) *Positive Accounting Theory*, Englewood Cliffs: Prentice Hall.

Weinrib, E. J. (1988) 'Legal Formalism: On the Immanent Rationality of Law', *The Yale Law Journal*, Vol. 97, pp. 950-1016.

Westwick, C. A. (1980) 'The Lessons to be Learned from the Development of Inflation Accounting in the UK', *Accounting and Business Research*, Autumn, pp. 353-373.

Willmott, H., Cooper, D. and Puxty, T. (1993) 'Maintaining Self-regulation: Making "Interests" Coincide in Discourses on the Governance of the ICAEW', *Accounting, Auditing & Accountability Journal*, Vol. 6, pp. 68-93.

Whittington, G. (1983) *Inflation Accounting: An Introduction to the Debate*, Cambridge: CUP.

Whittington, G. (1993) 'Corporate Governance and the Regulation of Financial Reporting', *Accounting and Business Research*, Vol. 23, pp. 311-319.

Whittington, G. (1994) 'The LSE Triumvirate and its contribution to price change accounting', in Edwards, J. R. (ed) *Twentieth-Century Accounting Thinkers*. London: Routledge/ICAEW.

Zeff , S. A. (editor) (1976) *Asset Appreciation, Business Income and Price-Level Accounting: 1918-1935*. Arno Press Collection.

Zeff, S. (1978) 'The Rise of Economic Consequences', *Journal of Accountancy*, December, pp.56-63.

Zeff, S. A., van der Wel, F. and Camfferman, K. (1992) *Company Financial Reporting - a historical and comparative study of the Dutch regulatory process*. Amsterdam: North-holland.

ACCOUNTING REGULATIONS

Accounting Standards Steering Committee, *Inflation and Accounts*, 1971

Aktiengesetz (1965).

Companies Act 1989.

Council Directive 78/660/EEC of 25 July 1978 (Fourth Directive), O.J. No. L 222 of 14 August 1978.

Council Directive 83/349/EEC of 13 June 1983 (Seventh Directive), O.J. No. L 193 of 18 July 1983.

Decree 86-221.

Decreto legislativo 9 aprile 1991, n.127. Attuazione delle direttive n. 78/660/CEE e n.83/349/CEE in materia societaria, relative ai conti annuali e consolidati, ai sensi dell'art.1, comma 1,della legge 26 marzo 1990, n.69.

Decreto-Lei n. 238/91 de 2 de Julho 1991.

Danish Accounting Standard No. 9 (1994).

Decreto-Lei n. 238/91 de 2 de Julho 1991.

Documenti della Commissione per la Statuizione dei Principi Contabili, "Conversione in Moneta Nazionale delle Operazioni e delle Partite in Moneta Estera" (Settembre 1988).

ED 42 *Accounting for Special Purpose Transactions,* 1988

ED 49 *Reflecting the Substance of Transactions in Assets and Liabilities,* 1990

ED 50 *Consolidated Accounts.* August, 1990.

ED 51 *Accounting for Fixed Assets and Revaluations*, 1990

European Commission (1995) *Paper of the Accounting Advisory Forum on Foreign Currency Translation.* Luxembourg: Office for official publication of the European Communities.

FAS 52 - Statement of Financial Accounting Standards No. 52 "Foreign Currency Translation" (1981).

Financial Accountants Standards Board, (FASB, 1978) *Objectives of Financial Reporting by Business Enterprises* (Statement of Financial Accounting Concept No.1).

FRS 2 *Accounting for Subsidiary Undertakings*. July 1992.

FRS 5 *Reporting the Substance of Transactions*. April 1994.

Handelsgesetzbuch 1985.

International Accounting Standards Committee (IASC, 1989) *Framework for the Preparation and Presentation of Financial Statements*, IASC: London.

IAS 21 - International Accounting Standard No. 21 "Accounting for the Effects of Changes in Foreign Exchange Rates" (1983).

IAS 21, revised "The Effects of Changes in Foreign Exchange Rates" (1993).

Law 2190/1920 (Greek Company Law, 1990).

Loi No. 66-537, 24 Juillet 1966.

Loi No. 85-11, 3 Janvier 1985.

Lov om visse selskabers aflæggelse af årsregnskab m.v. (Regnskabslov) (Annual Accounts Act).

PCG, p.II 12; PCG p.II 155-157 (1986).

PGC, quinta parte, Normas de Valoracion (1990).

Raad voor de Jaarverslaggeving 1.03.906-36.

Real Decreto 1815/1991, de 20 de diciembre, por el que se aprueban las normas para la formulació de las cuentas anuales consolidadas, BOE, 27 de diciembre 1991.

Royal Decree of 6 March 1990 (Consolidation Decree with Report to the King).

SSAP 20 Accounting Standard No. 20 "Foreign Currency Translation" (1983).

APPENDIX

SAMPLE COMPANIES

French sample companies (22)

1   Accor (87, 93, 95)
2   Alcatel Alsthom (87, 93, 95)
3   Béghin Say (87, 93, 95)
4   Bioblock Scientific (93,95)
5   BIS (87, 93, 95)
6   BSN (87, 93)
7   Carnaud Metalbox (93, 95)
8   Club Med (87, 93, 95)
9   Elf Acquitaine (87, 93, 95)
10   Eurotunnel (93, 95)
11   Henri Maire (93, 95)
12   Lafarge Coppee (87, 93, 95)
13   LVMH (87, 93, 95)
14   Lyonnaise des Eaux (87, 93, 95)
15   Pernod Ricard (87, 93, 95)
16   Piscines Jean Desjoyaux (93, 95)
17   PSA (87, 93, 95)
18   Remy Cointrau (93, 95)
19   Saint Gobain (87, 93, 95)
20   Thomson (87, 93, 95)
21   Tivoly (93, 95)
22   Total (87, 93, 95)

German sample companies (23)

23   Asko (87, 93, 95)
24   Babcock (87, 93, 95)
25   BASF (87, 93, 95)
26   Bayer (87, 93, 95)
27   BMW (87, 93, 95)
28   Computer 2000 (93, 95)
29   Continental (87, 93, 95)

30   Daimler Benz (87, 93, 95)
31   Degussa (87, 93, 95)
32   Hoechst (87, 93, 95)
33   Kaufhof (87, 93, 95)
34   Klöckner Humboldt-Deutz (87, 93)
35   Linde (87, 93, 95)
36   MAN (87, 93, 95)
37   Mannesmann (87, 93, 95)
38   RWE (87, 93, 95)
39   Schering (87, 93, 95)
40   Siemens (87, 93)
41   Thyssen (87, 93, 95)
42   Veba (87, 93, 95)
43   VEW (87, 93, 95)
44   Volkswagen (87, 93, 95)
45   Wella (87, 93, 95)

Dutch sample companies (20)

46   Akzo (87, 93, 95)
47   Bols Wessanen (87, 93, 95)
48   DAF (93, 95)
49   DSM (93, 95)
50   Elsevier (87, 93)
51   Heineken (87, 93, 95)
52   Hoogovens (87, 93, 95)
53   Hunter Douglas (87, 93, 95)
54   KLM (87, 93, 95)
55   KNP BT (87, 93, 95)
56   Oce van Grinten (87, 93)
57   Otra (87, 93, 95)
58   Phillips (87, 93, 95)
59   Royal Dutch (87, 93, 95)
60   Royal Nedlloyd (93, 95)
61   Royal Pakhoed (87, 93, 95)
62   Stork (87, 93, 95)
63   Unilever (87, 93, 95)
64   van Ommeren (87, 93, 95)
65   Wereldhave (87, 93, 95)

UK sample companies (44)

66	Albert Fisher (93, 95)
67	Allied (87, 93, 95)
68	Bass (87, 93, 95)
69	BAT (87, 93, 95)
70	BET (93, 95)
71	Blenheim (93, 95)
72	Body Shop (93, 95)
73	Bowater (87, 93, 95)
74	Boxmore (93, 95)
75	Bridgend Group (93, 95)
76	British Gas (87, 93, 95)
77	British Petroleum (87, 93, 95)
78	British Telecom (87, 93, 95)
79	BTR (87, 93, 95)
80	Cable & Wireless (87, 93, 95)
81	Charter (87, 93, 95)
82	Courtaulds (87, 93)
83	Euromoney Publications (87, 93, 95)
84	Fisons (87, 93)
85	GEC (87, 93, 95)
86	GNK (87, 93, 95)
87	Glaxo (87, 93, 95)
88	Grand Metropolitain (87, 93, 95)
89	Great Universal Stores (87, 93, 95)
90	Guiness (87, 93, 95)
91	Hanson (87, 93, 95)
92	ICI (87, 93, 95)
93	Ladbroke (93, 95)
94	Lamont (93, 95)
95	Laura Ashley (93, 95)
96	Marks & Spencer (87, 93, 95)
97	MB Caradon (93, 95)
98	Perkins Food (93, 95)
99	Pilkington (93, 95)
100	P&O (87, 93, 95)
101	Rothmanns (87, 93, 95)
102	RTZ (87, 93, 95)
103	Saatchi & Saatchi (87, 93)
104	Scottish & Newcastle (93, 95)
105	Sears (87, 93, 95)

106   Sema (93, 95)
107   Thorn EMI (87, 93, 95)
108   Tiphook (93, 95)
109   Whitbread (87, 93, 95)

Danish sample companies (5)

110   Danisco (93, 95)
111   East Asiatic Company (87, 93, 95)
112   Great Nordic (87, 93, 95)
113   ISS (93, 95)
114   Novo Nordisk (87, 93, 95)

Belgian sample companies (10)

115   Cockerill Sambre (93, 95)
116   Compagnie Internationale des Wagons-Lits (87, 93, 95)
117   Electrabel (93, 95)
118   Finoutremer (93, 95)
119   Geveart ((87, 93, 95)
120   Petrofina (87, 93)
121   Sipef (87, 93, 95)
122   SNCB (87, 93, 95)
123   Societe Generale de Belgique (87, 93, 95)
124   Solvay (87, 93, 95)

Irish sample companies (9)

125   Abbey (87, 93)
126   Clondalkin (87, 93, 95)
127   James Crean (87, 93, 95)
128   CRH (87, 93, 95)
129   Fitzwilton (87, 93, 95)
130   Independent Newspaper (87, 93, 95)
131   Jefferson Smurfit (87, 93, 95)
132   Ryan Hotels (87, 93, 95)
133   Waterford Wedgwood (87, 93, 95)

Italian sample companies (10)

134　Benetton (87, 93, 95)
135　Fiat (87, 93, 95)
136　Montedison (87, 93, 95)
137　Olivetti (87, 93)
138　Pirelli (87, 93, 95)
139　Raggio di Sole Finanziari (93, 95)
140　Saipem (87, 93, 95)
141　SIP (Telecom Italia) (87, 93, 95)
142　Sirti (87, 93, 95)
143　SME (93, 95)

Spanish sample companies (11)

144　Acerinox (87, 93, 95)
145　Aragonesas (93, 95)
146　Endesa (87, 93, 95)
147　Metrocacesa (93, 95)
148　Pycra (87, 93, 95)
149　Repsol (87, 93, 95)
150　Sevillana de Electricidad (87, 93, 95)
151　Tabacalera (87, 93, 95)
152　Telefonica (87, 93, 95)
153　Union Fenosa (87, 93, 95)
154　Uralita (93, 95)

BETRIEBSWIRTSCHAFTLICHE STUDIEN
RECHNUNGS- UND FINANZWESEN, ORGANISATION UND INSTITUTION

Die Herausgeber wollen in dieser Schriftenreihe Forschungsarbeiten aus dem Rechnungswesen, dem Finanzwesen, der Organisation und der institutionellen Betriebswirtschaftslehre zusammenfassen. Über den Kreis der eigenen Schüler hinaus soll originellen betriebswirtschaftlichen Arbeiten auf diesem Gebiet eine größere Verbreitung ermöglicht werden. Jüngere Wissenschaftler werden gebeten, ihre Arbeiten, insbesondere auch Dissertationen, an die Herausgeber einzusenden.

Band 21   Stefan Lange: Die Kompatibilität von Abschlußprüfung und Beratung. Eine ökonomische Analyse. 1994.

Band 22   Hans Klaus: Gesellschafterfremdfinanzierung und Eigenkapitalersatzrecht bei der Aktiengesellschaft und der GmbH. 1994.

Band 23   Vera Marcelle Krisement: Ansätze zur Messung des Harmonisierungs- und Standardisierungsgrades der externen Rechnungslegung. 1994.

Band 24   Helmut Schmid: Leveraged Management Buy-Out. Begriff, Gestaltungen, optimale Kapitalstruktur und ökonomische Bewertung. 1994.

Band 25   Carsten Carstensen: Vermögensverwaltung, Vermögenserhaltung und Rechnungslegung gemeinnütziger Stiftungen. 1994. 2., unveränderte Auflage 1996.

Band 26   Dirk Hachmeister: Der Discounted Cash Flow als Maß der Unternehmenswertsteigerung. 1995. 2., durchgesehene Auflage 1998. 3., korrigierte Auflage 1999. 4., durchgesehene Auflage 2000.

Band 27   Christine E. Lauer: Interdependenzen zwischen Gewinnermittlungsverfahren, Risiken sowie Aktivitätsniveau und Berichtsverhalten des Managers. Eine ökonomische Analyse. 1995.

Band 28   Ulrich Becker: Das Überleben multinationaler Unternehmungen. Generierung und Transfer von Wissen im internationalen Wettbewerb. 1996.

Band 29   Torsten Ganske: Mitbestimmung, Property-Rights-Ansatz und Transaktionskostentheorie. Eine ökonomische Analyse. 1996.

Band 30   Angelika Thies: Rückstellungen als Problem der wirtschaftlichen Betrachtungsweise. 1996.

Band 31   Hans Peter Willert: Das französische Konzernbilanzrecht. Vergleichende Analyse zum deutschen Recht im Hinblick auf die Konzernbilanzzwecke und deren Grundkonzeption. 1996.

Band 32   Christian Leuz: Rechnungslegung und Kreditfinanzierung. Zum Zusammenhang von Ausschüttungsbegrenzung, bilanzieller Gewinnermittlung und vorsichtiger Rechnungslegung. 1996.

Band 33   Gerald Schenk: Konzernbildung, Interessenkonflikte und ökonomische Effizienz. Ansätze zur Theorie des Konzerns und ihre Relevanz für rechtspolitische Schlußfolgerungen. 1997.

Band 34   Johannes G. Schmidt: Unternehmensbewertung mit Hilfe strategischer Erfolgsfaktoren. 1997.

Band 35   Cornelia Ballwießer: Die handelsrechtliche Konzernrechnungslegung als Informationsinstrument. Eine Zweckmäßigkeitsanalyse. 1997.

Band 36   Bert Böttcher: Eigenkapitalausstattung und Rechnungslegung. US-amerikanische und deutsche Unternehmen im Vergleich. 1997.

Band 37   Andreas-Markus Kuhlewind: Grundlagen einer Bilanzrechtstheorie in den USA. 1997.

Band 38   Maximilian Jung: Zum Konzept der Wesentlichkeit bei Jahresabschlußerstellung und -prüfung. Eine theoretische Untersuchung. 1997.

Band 39   Mathias Babel: Ansatz und Bewertung von Nutzungsrechten. 1997.

Band 40   Georg Hax: Informationsintermediation durch Finanzanalysten. Eine ökonomische Analyse. 1998.

Band 41   Georg Schultze: Der spin-off als Konzernspaltungsform. 1998.

Band 42   Christian Aders: Unternehmensbewertung bei Preisinstabilität und Inflation. 1998.

Petra Lietz / Dieter Kotte

The importance of economic literacy

Frankfurt/M., Berlin, Bern, Bruxelles, New York, Oxford, Wien, 2000.
XV, 142 pp., num. tab. and graph.
ISBN 3-631-36161-0 / US-ISBN 0-8204-4740-4 pb. DM 54.–*

In the world of globalization, international markets and world-wide competition it is important for students to be well informed about the underlying economic concepts. Knowledge about economics, termed 'economic literacy', has become as important as being literate in reading, writing and arithmetic. For each country and educational system the importance of economic literacy is tied to educating its youth to be capable of understanding, thinking and acting according to basic economic principles. Based on the Australian setting this book sheds light on the growing importance of economic literacy as reflected in the States' curricula and as measured in a recent survey conducted across Queensland.

Contents: Review of economic literacy world-wide – Gender differences in Economics – Content analysis of Economics curricula – Levels of economic literacy – Economics as a school subject – Economic Literacy Survey – Queensland 1998 – The internet and data collection – Literacy benchmarking using Rasch scaling – Student's attitudes towards economics – Successful teaching strategies in Economics – School resources and Economic literacy – Policy recommendations – Hierarchical linear models – Path analysis

Frankfurt/M · Berlin · Bern · Bruxelles · New York · Oxford · Wien
Auslieferung: Verlag Peter Lang AG
Jupiterstr. 15, CH-3000 Bern 15
Telefax (004131) 9402131

*inklusive Mehrwertsteuer
Preisänderungen vorbehalten
Homepage http://www.peterlang.de